THE
GOSPEL
AND
CONTEMPORARY
PERSPECTIVES

BIBLICAL FORUM SERIES
VOLUME 2

THE GOSPEL
AND
CONTEMPORARY PERSPECTIVES

DOUGLAS MOO
General Editor

kregel
PUBLICATIONS

Grand Rapids, MI 49501

The Gospel and Contemporary Perspectives

Published by Kregel Publications, a division of Kregel, Inc., P.O. Box 2607, Grand Rapids, MI 49501. Kregel Publications provides trusted, biblical publications for Christian growth and service. Your comments and suggestions are valued.

Cover design: Alan G. Hartman
Book design: Nicholas G. Richardson

Library of Congress Cataloging-in-Publication Data
Moo, Douglas J.
  The Gospel and contemporary perspectives / Douglas J. Moo, gen. ed.
    p.   cm. — (The trinity journal series)
  Articles reprinted from Trinity journal.
  Includes bibliographical references.
  1. Bible. N.T. Gospels—Criticism, interpretation, etc. 2. Church and the world. 3. Apologetics. I. Moo, Douglas J. II. Trinity journal. III. Series.
BS2555.2.G565   1997   230'.04624—dc21   96-40920
                                                CIP
ISBN 0-8254-3348-7

Printed in the United States of America
1 2 3 4 5 / 01 00 99 98 97

CONTENTS

ANOTHER GOSPEL:
THE "HEALTH AND WEALTH GOSPEL"

DEFENDING THE GOSPEL

PROCLAIMING THE GOSPEL

CONTRIBUTORS

J. Daryl Charles
  Resident Scholar, Wilberforce Forum, Reston, Virginia

Douglas Groothuis
  Assistant Professor of Philosophy of Religion and Ethics,
  Denver Seminary, Denver, Colorado

Paul Helm
  Professor of Philosophy of Religion, Kings College, London

Dennis Hollinger
  Adjunct Professor of Christian Ethics, Eastern Baptist Seminary,
  Philadelphia, Pennsylvania

Walter C. Kaiser, Jr.
  Colman M. Mockler Distinguished Professor of Old Testament,
  Gordon-Conwell Theological Seminary, South Hamilton,
  Massachusetts

David L. Larsen
  Former Professor of Homiletics, Trinity Evangelical Divinity
  School, Deerfield, Illinois

Douglas J. Moo
  Professor and Chairman of the Department of New Testament,
  Trinity Evangelical Divinity School, Deerfield, Illinios

J. P. Moreland
  Professor of Philosophy, Talbot School of Theology at Biola
  University, LaMirada, California

Harold A. Netland
  Professor of Missions and Director of the Ph.D. program in
  Intercultural Studies, Trinity Evangelical Divinity School,
  Deerfield, Illinois

John Piper
  Senior Pastor, Bethlehem Baptist Church, Minneapolis, Minnesota

7

Thomas E. Schmidt
  Associate Professor of Religious Studies, Westmont College,
  Santa Barbara, California

Victor L. Walter
  Pastor, Cheyenne Evangelical Free Church, Cheyenne, Wyoming

PREFACE

The name *evangelical* means "committed to the Gospel." In Christ, we believe, God has revealed His "good news" for all people. And we also believe that it is only in the Gospel that we discover ultimate truth about God, human beings, and the world. Explaining and defending the Gospel is therefore central to the Christian mission. In this volume, we reproduce articles from *Trinity Journal* that focus on the Gospel.

Challenges to the Gospel come both from within the Christian movement and from without. Our first five chapters deal with a challenge from within: the "Health and Wealth Gospel." This particular version of Christian teaching holds that God has promised in His Word that every Christian, through faith, can be both materially prosperous and physically sound. Preachers of this message continue to attract quite a following. Yet, as the chapters we publish here argue, the "Health and Wealth Gospel" is, indeed, "another gospel"—a serious departure from the Good News of God in Christ.

In the second section of the volume we include chapters that tackle challenges to the Gospel from without. Our time is one in which many people think that truth is relative, that what is "true" for one person or one ethnic group might not be "true" for another. In this belief is found a new challenge to Christians who believe that Christ is "the way, *the truth,* and the life." The authors of these chapters are seeking to give Christians the philosophical tools they need to give to people in our culture a "reasoned account" of the truth that we hold.

The Gospel is above all meant to be proclaimed. A volume on the Gospel without something about preaching would therefore suffer from a glaring gap. And so our volume concludes with exhortations from two different preachers to give ourselves to the task of proclamation. May we commit ourselves afresh to the defense and propagation of the Gospel!

Douglas J. Moo

ABOUT *TRINITY JOURNAL*

TRINITY JOURNAL is the faculty-sponsored journal of Trinity Evangelical Divinity School of Trinity International University in Deerfield, Illinois. Today Christian readers can choose from a flood of books, journals, and magazines, and we think that *Trinity Journal* has a special place in this flood of material. Our mission is to bring the very best of evangelical scholarship to the working pastor, missionary, and informed layperson. While much is written on what Christians believe, how Christians should act, how Christians should view social issues, etc., we believe that it is extremely important that Christians understand where these beliefs come from—the Word of God. We are not content with just tradition and majority opinion. We believe that the Word of God should be the solid basis and foundation for our beliefs, our teachings, and our very lives.

Trinity Journal's purpose is to present excellently researched and well-written scholarship that not only challenges one's thinking but also challenges one to a more holy walk with God. If we are to follow God more closely, we need to have a firm hold on His Word and a deep understanding of His will. If *Trinity Journal* is instrumental in serving God's people in this way, we will have met our purpose . . . to God be the glory.

If you would like to subscribe, please write to:

Trinity Journal
Attn: Business Manager
2065 Half Day Road
Deerfield, IL 60015

ANOTHER GOSPEL: THE "HEALTH AND WEALTH GOSPEL"

CHAPTER ONE

ENJOYING GOD FOREVER: A HISTORICAL/SOCIOLOGICAL PROFILE OF THE HEALTH AND WEALTH GOSPEL

Dennis Hollinger

E njoying God forever! This partial response to the opening question of the Westminster Catechism would seem to describe the contemporary health and wealth gospel movement. The 1647 Catechism begins with the question: "What is the chief end of man?" The catechist responds, "Man's chief end is to glorify God and to enjoy Him forever." Throughout the church's history certain groups and movements have tended to overemphasize one dimension of this response at the expense of the other. The health and wealth gospel appears to be a case in point. By accentuating the goodness of God (which is activated by a believer's faith), the movement's adherents are inclined to focus primarily on enjoying God over glorifying God. Evidence for the theme of enjoyment is seen in the promises of healing, financial prosperity, and general well-being.

The health and wealth gospel is an identifiable religious movement comprised of distinct teachings, key preachers, a particular clientele, conferences, massive publications, media ministries, local congregations that identify with the teachings and preachers, educational institutions, and a loosely knit organization called the International Convention of Faith Churches and Ministries (ICFCM). Adherents have often labeled themselves "Word" or "Word of Faith Churches" as well as "faith movement." Critics have utilized such phrases as "name it and claim it," "the gospel of prosperity," and "the health and wealth gospel." Among the major leaders are Kenneth Hagin, Kenneth and Gloria Copeland, Jerry Savelle, and Fred Price—people with substantial followings not only in the United States but also in parts of Europe and the Third World. All share a common commitment to spreading the Word of God, a Word that they believe has been distorted and unheeded with regard to faith, healing, and prosperity.

The themes of the movement are certainly not new. The emphasis, for example, on financial prosperity as a fruit of true Christian commitment, prayer, or faith has precedence within Christian history. During the Gilded Age in late nineteenth-century America, numerous clergy espoused the notion that right thinking and right living could unlock the doors to bountiful wealth. William Lawrence (1858–1941), an Episcopalian bishop of Massachusetts, taught that "in the long run, it is only to the man of morality that wealth comes. . . . Godliness is in league with riches."[1]

13

What is new among the contemporary faith teachers is the particular way in which they have packaged and framed their beliefs. Their roots and ideas can certainly be found in prior movements and historic figures, but the health and wealth gospel represents a new and distinct religious movement that is flourishing amidst the controversy which surrounds it. Though the movement is primarily Pentecostal in its orientation, its impact is now being felt beyond the boundaries of traditional Pentecostalism and the new charismatic movement.

This chapter seeks to give an historical and sociological overview of the faith movement. After a brief overview of its major themes, we will survey the key figures of the movement and its historic roots. Finally, the chapter will attempt to provide sociological analysis as to why the health and wealth gospel has emerged and flourished in twentieth-century America.

I. MAJOR THEMES

According to Bruce Barron, in his well-balanced book, *The Health and Wealth Gospel*, there are three main themes that set the movement apart from traditional Christian understandings: healing, prosperity, and positive confession.[2] The faith teachers themselves are quick to point out that these are not the primary themes of Christian faith and that they must be understood in light of traditional Christian doctrines. Kenneth Hagin, Jr., in a personal letter to me rejected any cultic or heresy labels and stated, "Our major tenets of faith are held in common by those in the evangelical world—beliefs such as the virgin birth and deity of our Lord Jesus Christ, the absolute necessity of the new birth through faith in the atoning work of Jesus on the cross, and other fundamental doctrines of the church."[3] Nonetheless, the themes of healing, prosperity, and public confession are highly significant for faith preachers and their followers and are clearly at the heart of the controversy surrounding the movement.

The themes themselves are generally understood to have their source in the Abrahamic covenant with its promise of great blessing. In the Old Testament these blessings included health and wealth to those who were faithful to God. The atonement of Christ is seen to extend these blessings to all people on the basis of Galatians 3:13–14, "Christ redeemed us from the curse of the law . . . that the blessing of Abraham might come to the Gentiles through Christ" (NIV). As Kenneth Copeland puts it, "You are an heir to the blessing which God gave to Abraham. This blessing, found in the 28th chapter of Deuteronomy, covers every area of your existence: spirit, soul, body, financially, and socially."[4] Not only does Christ's atonement extend Abraham's blessings to us, it also overturns the curse of the law, which included both poverty and sickness. It is from this framework that the faith teachers espouse healing, prosperity, and positive confession.

A. Healing

The healing power of God is by no means a novel teaching. Christian theologians, preachers, and movements down through history have articulated in varying forms doctrines of healing. What sets the health and wealth gospel apart from mainstream Christian understanding is its emphatic insistence that God always intends to heal and that healing is assured if Christians have the faith to believe it. Most of the movement's teachers do not totally negate the role of the medical profession but insist that divine healing is a higher way. As Fred Price put it, "Doctors are fighting the same enemies that we are, the only difference is they're using toothpicks and we are using atomic bombs."[5] One exception to a secondary acceptance of medical help was the late Hobart Freeman, who while not being closely connected organizationally to the other faith preachers, nevertheless shared with them similar teachings. Freeman forbade any medical help for his followers, including eyeglasses, and came to the national spotlight when it was reported that by 1984 over ninety unnecessary deaths had occurred in his Faith Assembly movement.[6]

The faith teachers believe that "healing is just as much a part of the plan of redemption as salvation, the Holy Spirit and heaven as your eternal home."[7] Since healing is perceived to be accomplished through Christ's atonement, it is activated by faith alone. While the laying on of hands has been utilized in their healing campaigns, these preachers are quick to note that there is no power of healing in this symbolic act. Rather the ritual is a point of contact with someone who has faith in order to activate the faith of the person in need. The health and wealth gospel's doctrine of healing is clearly stated by Jerry Savelle:

> Not only is it God's will to heal, it is God's will to heal all! Satan is the author of sickness and disease.
>
> By the authority of His Word, God has made provision for our healing. It is not the will of God that anyone be sick with any sickness or disease or pain whatsoever from hangnails to tuberculosis![8]

B. Prosperity

The doctrine of prosperity, while the most controversial of the movement's teachings, has certainly been a major factor in its popularity. The concept is understood in broad terms: "Prosperity is the condition of being successful and thriving in all areas: spiritually strong, physically strong (healthy), and mentally solid."[9] But there is no question that for the faith adherents financial prosperity is a divine promise signifying God's blessing upon those whose faith is great enough to expect it.

Since material wealth was part of the Abrahamic covenant and since Christ has overturned the curse of the law which included poverty, Christians are said to have a right to claim prosperity. Moreover, says Fred Price, "If the Mafia can ride around in Lincoln Continental town cars, why can't Kings's Kids?"[10] The adherents of the movement find further support in the New Testament with passages like the KJV rendition of 3 John 2, "Beloved, I wish above all things that thou mayest prosper and be in health, even as thy soul prospereth."

Some of the faith preachers advocate a "success formula," which they assert to be a universal or cosmic law. Essentially, the formula claims that financial success will come to those who have the faith to believe it and who are themselves a giving people. Since it is a universal law, it applies even to non-Christians who practice its principles. Speaking of a nonbeliever, Kenneth Hagin writes, "God didn't bless him because he was a sinner. He received God's blessing because he honored God. God has a certain law of prosperity and when you get into contact with that law . . . it just works for you—whoever you are."[11]

Part of the "success formula" is the promise of a hundredfold return based on Mark 10:29–30, "No one who has left home or brothers or sisters or mother or father or children or fields for me and the gospel will fail to receive a hundred times as much in this present age (homes, brothers, sisters, mothers, children and field—and with them, persecutions) and in the age to come, eternal life" (NIV). Commenting on this passage Gordon Lindsay of Christ for the Nations Institute in Dallas says, "There can be no mistake, the promise includes temporal wealth. . . . How much? An hundredfold! In other words he who gives up thousands in following Christ is eligible to receive hundreds of thousands."[12] In similar fashion Kenneth Copeland asks, "Do you want a hundredfold return on your money? Give and let God multiply it back to you."[13]

Many of the faith teachers emphasize that God brings financial reward not for selfish or greedy personal indulgence but rather for the purposes of generosity toward others and the propagation of the Gospel. As Gloria Copeland puts it, "Don't just believe God to meet your needs. Believe Him for a surplus of prosperity so that you can help others. We here in America are a blessed people financially. We have been called to finance the gospel to the world." Kenneth Hagin, Jr., has responded with disgust toward those who follow the movement in order to get wealthy. Speaking to a gathering of students at his Rhema Bible Training Center he stated boldly, "If you came to this school with the idea that it is going to help you get more faith so you can have Cadillacs, I want you to resign today."[14]

In recent years further qualifications have been placed on the prosperity theme. For example, since 1985 Kenneth Copeland has acknowledged that prosperity is relative and in many contexts throughout the world may come in the forms of bountiful rain and plenty of food.[15] Others have admitted that their teachings have been taken by followers to overshadow the main tenets of the Christian faith. Despite such confessions the movement continues to articulate the theme of prosperity in a "kingdom context," for prosperity they believe is clearly promised in the pages of Scripture. As Jerry Savelle puts it, "If I am not prospering, . . . it is not God's fault, nor the fault of the Word of God—it is my fault."[16]

C. Positive Confession

According to the faith movement, healing and prosperity are primarily realized through evoking the third distinctive theme, positive confession. This concept can best be understood as a statement, made in faith, that lays claim to God's provisions and promises. To be healed, for example, people must pray in faith with a positive affirmation that they are healed, even if the symptoms of illness linger on. Since it is "with your mouth that you confess and are saved" (Rom. 10:10), it is with similar confession that humans can experience and enjoy God's other provisions. Positive confession is also seen to be grounded in Mark 11:23–24, "I tell you the truth, if anyone says to this mountain, 'Go, throw yourself into the sea,' and does not doubt in his heart but believes that what he says will happen, it will be done for him. Therefore I tell you, whatever you ask for in prayer, believe that you have received it, and it will be yours" (NIV).

It is from this theme that the popular phrase, "Name it and claim it," is derived. In a widely circulated booklet Kenneth Hagin unabashedly affirms,

"You can have what you say." Hagin goes on to note that people's "words give them away. You can locate people by what they say. Their confession locates them."[17] Though Hagin puts some limits on what we can request from God, he also speaks forthrightly of writing your own ticket with God. He asserts that God has given to him four simple steps—say it, do it, receive it, and tell it— which will enable anyone to receive from God what they confess.[18] Kenneth Copeland describes this theme in terms of commanding God:

> As a believer, you have a right to make commands in the name of Jesus. Each time you stand on the Word, you are commanding God to a certain extent because it is His Word. Whenever an honest man gives you his word, he is bound by it. It is not necessary to order him around because a truly honest man will back his word. When you stand on what he has said, he is commanded to do it.[19]

Positive confession then is the vehicle through which God's promises are effected for the faith preachers. To pray "If it be God's will" reflects a lack of faith and positive confession. Charles Capps, a retired farmer and now a leading exponent of the movement, states, "You have to believe that those things you say—everything you say—will come to pass. That will activate the God kind of faith within you, and those things which you say will come to pass."[20]

II. MAJOR FIGURES OF THE MOVEMENT

There are clearly identifiable leaders within the health and wealth gospel movement. They are regarded by adherents as the teachers, inspirers, and figureheads of this clearly demarcated religious entity.

A. Kenneth Hagin, Sr.

Kenneth Hagin has generally been acknowledged to be "the father of the faith movement" and "the granddaddy of the faith teachers."[21] Though younger faith preachers may outdo him in preaching, he is the indisputable leader of the movement. Almost all the other faith preachers point in some way to the profound influence of Kenneth Hagin for their own spiritual development, understanding of faith teachings, and call to ministry. Historian David Harrell describes Hagin as "an able preacher with a homey and humorous Texas style" who has "always been more a student and teacher than platform performer."[22]

Born on August 20, 1917 with a congenital heart defect and weighing less than two pounds at birth, young Hagin faced a life of hardship and unhappiness. His physicians said that he didn't have a chance in a million to live a long life. Hagin's physical incapacities were compounded at age six by his father's desertion of the family and the subsequent nervous breakdown of his mother. At age sixteen, after being essentially an invalid his whole life, Kenneth experienced a miraculous healing. He immediately began preaching as a Baptist evangelist in the rural and small-town areas of his native Texas. After receiving "the baptism of the Holy Spirit" in 1937, Hagin was licensed with the Assemblies of God and served various of their churches in Texas until 1949. At this point he began an independent healing ministry as part of the post-World War II healing revival, a movement which included persons such as Oral Roberts, William Branham, and

A. A. Allen. The ministry of Hagin at this juncture was never popular, as he seemed to lack the flair of other healing evangelists.

During the 1960s Hagin's ministry began to flourish as his healing emphasis was supplemented by themes of faith, prosperity, and positive confession. Radio programs, conferences, a monthly magazine, and then in 1974 the founding of Rhema Bible Training Center (under the direction of his son Kenneth, Jr.) helped to establish Hagin's ministry as the hub of the faith movement. By 1982 there were over eleven thousand students enrolled in Hagin's correspondence courses and today there are over fifteen hundred students at the Rhema Bible Training Center in Tulsa. He has traveled throughout the world preaching his faith message and by all accounts is the leader of the movement.

B. Kenneth and Gloria Copeland

Kenneth and Gloria Copeland have developed a worldwide faith ministry that has won them significant influence and popularity among the health and wealth gospel followers. Converted in 1962, the Copelands experienced a rather uneventful life until 1967 when they headed to Oral Roberts University. "With only a dime in his pocket, Kenneth Copeland enrolled there believing that his commitment to the Lord . . . would help sustain him."[23] Since Kenneth was a trained pilot, he quickly landed a job on the flight crew for Oral Roberts's cross-country crusade flights. Through this experience he gained firsthand experience in faith-healing ministries. It was not Roberts, however, that had the greatest influence on the Copelands, but Kenneth Hagin. After hearing a Hagin tape in 1967 they began to devote themselves assiduously to his teaching and a year later began their own ministry.

The Copelands carry on an extensive work through conferences, television, satellite, books, and tapes. Their monthly magazine, *The Believer's Voice of Victory*, is said to have a circulation of seven hundred thousand. The Copelands' rising prominence is enhanced by their dynamic oratory skills and by Kenneth's popularity as a singer. While healing is a part of the Copeland ministry, the primary focus appears to be on laying claim by faith to the special rights and privileges of Christians, especially the material ones. As Kenneth Hagin gets on in years it would appear that the mantle of leadership will fall on Kenneth Copeland. In fact, McConnell claims that already "Copeland is now the ex officio leader of the Faith movement. Nevertheless, at least in spiritual matters, when Hagin speaks, Copeland still listens."[24]

C. Jerry Savelle

Jerry Savelle received a call to ministry at age twelve while watching the healing ministry of Oral Roberts on television.[25] It was not until 1969, however, that Savelle began to experience spiritual renewal and went into the ministry. The impetus for change came through the preaching of Kenneth Copeland. Savelle, having overcome financial, spiritual, and emotional stress, joined the Copelands' ministry as an associate evangelist.

Eventually Savelle formed his own organization, the World Outreach Center, located in Forth Worth, Texas. He carries on an extensive preaching ministry, distributes nearly three hundred thousand copies of his own tapes and books each year, and is the founder of Overcoming Faith Center Churches, Medical Center, and Bible Training Center in Kakamega, Kenya. The thematic focus of his ministries, which now extend to thirty-six different countries, is very similar to that of Copeland and Hagin, with the addition of strong evangelistic concerns.

D. Fred Price

Fred Price is the most prominent of a growing number of black faith preachers. After years of spiritual lethargy Price claimed that his contact with Hagin's teachings changed his life. He declares that "Kenneth Hagin has had the greatest influence upon my life of any living man."[26] In 1970 he began a church near Los Angeles called the Crenshaw Christian Center, a center at which Kenneth Hagin is still a frequent speaker. Price's church has grown from one hundred and fifty members in 1972 to over fourteen thousand members. His flamboyant preaching style and colorful language has made him a popular preacher in the faith movement circuit as well as on his own television program.

E. Other Leaders

Several other preachers in the health and wealth gospel movement deserve brief mention. Charles Capps, a former farmer from Arkansas, is particularly known as a teacher of positive confession. Robert Tilton of Dallas became increasingly popular through his TV program Success-N-Life as well as through his Word of Faith Satellite Network, which beamed his seminars and revivals into nearly two thousand churches (although he is now embroiled in legal difficulties and scandals). Marilyn Hickey, one of a number of women preachers in the movement, is known for her radio program accentuating keys to prosperity.

There are other preachers who herald a gospel of prosperity but should be seen as distinct from the faith movement. Most notable is Rev. Frederick J. Elkerenkoftter II, better known as Rev. Ike. Originally a storefront preacher in Boston, Rev. Ike now preaches and beams his TV broadcasts from Harlem. Over the years he has shifted away from Christian-oriented preaching and now embraces what he calls "Science of the Mind." He is particularly known for his pithy prosperity slogans: "You can't lose with the stuff I use," and "The lack of money is the root of all evil."[27]

III. HISTORICAL ROOTS OF THE MOVEMENT

The contemporary health and wealth movement flows historically from two primary tributaries: Pentecostal healing revivalism and the influence of E. W. Kenyon (1867–1948), a New England preacher-educator who apparently imbibed the waters of nineteenth-century New Thought metaphysics. McConnell's *A Different Gospel* attempts to undermine the Pentecostal influence, giving primacy to the "Kenyon Connection." My own conclusion, however, is that we cannot minimize the role of the healing revivalist tradition.

A. Pentecostal Healing Revivalism

Pentecostalism in America is generally recognized as having emerged with the Azusa Street Revival in Los Angeles in 1906. Expanding on the earlier holiness emphases on a second work of grace and entire sanctification,

Pentecostalism stressed the need for a baptism of the Holy Spirit evidenced by speaking in tongues. Healing and other miraculous signs were at the heart of the movement from its earliest days. Numerous faith healers traveled the Pentecostalist circuit with a message that faith and the touch of the healer could evoke a miracle from God.

It was not, however, until after World War II that a distinct healing revival movement emerged. David Harrell describes it this way:

> Since World War II, hundreds of ministers, most of them in the 1950s coming from the ranks of classical pentecostalism but later from a variety of backgrounds, established independent evangelistic associations. These associations lived or died with the charisma of the evangelist, and some became multimillion dollar organizations. Taken together, they were a powerful independent force in modern American religion and won the religious loyalty and financial support of millions of Americans. Little understood by the public, the faith healing revivalists were the main actors in the postwar pentecostal drama.[28]

Among the key figures of this movement were William Branham, Oral Roberts, Jack Coe, A. A. Allen, Gordon Lindsay, and T. L. Osborn. The ministry of these and similar healing revivalists received coverage in *The Voice of Healing*, a magazine which more than any other vehicle tied the entire movement together. The revivalists were essentially of one mind with regard to healing—God always intends to heal, and it is up to the faith of the believer, activated by the laying on of hands or by anointed cloths, to bring God's promise to fruition.

The theme of prosperity is found early on in the healing revival movement. Already in the 1930s Thomas Wyatt made prosperity the foundation of his ministry.[29] In the 1950s the controversial A. A. Allen began to accentuate the financial blessing theme. Allen, who eventually died from alcoholism, was fond of telling a story about a $410 printing bill which he couldn't pay. He had only a few one-dollar bills in his pocket when suddenly the bills were transformed to twenties and the need was met. In 1963 Allen claimed to have received a revelation directly from God: "I am a wealthy God! Yea, I am not poor. . . . But I say unto thee, claim my wealth in thy hand, yea, in thy purse and in thy substance. For behold, I plan to do a new thing in the earth!"[30]

In 1947 Oral Roberts "discovered" 3 John 2 with its perceived emphasis on prosperity. Commenting on the passage, he said to his wife, "Evelyn, we have been wrong. I haven't been preaching that God is good. And Evelyn, if this verse is right, God is a good God." David Harrell notes that from this point the Robertses began to explore the implications of such a message not only for a new car, house, etc., but also for their larger worldwide ministry.[31]

The prosperity theme of the revivalists was often placed in the service of fund-raising, and therein emerged considerable controversy. Already in the early 1950s the Assemblies of God leadership began to raise questions about such fund-raising efforts and their corresponding themes of prosperity. By 1953 the denomination's *Pentecostal Evangel* stopped printing the revivalists' reports, and three years later their General Presbytery issued a strongly worded statement against questionable fund-raising techniques and promises of financial reward.[32] Clearly then, the emphasis on prosperity among contemporary faith teachers is nothing new.

By the late 1950s, as the healing revival movement began to wane, a new movement was about to be born—the new charismatic movement. This burgeoning religious force came to replace the old-style Pentecostalism in popularity and influence. Some of the old-time healing revivalists made the transition to a less separatistic and less legalistic expression of faith; others did not. Among those who made the transition was Kenneth Hagin. As Barron sees it, the faith teachers "owe their success largely to their transformation from Pentecostal to charismatic."[33] The contemporary health and wealth gospel emphasis is linked to the older Pentecostal healing revivalism both through ideas (healing, faith, prosperity) as well as through individuals who bridged the two movements, such as Kenneth Hagin.

Another significant figure to make that transition was Oral Roberts. Of interest at this point is his role in the faith movement. There are clear links between Roberts and the faith teachers, but striking differences as well. We have already noted that in 1947 Roberts got excited over the 3 John 2 passage with its perceived implications for prosperity. In 1954 he introduced the "Blessing-Pact," with a promised financial blessing for those who gave one hundred dollars to his ministry. A year later he published *God's Formula for Success and Prosperity,* and in the 1970s he began teaching his "seed-faith" concept. According to this concept the Old Testament tithe (give because you owe it to God) was replaced in the New Testament with giving in order to expect a blessing. God will supply, said Roberts, not just the bare essentials of life but will give abundantly to those who give.

Not only have some of Roberts's ideas seemed similar to those of the faith teachers; he has had intimate contact with them. Roberts has often attended and preached at Kenneth Hagin's annual camp meeting and has invited numerous of the faith teachers to preach at Oral Roberts University. Controversy over their message peaked in 1980 when Fred Price was preaching at ORU and a theology professor shouted no in response to Price's teaching. Roberts was incensed by the protest and demanded an apology from the professor.[34]

Despite personal interactions and similar ideas Oral Roberts seems to have distanced himself from the movement at certain points and is continuing to distance himself as the controversy intensifies. Roberts, for example, does not teach that God will always heal if one only believes and positively confesses. His own City of Faith blends medical healing with faith. In an article on faith healing in *Christianity Today* Rodney Clapp notes, "In visiting places like . . . Oral Roberts's City of Faith hospital, I detected the unfolding of what I call a centrist view of healing."[35] It is also significant to note that some of the sharpest critiques of the faith movement have come from within the university—theology professor Charles Farah's *From the Pinnacle of the Temple* and McConnell's *A Different Gospel,* originally a master's thesis at ORU. Roberts, like other faith teachers, bridged the gap between the older Pentecostal healing movement and the newer charismatic expression. At best, however, his link to the health and wealth gospel remains tentative.

B. The Role of E. W. Kenyon

It might appear unlikely that a New England preacher-educator with no organizational or personal links to Pentecostalism could influence a movement such as the health and wealth gospel. But there is undeniable evidence that E. W. Kenyon has played a formative role in the ideas propagated by faith preachers. McConnell (*A Different Gospel*) demonstrates how Kenyon's ideas have shaped the thought of faith teachers and how Kenyon himself had been strongly influenced by New Thought metaphysics or Science of the Mind, a philosophy quite prevalent in late nineteenth-century New England. McConnell goes on to argue that "because of Kenyon's historical connection to the metaphysical cults, the modern Faith movement teaches doctrines that are neither biblical nor orthodox. In other words, because the historical root is cultic, the theological fruit is cultic as well."[36] McConnell can be vitriolic at times and is reluctant to acknowledge Pentecostal healing revivalism as one of the roots of the faith movement, but his work is extremely valuable in documenting the "Kenyon connection."

Born on April 24, 1867, in Saratoga County, New York, Essek William Kenyon became a self-educated student and avid supporter of education. He never earned a degree but attended various institutions in New Hampshire and Boston. Though he was raised a Methodist, Kenyon joined the Baptists following his conversion during late adolescence. He became an evangelist and through his preaching helped start a number of Baptist churches in rural New England. Kenyon's zeal for education led him to found Bethel Bible Institute in Spencer, Massachusetts, a school that eventually became Barrington College (now merged with Gordon College). He was the superintendent and driving force behind Bethel from 1900 to 1923 but eventually resigned from the school amid a swirl of controversy that was never made public. From there Kenyon moved to the west coast where he pastored several churches, served as an itinerant evangelist, carried on a radio program, and wrote books and pamphlets until his death in 1948.

While living in Boston in the 1890s, Kenyon attended the Emerson College of Oratory, a school that was closely connected with New Thought metaphysics. "New Thought was the brainchild of Phineas P. Quimby (1802–66), . . . and it is generally agreed by scholars of the metaphysical cults that Mary Baker Eddy, the founder of Christian Science, was heavily dependent on the writings of P. P. Quimby, by whom she received a healing and under whom she later studied."[37] A broad movement involving numerous metaphysical groups, New Thought accentuated among other things the immanence of God, the primacy of the mind as a cause of all effects, freedom from disease and poverty, the divine nature of humans, and the role of incorrect thinking in all sin and disease. McConnell believes that though Kenyon at times critiqued the New Thought movement, he nonetheless drank deeply at its wells through his studies at Emerson College as well as through contacts with various people in Boston who had propensities in that direction. He writes, "Because he had no theological background in . . . the Holiness-Pentecostal tradition, in formulating his 'new type of Christianity' of healing and prosperity, Kenyon drew from the only background in these areas that he did have: metaphysics."[38]

Kenyon's preaching reverberated with themes we have noted in the health and wealth gospel: healing, prosperity, and positive confession. Of the latter, for example, Kenyon thought that what one confesses with the lips controls one's inner being. In fact Kenyon is the source of the popular phrase in the faith movement, "What I confess, I possess."[39] Teaching that sickness is spiritual, not physical, Kenyon stated, "I know that I am healed because He said that I am healed and it makes no difference what the symptoms may be in the body. I laugh at them, and in the Name of Jesus I command the author of the disease to leave my body."[40] He also emphasized prosperity but was less materialistic in his understanding of it than the current faith movement.

Kenyon was not a Pentecostalist and even saw destructive tendencies in Pentecostal teaching. Nonetheless, various Pentecostal healing revivalists of the 1940s and 1950s had read Kenyon's works and at times quoted from him. As the metamorphosis evolved from old-time healing revivalism to the new faith movement, one person more than any other propagated certain of Kenyon's emphases—Kenneth Hagin. Hagin has on occasion acknowledged his appreciation of Kenyon's writings,[41] but McConnell shows far more extensive borrowing from Kenyon than Hagin admits. In fact McConnell documents extensive plagiarism by Hagin from Kenyon. His book contains four pages of column-by-column comparison of Kenyon and Hagin quotes and the evidence is overwhelming—it is virtually word for word borrowing without any acknowledgment. Hagin's plagiarism is contained in numerous articles and books over a period of eight years.[42]

The use of Kenyon by the faith teachers has not gone unnoticed by those who were once close to the evangelist-educator. Speaking of the faith movement's little-acknowledged use of her father's ideas, Kenyon's daughter, Ruth Kenyon Houseworth, said, "His first book was printed in 1916, and he had the revelation years before that. These that are coming along now that have been in the ministry for just a few years and claiming that this is something that they are just starting, it makes you laugh a little bit."[43] Similarly, John Kennington, a pastor in Oregon who knew and on occasion ministered with Kenyon, states, "Today Kenyon's ideas are in the ascendancy. Via the electronic church or in the printed page I readily recognize not only Kenyon's concepts but at times recognize pure plagiarism, for I can almost tell you book, chapter, and page where the material is coming from."[44]

The role of E. W. Kenyon in the health and wealth gospel is undeniable. Though Kenyon's link with the New Thought movement needs further historical investigation, McConnell's attempt to show the connection seems quite persuasive.

IV. A SOCIOLOGICAL ANALYSIS

Why has the faith movement flourished at this time? What social and cultural factors have helped shape the forms and particular expressions of this religious phenomenon? To ask these and other sociological questions is not to comment on the theological validity of such a movement. All religious expressions are manifest within historical settings and are to some measure, whether for good or ill, shaped by their sociocultural contexts. In this brief sociological analysis I intend only to suggest some possible human explanations for the popularity, forms, and emphases of the health and wealth gospel. As of yet there are not statistical analyses of the health and wealth gospel followers to discern their religious, educational, and social class backgrounds nor data to assess the influence beyond the boundaries of the movement per se. Thus only hypotheses can be suggested. The following are only representative of the kinds of sociological explanations that might be offered to explain the movement's development. Others could undoubtedly be added to the list.

A. Deprivation Theory

One possible explanation for the popularity and particular emphases of the faith movement is what sociologists call deprivation or relative deprivation theory. It hypothesizes that "people join sects because they seek to redress the lack of deference and esteem they feel is rightfully theirs."[45] The deprivation or marginality perceived by such people may be economic, cultural, or psychological, but joining a particular religious group is one way to establish one's niche within society. By itself the theory is an insufficient explanation for human behavior, for it does not account for a number of realities: why people join one movement over another, why some people look to religion and others do not, and why the most disadvantaged in society often refuse to join organized religious groups at all. But deprivation can be seen as one salient factor among others for explaining religious behavior and expression.

Though no data are available at this time on the socioeconomic status of faith teaching followers, the assumption of most observers is that they come from the ranks of working-class people who are seeking to find a psychological, economic, and cultural home in middle America. If that is indeed the case, we can understand why such persons would be attracted to a movement that promises, in the words of Kenneth Hagin, that God "wants His children to eat the best, He wants them to wear the best clothing, He wants them to drive the best cars, and He wants them to have the best of everything."[46]

It is also significant that almost all of the movement's leading preachers either grew up in poverty and hardship or at least at some point in their lives experienced destitution and feelings of powerlessness. R. O. Corvin, an influential Pentecostal leader and educator since World War II, gives some feel for the background from which many of the leaders emerged:

> Persecution against Pentecostals was both real and imaginary. Preachers who identified themselves with the churches entered the arena of life fighting. . . . They preached in school houses, under brush arbors, in store buildings, on street corners, under tents, in homes, on radios. They built inferior frame structures and large tabernacles.[47]

Coming from such marginal contexts, the faith preachers have often despised their early poverty and deprivation. A gospel of economic and physical well-being was appealing to such persons and continues to provide hope for the thousands of followers who seek release from a life of sociocultural disenfranchisement.

B. American Cultural Themes

Another possible explanation for the rise of this movement stems from cultural themes that are deeply embedded in American society. Notions of wealth and health (physical well-being) have long and powerful histories in this society, and it is therefore understandable that at times these values have become integral parts of religious expression. Like deprivation, these contextual themes alone cannot account for a movement, but they coalesce along with other explanatory variables.

Americans have historically been concerned with physical well-being, a passion that likely contributed in part to the rise of New Thought metaphysics (including Christian Science) in the nineteenth century. Two recent books describe the current American preoccupation with wellness and our bodies: *Worried Sick: Our Troubled Quest for Wellness* by Arthur J. Barsky and *Bodies: Why We Look the Way We Do (And How We Feel About It)* by sociologist Barry Glassner. Barsky, a professor of psychiatry at Harvard Medical School, observes that "because health has become synonymous with overall well-being, it has become an end in itself, a paramount aim of life."[48] Could it be that the health and wealth gospel is a reflection of such an ethos?

Similarly, wealth and prosperity have been part of the American character for centuries. Some of the earliest European descriptions of the New World focused primarily on its wealth and economic opportunity. In *Eastward Ho*, a comedy written in 1605, one of the characters says of Virginia, "I tell thee, gold is more plentiful there than copper is with us. . . . Why, man, all their dripping pans are pure gold: and all their chains with which they chain up their streets are massy gold."[49] Summarizing our whole history David Potter writes:

> The factor of abundance, which we first discovered as an environmental condition and which we then converted by technological change into a cultural as well as a physical force, has not only influenced all the aspects of American life in a fundamental way but has also impinged upon our relations with the peoples of the world.[50]

Countless other analysts have described the profound impact that the pursuit of wealth and prosperity have had on American social character. It would appear that the contemporary faith movement is another chapter in that cultural history.

The thrust of the health and wealth gospel is also a reflection of another American cultural theme, individualism. In Robert Bellah's widely read *Habits of the Heart,* personal fulfillment and financial success are portrayed as major expressions of the American ethos of individualism. "Americans tend to think of the ultimate goals of a good life as matters of personal choice. The means to achieve individual choice, they tend to think, depend on economic progress."[51] Such attitudes have become commonplace in American religion with its privatized, therapeutic bent, which often seeks not the good of others but primarily the good of the self. Its narcissistic tendencies are well captured by Bellah in an interview with a young nurse named Sheila: "My faith has carried me a long way. It's Sheilaism. Just my own little voice. . . . It's just try to love yourself and be gentle with yourself."[52] While the faith movement tends to stand over against American culture at one level, at another level it may well have acquiesced to the lure of American individualism and personal success. For it is the enjoyment of God, not the glory of God, that seems to have captivated the hearts and minds of the faith-teaching followers.

C. The Fund-Raising Factor

There is a rather pragmatic factor that has likely played a significant role in the prosperity emphasis of the faith teachers—their need to raise money to maintain their ministries. As Barton has noted, "Many well-known faith teachers do not pastor a church of their own, so they have no list of members whose donations they can count on receiving consistently. If they do not continue to successfully solicit contributions and sell their books and tapes, they have no guaranteed income against which to borrow."[53] The competition is fierce and the cost of TV programs, satellite networks, and travel is immense. In such a context the temptation to accentuate economic promises for giving to God (via their particular ministry) is overwhelming. From a functionalist perspective, the selected theological distinctives of the movement serve to ensure their financial solvency.

As noted earlier, fund-raising tactics that included financial promise received attention and critique already in the 1950s by the leadership of the Assemblies of God. Though some of the faith preachers have attempted to moderate their appeals, others have not. One young health and wealth gospel preacher told his audience:

> Now there are fifteen people here tonight in this tent . . . because God has told me that he is going to give you an unlimited blessing. God told me that. God is going to speak to fifteen people to write a check even if you have to postdate it for thirty days, God is going to talk to fifteen people to write a check or give $300. . . . Now, if you don't believe he can do it for you, then you're not going to be one of them.[54]

Most faith preachers are not quite so overt, but the covert message can be read between the lines. One can only speculate what would happen to the movement if promises of prosperity and health were suddenly removed.

V. CONCLUSION

Enjoying God forever! Proclaimers of the health and wealth gospel appear to be doing just that, at least for the moment. This dynamic and flourishing movement has played a more significant role in shaping the American religious landscape than has been previously acknowledged. Key teachings and tenets have subtly infiltrated the thought and vocabulary of preachers and lay persons not otherwise identified with the movement. Statements like, "You can't outgive God" and "God doesn't want his people to go second class," reverberate well beyond the formal boundaries of the movement itself.

The future of the health and wealth gospel is hard to predict. There are signs that certain leaders are beginning to moderate some of their teachings in response to widespread criticism. Simultaneously, new preachers and teachers with even more crass approaches are appearing on the scene. What can be said from a sociological standpoint is that the health and wealth gospel resonates in profound ways with some of the deeply embedded cultural themes of American society. Therein lies much of its success.

CHAPTER TWO

THE OLD TESTAMENT CASE FOR MATERIAL
BLESSINGS AND THE CONTEMPORARY BELIEVER

Walter C. Kaiser, Jr.

Can the Old Testament be interpreted as advocating a prosperity gospel of wealth, health, and success? Are such passages as Leviticus 26, Deuteronomy 26, and Psalm 37 fairly understood as supporting a theology of affluence? Can we revise the proverb to say, "Early to faith and early to obedience, makes a person healthy, wealthy, and wise"? Regardless of anything else?

Such questions are being answered affirmatively by an increasingly large number of evangelicals and some positive thinkers. In fact the promise of wealth, health, and success is too tempting for many to resist. Unfortunately, this so-called gospel of success tries to appeal to biblical authority and examples. Prominent among the lists of alleged biblical prooftexts are a number of passages from the Old Testament.

These challenges, apart from any other reasons, are more than adequate to call the academic and believing community to express what is the Old Testament case for the legitimate enjoyment of the material aspects of our culture. There is, of course, a theology of culture in the Old Testament. It is grounded in our positive affirmation and God's approbation of the created order. There is also a holistic approach to the spiritual and material aspects of reality.

The sad fact is that few have ventured into those portions of Scripture that call for a balanced approach to the questions of wealth, health, and success. Instead, success, and the determined quest for it alone, is spoiling America's "worldly evangelicals."[1]

It is important that we first understand who the advocates of the prosperity gospel are and what it is that they are claiming. The prosperity gospel does not appear to belong to any particular denominational group or brand of theology; in fact, it is so broadly spread over the American scene that it defies any easy categorization theologically. At times it has the emphasis of the possibility or positive thinking of a Robert Schuller and a Norman Vincent Peale. At other times it appears to be the private preserve of faith-healing groups. But more than all of these it rests on our culture's heavy involvement with an affluent suburban Christianity.

Some of the more visible personalities in this broadly based group include Kenneth Hagin, pastor of the Rhema Bible Church in Tulsa, Oklahoma; Kenneth and Gloria Copeland from Fort Worth, Texas; Charles Capps, a pastor from Oklahoma; Robert and Marte Tilton, co-pastors of the Word of Faith Church in

Farmers Branch, Texas; and Charles and Frances Hunter, faith-healers and founders of the City of Light, Kingwood, Texas.[2] Lesser lights include John Osteen, pastor of LaPewood Church in Houston, Texas; and Jerry Savelle, an evangelist and former associate of Kenneth Copeland.

Among the favorite Old Testament texts of this group are these (all cited from AV):

They that seek the Lord shall not want any good thing (Ps. 34:10).

Let them shout for joy and be glad that favor my righteous cause; yea, let them say continually, let the Lord be magnified, which hath pleasure in the prosperity of his servant (Ps. 35:27).

I have been young, and now am old; yet have I not seen the righteous forsaken, nor his seed begging bread (Ps. 37:25).

This book of the law shall not depart out of your mouth: but thou shalt meditate therein day and night, that thou mayest observe to do according to all that is written therein, for then thou shalt make thy way prosperous, and then thou shalt have good success (Josh. 1:8).

If they obey and serve Him, they shall spend their days in prosperity, and their years in pleasures (Job 36:11).

If thou wilt diligently hearken to the voice of the LORD thy God, and wilt do that which is right in his sight, and wilt give ear to his commandments, and keep his statutes, I will put none of these diseases upon thee, which I have brought upon the Egyptians: I am the LORD that healeth thee (Ex. 15:26).

Who forgiveth all thine iniquities; who healeth all thy diseases (Ps. 103:3).

Surely he hath borne our griefs, and carried our sorrows; yet we did esteem him stricken, smitten of God, and afflicted. But he was wounded for our transgressions, he was bruised for our iniquities: the chastisement of our peace was upon him; and with his stripes we are healed (Isa. 53:4–5).

In its most developed form, the gospel of prosperity asserts that God has set up certain laws and principles in His universe. Among these are His laws on wealth and health. What the believing child of God needs to do is to learn these principles from texts such as those we have just quoted from the King James Version (a favorite translation with this group) and then to set these laws into motion by speaking them with our own mouths, for everything we say will come to pass! On this model, the spoken word (Greek ῥῆμα) has a residual power within it that we only need utilize according to the principles that God vested in His world.

An alternative model focuses on Paul's triumphant note that "Christ redeemed us from the curse of the law" (Gal. 3:13). Curiously, we are assured that this curse is equated with the curses in Deuteronomy 28:15–68 (which embraces sickness, poverty, and death). What the redeemed person needs to realize is that with his or her personal salvation has come a release from all poverty, sickness, or even the second death!

But there is more. Not only were believers redeemed from the curse of the law, as defined above; they were also promised all the blessings of Abraham since we too are now Abraham's seed! Since God promised that He was going to make Abraham prosperous and rich, we too are going to enjoy the same benefits!

A third popular model appears to have revised its estimate of sin as defined biblically. For some of the advocates of this health, wealth, and prosperity theology, sin is "any act or thought that robs myself or another human being of his or her self-esteem."[3] In the new birth, a new positive self-esteem replaces the former negative inferiority complex. With a new sense of self-esteem, individuals are now free to go for the stars: anything is now possible. God wants to see us succeed; that is why He has promised to crown our efforts with success.

In addition to these contemporary gospel-of-affluence evangelists, the charge has frequently been leveled against the Old Testament that it too fosters a type of eudaemonism. Eudaemonism is that ethical position that stresses that goodness, happiness, and material rewards always come from satisfactory ethical actions. Rather than focusing on the rightness of an ethical action, the charge made against the Old Testament by some of its critics is that the Old Testament gives as its main motive for many, if not most, ethical actions, a desire to achieve material prosperity and success. Such a charge, if true, would expose the Old Testament to the accusation that it is governed more by utilitarian and pragmatic outcomes such as pleasure, wealth, and health than it is governed by principles and the standard of the person and being of God. This is commonly referred to as "Deuteronomic theology," or the "retributive motive." Any complete consideration of our topic must include a discussion of this charge as well, for it would appear from this charge that the gospel of affluence and the Old Testament ethic of eudaemonism are very much related; one turns it into a positive asset while the other finds it to be a negative blot on the Old Testament's record.

I. THE OLD TESTAMENT VIEW OF EUDAEMONISM

The argument has been repeated so frequently that it now passes for fact: the motive for ethical action in the Old Testament was the desire for material prosperity and the anxiety to escape disaster. But if that charge is true, how could an ethical theory that purports to come from God define ethical obligation solely by reference to personal well-being? Could such revelation assume that the ultimate motive for ethical behavior was merely self-interest, concern only for one's well-being?

A. The Problem of Defining Eudaemonism

There are so many problems with such a materialistic motivation for ethics that one hardly knows which problem to tackle first. Perhaps it would be best to start with a definition of the word itself. The Greek word εὐδαιμονία is widely and generally rendered "welfare" (German *Wohlfahrt*), but welfare is not to be automatically regarded as identical with happiness. Even though some ethicists define happiness as a technical equivalent of welfare, this definition involves an unnatural divorce from the commonly accepted connotation that happiness bears in ordinary speech, i.e., pleasure as an essential, if not one of the predominate, ingredients of life. It would be more appropriate to call such a high emphasis on pleasure "hedonism."

What ethical motivation does the Old Testament advocate? One thing for sure, it did not advocate personal welfare above the welfare of the nation. The top motive for ethical decision featured what it meant to be a "holy *people*" of God, not a desire for personal prosperity or the desire personally to avoid disaster and suffering.

B. The Nature of God

The starting point for understanding Old Testament ethics is the nature of God. The norm for all ethical decision is nothing less than the character of God as it is expressed in His "holiness." God is "wholly" distinct and, in that sense, is "set apart" from all that is common, profane, or contrary to His nature and character. This norm is set forth in Jeremiah 9:23–24:

> Let not the wise man boast of his wisdom
>   or the strong man boast of his strength
>   or the rich man boast of his riches,
> but let him who boasts boast about this:
>   that he understands and knows me,
>   that I am the LORD, who exercises kindness,
>   justice and righteousness on earth,
>   for in these I delight.

To "know" God personally meant that a person would strive to do the good set forth in God's character and being. Each individual was to be holy as the Lord was holy.

Holiness was so much a part of Old Testament life that it was impossible to exclude anything from the potential sphere of its influence. The central challenge of life was "Be holy, because I [the LORD] am holy" (Lev. 11:45). Hence, we perceive Old Testament ethics to be deontological (from the Greek word δέον, which stresses the "ought" or "binding" nature of the rightness of an action. What makes something "right" then is not its results but the specific command or character of God).[4]

The case for holiness is to be found at three levels: (1) the explicit statements in the "Law of Holiness" (Lev. 18–20); (2) the definition of holiness as a term that is practically equivalent to the complete "Godhead" in all His attributes as a standard for what is spiritual, moral, and ethical; and (3) the norm for what is the good, just, right, and appropriate standard of acting and being. It is this *imitatio Dei* that captures the mainspring of Old Testament ethics, "Be holy, because, I, the LORD your God, am holy."

C. The Case for Motives in Old Testament Ethics

The first scholar who directed the world of biblical scholarship to the issue of motives in the Old Testament was Berend Gemser. He defined motives as "grammatically subordinate sentences [or clauses] in which the motivation for a commandment is given."[5] Gemser arranged the contents of these clauses around four categories of motivation: (1) explanatory appeals to common sense of the hearer; (2) ethical appeals to conscience or ethical sentiments; (3) religious and theological appeals grounded in the nature and will of God; and (4) historical appeals to God's great acts in history on behalf of His people.

It is clear that Old Testament morality is governed by more than mere outward acts; it is also concerned with internal motivation. Even though B. D. Eerdmans contested this point in 1903 when he asserted that "Old Testament ethics do not meddle with the inner thoughts of men,"[6] Gemser responded by pointing to some thirty-six places where the Hebrew text linked ethical judgments with the inner thoughts and motivations of the heart.

D. Motivation in Proverbs

Few books have been assailed more frequently for suggesting a profit, success, or materialistic motivation for right action than the book of Proverbs. R. N. Gordon listed some 133 references in Proverbs where, as one of six motivators to ethical behavior, material inducements or punishments were used to obtain compliance with the injunctions of the book. However, in Gordon's view the ultimate motive in Proverbs was *life*. Said Gordon

> In a sense many of the other motives can be combined to make up *life*, when *life* is understood as a full, satisfying useful, integrated and enjoyable existence. . . . Many of the quotations which have hitherto been referred to as "utilitarian and eudaemonistic" and which are prompted by a desire for worldly and materialistic success and motivated by selfish ends, can be re-interpreted as part of a search for a wholeness in life in which these goals are necessary amongst others.[7]

Since all of life is proclaimed as a "gift," material benefits were regarded as no greater inducement than was life itself. Nor were material blessings of life looked upon as being greater in value than the rewards of wisdom and life themselves.

It is a distinctively twentieth-century obsession that fixes so singularly on the material aspects of life. The Old Testament writers recommended that humans fix their eyes on "the fear of the LORD" as the beginning point for all greatness and wealth (see, e.g., Prov. 1:7).

This same fear of the Lord also taught Israel and Judah to focus on the group, the nation as a whole, rather than on a rugged individualism that we find so frequently in twentieth-century Western societies. It was in Israel's corporate calling to be the people of God, a holy nation, a royal priesthood that the promises made in Leviticus 26, Deuteronomy 28, and in many psalms find their locus. Not individual but corporate blessing—the land, its productivity, its increase in the flocks and herds, and the wealth that accompanied it—constitutes "life" in these texts.

E. The Purpose of Material Blessings

Material blessings in the Old Testament were used by God for various ends. First of all they were given that God might confirm his covenant promise to build a mighty nation. "But remember the LORD your God, for it is he who gives you the ability to produce wealth and so confirms his covenant which he swore to your forefathers as it is today" (Deut. 8:18).

This covenant was not to be selfishly squandered; it was to be shared with the nations. Likewise the blessings that were derived from that special relationship were in turn to be used as teaching tools—both in their positive and negative examples! "The LORD will send a blessing on your barns and on everything you put your hand to. . . . Then all the peoples on earth will see that you are called by the name of the LORD and they will fear you" (Deut. 28:8, 10). But, "All these curses will come upon you. They will pursue you and overtake you until you are destroyed, because you did not obey the LORD your God . . . because you did not serve the LORD your God joyfully and gladly in the time of prosperity" (Deut. 18:45, 47). Thus the material blessings were given to Israel to teach the other nations that it was God, not the might of the Jews' own hands, that was producing the wealth they had garnered.

II. THE OLD TESTAMENT VIEW OF THE PROSPERITY GOSPEL

Is success, prosperity, wealth, and happiness guaranteed for all of God's people today in the same way that God blessed some of the great worthies in Old Testament times? Can we contemporary believers "corner the market" on success if we meet God's conditions for doing so?

Things have certainly turned around since the early 1970s when the poorer a Christian seemed to be, the more spiritual he or she was. This remarkable reversal is related to new interpretations of several key conceptions: the divine power of words, the divine promise of wealth, the divine curse of poverty, the divine promise of healing, and the divine promise of success.

A. The Divine Power of Words

How does one enter into this experience of divine health, wealth, and success according to those who preach the gospel of prosperity? Counseled Kenneth E. Hagin, "In my vision, Jesus said, 'Positive or negative, it is up to the individual. According to what the individual says that shall he receive.'"[8] Now if we think that Kenneth Hagin might mean these words in some figurative way he is even more explicit in saying that "When you make a positive confession of faith it creates the reality."[9] The reason things work this way is supplied by Sid Roth: "Since words are the building blocks of creation, we must be very careful what we say. Words not only create, they can also destroy."[10]

The same power of the "word" that, it is alleged, we find in Romans 10:9–10 —"if you confess with your mouth 'Jesus is Lord' . . . you will be saved"—is said to apply to physical reality. According to this view, words are able to create their own fulfillment. Just as God's faith-filled words spoke the universe into being, so our faith-filled words contain a similar inherent power. And it is this power which God chooses to recognize and use.

The Scriptures however, do not support such an exaggerated emphasis on a positive confession. It would appear to subordinate the sovereignty of God to human words. The effect of this would be to make God our servant and to render prayer unnecessary, since all that we spoke with our tongue by way of positive confession would become reality.

Hagin claimed that this truth came to him in a vision in 1953. But this vision must accord with Scripture, for that is one of the tests given in Deuteronomy 13 and 18 for a false prophet. All attempts to invent new truth that goes beyond Scripture must be labeled for what they really are: heretical.

But what of the supposed power of words in biblical writings? According to a number of Old Testament scholars, the spoken word in ancient Israel ". . . is never an empty sound but an operative reality whose action cannot be hindered once it has been pronounced. . . ."[11] These words are likened by these scholars to missiles with time fuses, grenades buried in a plowed field, or bombs that have been shot into enemy territory, which remain dangerous and effective for a long time to come.[12]

Thiselton points out that almost all of these Old Testament theologians go back to three classic studies: O. Grether, *Name und Wort Gottes im Alten Testament* (1934); L. Dürr, *Die Wertung des göttlichen Wortes im Alten Testament und im antiken Orient* (1938); and V. Hamp, *Der Begriff 'Wort' in den arammäischen Bibelübersetzungen* (1938).[13] Eventually both Old Testament and New Testament theologians took up this emphasis on the power of the spoken word.

The dynamic power of Old Testament words was said to be illustrated in such passages as Jeremiah 1:9–10: "I appoint you over nations and kingdoms to uproot and tear down, to destroy and to overthrow, to build and to plant"; Jeremiah 23:29: "'Is not my word like fire,' declares the LORD, 'and like a hammer that breaks the rock in pieces?'"; and Isaiah 55:10: "So is the word that goes out of my mouth: it will not return to me empty but will accomplish what I desire and achieve the purpose for which I sent it."

This emphasis is not restricted to the prophets or to mere poetic personification, argue prosperity advocates. The psalmist pictures the God of creation as saying "He spoke and it came to be; he commanded, and it stood firm" (Ps. 33:9); "He sent forth his word and healed them" (107:20); "He rebuked the Red Sea and it dried up" (106:9); "At your rebuke the waters fled, at the sound of your thunder they took to flight" (104:7).

Even when the patriarch realizes that he has been tricked and has given his blessing to the wrong son, Isaac laments "I have made [Jacob] lord over you [Esau] and have made all his relatives his servants and I have sustained him with grain and new wine. So what can I possibly do for you, my son?" (Gen. 27:37). Similarly Balaam tells Balak, "I have received a command to bless; [God] has blessed, and I cannot change it" (Num. 23:20).

However, these texts do not constitute an adequate basis for placing some type of magical power in the words themselves. Such a mistaken reification (the act of treating something as existing [from the Latin *res*, "thing"]) commits at least four basic mistakes, argues Anthony Thiselton.[14] For example, the fact that the Hebrew word דָּבָר can be translated both as "word" and "thing" does not mean that once a word is uttered it can become a thing which it is now impossible to push back into the mouth of the speaker! This is merely an example of polysemy (a diversity of meanings in the same word), a practice that appears in most languages. The causes for this phenomenon may be multiple, often arising more from historical accident than from some etymological basis. Thiselton illustrates his point by observing that just because "taste" in English, *gout* in French, *Geschmack* in German, and *gusto* in Italian all mean either "taste" in tasting food or else "taste" in aesthetic appreciation, it does not follow that good taste in society is connected with taste in the dining room. Even more significantly, this argument breaks down because most of the words that exhibit this alleged phenomenon of power are power-laden not due to the nature of the words themselves but because they are the words of God or of one of His prophets delivering His word. The authoritative one who delivers the words has power to effect what he says.

In the area of blessings and curses, a third mistake is committed, in Thiselton's judgment. It is not as if the words of blessing or curse as pronounced have power to do what they say in and of themselves; it is, rather, the fact that the appropriate person in the appropriate situation has spoken these words. A person without money, or a shipping company, possessing no influence, cannot go up to a great ship in a harbor and announce, "I name this ship *Queen Elizabeth III*." Those words have no effect and no power because they have been uttered by one who is the inappropriate person in an inappropriate situation, just as "I pronounce you husband and wife" has little force if the one pronouncing this "exercitive" has not been recognized by the state or some ecclesiastical body. The pronouncement is not automatically self-authenticating. True blessings and curses are actually prayers to God asking for God's gift to be bestowed. The words in themselves cannot be invested with a power as if they were separated from the source from which the result comes: namely, our Lord Himself.

Thiselton's fourth and final objection to this alleged power of the word is that language is not polarized around a "dianoetic" (i.e., words are known by their νοῦς = "thought") view of words versus a "dynamic" view of words. Such a view of language is too reductionistic and simplistic. Nothing is forcing us to choose between the view that says a word is only a vehicle for the purposes of intellectual self-expression and the view that says words appear as a material force.

Because of the strength of these four arguments, the view that there is some type of supposed power in the word as such must be abandoned. Blessings and curses were revocable; they are not controlled by humans apart from God. Neither the Hebrew דָּבָר nor the Greek ῥῆμα or λόγος gives any evidence for this thesis. Therefore, the simple uttering of the words of our mouths, be they words of a positive confession or words of a negative confession, cannot be linked with any type of magical power.

B. The Divine Promise of Wealth

The preoccupation of the gospel of affluence with material wealth is more of a sign of its sociological roots than of its biblical exegesis. In that regard, it runs counter to Paul's warning, "Do not conform any longer to the pattern of this world" (Rom. 12:1).

Current teaching on the biblical view of wealth is confusing to say the least. On the one hand we are being told "The New Testament condemns not just improper attitudes toward wealth, but also the mere possession of undistributed wealth."[15] On the other hand preachers like Brother Al and Reverend Ike urge us to "Serve God and get rich," for any who are living in poverty are living "a Satan-defeated life."

For Scripture, wealth in and of itself is not an evil but a gift of God. Wealth is not an end in itself for which a person must give all of his or her energies to achieve, for that would be an idolizing of the things of this world. Neither can the ills that sometimes accompany affluence be avoided merely by the removal of all these things, for some are either naturally or voluntarily poor but are proud of their poverty. Thus the same disease that afflicts some who idolize their possessions with a pride that replaces God Himself is shared with those who haughtily "thank God" that they have nothing to do with any of the stuff of this world and want all to recognize them for this virtue, which they hold as a badge of merit.

Few books of the Bible deal so fully with affluence and its problems as Deuteronomy. Moses warned that when the people were granted the gift of the good land into which the Lord their God was bringing them they might be tempted to forget the Lord (Deut. 8:17–18). The temptation would be to say that they had obtained all these good things by the works of their own hands (or, we could add, in the context of the gospel of affluence, by the positive confession of our mouths).

Deuteronomy 26 is especially significant in connecting Israel's obedience as a nation with God's spiritual and material blessings on that nation. Religion and the principles of economics were not separate realms, but they were bound together by the one and same Lord who promised that the nation would reap what it had sown.

Behind all of the Old Testament teaching on wealth was the principle that "The earth is the Lord's and everything in it" (Ps. 24:1). This meant that all things belonged to God, and He alone was the disposer of all that exists. Men and women were merely managers and stewards of what God had entrusted to them. The living God would hold all managers of His goods, large or small, accountable to Him for the way those goods were used and shared.

The mere possession of wealth was not in itself blameworthy or sinful; the problem lay in the use and in one's attitude toward what he or she possessed. Abraham was one of the great and wealthy men of antiquity; he had great possessions (Gen. 13:2, 6). Isaac, his son, had such wealth that he was the envy of the whole Philistine nation (26:12–14). Likewise, Jacob (28:13–15; 32:10), Job (Job 1:3; 42:10), and Solomon (1 Kings 3:13) enjoyed the same lap of luxury.

While the Old Testament prophets had much to say about wealth, they neither condemned wealth nor exalted poverty as a moral ideal. But like everything else in this world, great wealth could be abused—and it was.

This is not to say that the Old Testament was free of poverty or want. Neither did the writers of the Old Testament miss the fact that great wealth may result from unrighteous practices. Not all who deserve to be punished for the way they got their wealth or the way they failed to use it as good stewards of the grace of God immediately receive the swift divine judgment they and their misdeeds so richly deserved (e.g., Ps. 10). Yet it is the person who fears the Lord, delights in His commandments, and is generous with the poor who has riches in His house (112).

In Proverbs, wealth and the ability to gain riches are gifts that come from God but not without human industriousness and labor (Prov. 13:4; 14:23). Proverbs does emphasize the moral restraints that God has placed on gaining wealth. It is not to be achieved through deceit (21:6), or by using false balances (20:10), or by shifting boundary markers (22:28), or through oppression (23:10–11). Such wealth will prove to be a snare of death to those who touch it and a will-o'-the-wisp (21:6).

What is wrong, then, with the gospel of affluence theology? It is simply this: while wealth can be a blessing from God, it must not be overvalued. It cannot be made the sign of God's approval or the ultimate object of a believer's trust (11:28). When believers are arranging their values, they must remember that wisdom is more precious than jewels; nothing we could desire could compare with it (3:15).[16]

Thus it would appear that a legitimate concept of wealth and possessions has been taken and hyped to an exaggerated position without retaining the balance that it receives in its biblical context. The dangerous part of the logic of the affluent-gospel preachers is their assumption that if we are in God's will, we will be prosperous, no matter what! That is a heretical idea without scriptural foundation. This is not to say that poverty equals spirituality.[17] It does not!

Recently an attempt has been made to equate "the rich" in Proverbs with the oppressor. This is done by incorrectly assuming that Proverbs 22:2 and 29:13 are parallel passages.

> The rich and the poor meet together,
> The Lord is the maker of them all (22:2).

> The poor and the oppressor meet together,
> the Lord gives sight to the eyes of both of them (29:13, my translation).

G. W. Wittenberg[18] assumed that since the verbs, "meet together," were the same in both proverbs, and since both mentioned "the poor," then "the oppressor" of the second proverb must have replaced "the rich" of the previous proverb. Thus, according to Wittenberg, wealth was a desirable asset and a blessing so long as it was connected with the agriculturalist. But a change came in the book of Proverbs when a money economy (implied in those proverbs in the book which treat wealth from a negative point of view) was introduced along with the merchant class! Money acquired through commerce, trade, and other financial transactions, it was inferred, would dissipate rapidly. While this contrast between the agriculturalist and the merchant is not always clearly expressed in Proverbs, allowed Wittenberg, it can be deduced because of the substituted word *oppressor* where once "rich" had stood in an earlier proverb.

Years ago Milton Terry advised biblical exegetes to determine in every case whether the passages adduced as parallels were really parallel. He warned that there were many similarities of sentiment that were not actually parallel. Said he:

> Proverbs xxii,2, and xxix,13, are usually taken as parallels, but a close inspection will show that though there is a marked similarity of sentiment, there is no

essential identity or real parallelism. . . . Here the *man of oppressions* is not necessarily a rich man; nor is *enlightener of the eyes* an equivalent of *maker* in xxii,2. Hence, all that can be properly said of these two passages is, that they are similar in sentiment, but not strictly parallel or identical in sense.[19]

Thus we cannot follow Wittenberg in his reassigning the Proverbs to older and later materials and in his reevaluation of poverty and wealth. There is no evidence that the Israelite authors reacted against the Canaanite commercial practices of their day and thus reacted against all forms of wealth because of this bad experience.

The importance of grasping the biblical concept of prosperity and how it has been distorted today can hardly be overemphasized. For example, David Harrell assures us that the doctrine of prosperity has come to be "the most important new idea of the charismatic revival," a teaching that has "almost supplanted the earlier emphasis on healing."[20] Even though the Faith Movement did not originate this emphasis (McConnell has given abundant evidence that E. W. Kenyon is the real father of this emphasis[21]), it has gained some of its most vigorous exponents in this group in recent years. Their exorbitant claims for material prosperity have become one of the main reasons for the fantastic growth of the movement.

According to McConnell, the teachings of these aberrant faith teachers fall into two types: (1) an *"egocentric* teaching on prosperity," which promises prosperity from God for those who support the evangelist's ministry; and (2) a *"cosmic* teaching on prosperity," which centers on the alleged universal principles of material blessing that God has set in the universe.[22]

The personality cult of the leaders of the health, wealth, and prosperity syndrome is a fairly well recognized phenomenon today. What is less well known is the claim that God has established certain laws governing prosperity in His Word that function as certainly as such physical laws in the universe as gravity. However, in the case of the laws of prosperity, it is our faith that causes these laws to function. Thus some refer to the "seed of faith" while others prefer to hawk "success formulas." These so-called laws are set in motion by a positive mental attitude and a positive confession. One need only to say "whatever their li'l ol' heart desires" and it will happen! This is because of the alleged power of the word, a concept we have already found to be without any scriptural basis.

Not only does this concept verge on the use of occult powers, it openly espouses such! Ralph Waldo Trine, E. W. Kenyon's classmate, taught: "This is the law of prosperity. . . . To hold yourself in this attitude of mind is to set into operation subtle, silent and irresistible forces that will sooner or later actualize in material form that which is today merely an idea. But ideas have occult power, and . . are seeds that actualize material conditions."[23] While most faith teachers would reject the use of the occult, they must, as McConnell warned *"come to grips with the fact that those who began the practices of positive mental attitude and positive confession attributed their ability to acquire riches to psychic and occultic powers."*[24]

It is fairly easy to show from a New Testament point of view how the Faith Theology is a distorted view of "need." Prosperity teachers tend to equate "your

Father knows what you need before you ask" (Matt. 6:8) with "everything our li'l ol' heart wants." But Jesus pointed to only three needs: food, drink, and clothing (Matt. 6:8–32). Paul advised, "If we have food and clothing, with these we shall be content" (1 Tim. 6:8).

But the Old Testament presents a somewhat more difficult case, since many tend to grab at a phrase, clause, or sentence here or there without taking the trouble to isolate the context in which it was given. Especially vulnerable are the Proverbs. This book, however, "is no 'how-to-do-it' manual; it is a program of character-building, which is the devoted occupation of a lifetime. It is not meant for the casual tourist. . . ."[25] Wealth may be one of God's blessings, but it is only one. There are inherent dangers to possessing wealth and security, or divine approval must not be unilaterally linked with it. So far as Proverbs is concerned, the primary agenda in life is to attain wisdom and to live in the fear of the Lord. That goal supersedes all others.

C. The Divine Curse of Poverty

All too quickly do prosperity-gospel preachers link Paul's statement in Galatians 3:13, "Christ has redeemed us from the curse of the law," with the curses mentioned in Deuteronomy 28:15–68, which include sickness, poverty, and death.

Once again we are being told that we have parallel passages when we do not have anything of the sort. Paul's concern was with a right standing before God. The curse we were redeemed from was the eternal death to which our sins were leading us until the Messiah came and took the penalty of death, which our sins had earned, and hung upon a tree for us (an act which in itself showed the person so treated to be himself accursed [Deut. 21:22–23]). But this is an entirely different matter from Israel's failure to keep the moral law of God as a nation and for which it exposed itself to the increasingly more devastating judgments of God. These judgments were evidences that God still loved that nation and that He wanted it to return to Him. But in no way were they the start of God's final judgment for individual failure to believe on Him as one's redeemer. Only those who had already accepted the Man of Promise who was to come could be expected to live in the nation as one who obeyed the voice of God.

The book of Proverbs traces a realistic picture of the poor. Unfortunately, poverty earns very few friends (Prov 19:4). Even one's own relatives shun the poor (v. 7), with the further galling state of affairs in which the rich rule over the poor (22:7). The cry of the poor falls on deaf ears (18:23), and they are often the prey of all sorts of murderous hoodlums (30:14).

There are some practical pieces of advice, however. Solomon does not claim that those who are in the grip of poverty are there because of the grip of sin on their lives or because they have not "named it and claimed it [riches]." Some have gotten into the clutches of poverty through lazy hands (10:4; 12:24), ignoring correction and discipline (11:18; 13:18), stinginess and withholding aid to those in need (11:24; 22:16; 28:22), sleeping too much (10:5; 20:13; 24:33), wickedness (11:25), gluttony and drunkenness (23:20–21), and concealing sin (28:13). But to be fair, there are others who are poor who have not deserved what has happened to them. It is only because of the providential will of God that these people are poor (20:12; 22:2; 29:13). The poor are not to be judged (24:23; 28:21), exploited (22:22–23; 28:3), or mocked (17:5). Instead, those who are not poor are to speak up in behalf of the poor (31:8–9) and defend their rights.

Scripture gives no aid to the view that poverty is in all its forms a result of the judgment of God and an evidence that the persons so afflicted are outside the will of God. Such a universal categorization is a caricature of the biblical position.[26]

D. The Divine Promise of Healing

The assumption of advocates of the health and wealth gospel is that it is never the will of God for anyone ever to be sick. Healing comes through the exercise of faith. One must only "name it and claim it" or "believe it and receive it."

Believers under the influence of this "Gospel" are taught to talk to the disease. The mere commanding the disease with authority to be gone is sufficient to effect the healing itself.

When questioned about a biblical basis for such action, the assumed power of words will be reintroduced or such Old Testament passages as Isaiah 53 and Deuteronomy 28. Since we have already dealt with the alleged power of words at some length and the inappropriateness of contending that Galatians 3:13 has canceled out the curse of sickness threatened in Deuteronomy 28, we should focus on the Old Testament texts that are said to provide the promise of healing and the prospect of perpetual health.

Psalm 103:3 promises, "He forgives all my sins and heals all my diseases." But the psalmist uses a word for "diseases" that appears only three times in the entire Old Testament. In both Deuteronomy 29:22 and 2 Chronicles 21:19, it refers to distress that God sends as a judgment for sin. This is not to say that all sickness is retributive and the direct result of personal sin in one's life, for this is to argue the same way as Job's three "friends"—a procedure that brought the stern rebuke of God at the close of the book (Job 42:7). But it is to say that Psalm 103:3 cannot be used to claim that God heals all diseases.

The most frequently quoted passage, however, is Isaiah 53:4–5:

> Surely he took up our infirmities
> and carried our sorrows,
> yet we considered him stricken by God,
> smitten by him, and afflicted.
> But he was pierced for our transgressions,
> he was crushed for our iniquities;
> the punishment that brought us peace was upon him,
> and by his wounds we are healed.

As if to clinch the argument, Matthew cites this passage after a series of healings (8:16–17) saying that it happened so that what Isaiah the prophet spoke might be fulfilled.

However, the points that need to be demonstrated are these. Even if our Lord did perform a series of healing ministries as a fulfillment of what was spoken by Isaiah, was this more than a foretaste of the total restoration that was to come when our Lord returned the second time in all His glory? In other words, can it be shown that what was inaugurated during the earthly ministry of our Lord was meant to be continued in the absence of our Lord? We think not. Not everything that was won by our Lord in His atonement was fully realized immediately, for as Romans 8:22 observes, the whole creation is waiting for its release and final redemption at the second coming of our Lord.

If the redemption won for us on the cross by our Lord also provided full and complete release from all diseases from the first day we believed forward, how would death or even the slightest trace of debilitating disease have any effect over a Christian? To concede the point on the slightest appearance of disease or death would be to throw in doubt the whole case on which our salvation rested.

We conclude that there is healing in the atonement; we only contest how and when it is fully applicable. We think that believers will be finally delivered from the dread of disease only when our Lord has put all enemies under His feet, even death itself at the conclusion of the millennium (1 Cor. 15: 25–26).[27]

E. The Divine Promise of Success

The main passage which is leaned on for support of this promise is Joshua 1:8. Surely prosperity and success are offered in this text, but what kind of success and to whom is it offered?

The promise given to Joshua was the continuation of the Abrahamic covenant in which Israel was to inherit the land. The success was military, not specifically financial. The condition was the observance of the law of God.

The psalmist David likewise spoke of many benefits as coming from obeying the law of God, but he never listed material prosperity as one of them. God did promise wisdom, discernment, peace, insight, comfort, encouragement, and the like, but there was never an encouragement to delight in the law of the Lord in order to get rich or to obtain more possessions.

It is true, of course, that there are spiritual principles that are to be derived from texts like Joshua 1:8, but these must be in the same area as the abstract principle that stands behind the Old Testament illustration being offered in the context under consideration. To do otherwise would be to lapse into spiritualization and crude allegorizing of the text, devices that have proven to be most harmful to the church in the past. In this case, the principle would seem to be the centrality of the Word of God in the life of the community. The success that will come from adherence to that Word begins in the spiritual realm and then moves out to those areas featured in the covenant under discussion in this passage.

CONCLUSION

The message of health, wealth, and prosperity theologians is a bogus gospel. It cannot command the support of Scripture or of the believing community's previous experience of the work of the Holy Spirit.

In fact, it falls most tragically on the very texts and theological principles it wishes to establish. There is no basis for a so-called power of the word apart from the only One who can fill that word with power, our Lord Jesus Himself.

Neither can we affirm that the "curse" from which we have been redeemed (Gal. 3:13) are the "curses" (note the change to the plural) of Deuteronomy 28. The context of Galatians is soteriological whereas the context of Deuteronomy is national and experiential. The curses that Moses mentions were to be visited upon Israel as a judgment from God on those who claimed to be His own children. Nowhere does Scripture argue that all illness is the result of specific sin. And even if it did, that is not what Deuteronomy 28 is talking about.

We do believe in the power of the Word of God but not the power of our own words. We do believe in the blessing of possessions and wealth as a gift that may come in the providence of God but not in talking them into existence as an act of self-will. We do believe in healing as a gift from God; sickness, however, is not always a sign that a person is out of the will of God, and the use of medicine and doctors is not a sign of a lack of faith in God's ability directly to intervene apart from secondary agencies. And we do believe that God promised to carry out every aspect of His pledge to Abraham and David; but this does not mean that believers have a carte blanche and an automatic guarantee of success for whatever they attempt under any and all conditions.

The prosperity gospel is a cultural captive of our affluent, success-crazy society. We recommend that we return to God's standards for success, prosperity, health, and wealth. There are pieces of the truth in most of the claims made by those who espouse one aspect or another in the affluent gospel, but like most heresy, the false parts are accepted in the name of the small kernel of biblical truth found in each claim. What is needed is less prooftexting over random passages taken from here and there in the Scriptures. Instead, we need to develop large teaching passages on each of these themes and see what Scripture teaches in its wholeness, rather than in just an assortment of bits and pieces quoted randomly from texts with authoritative assurances that that is what the texts mean in these contexts. We need more teaching from the Word on this subject, not less. And a large part of the teaching on this subject will be found in that part of the canon where contemporary Christians and pastors are the weakest and most negligent in their preaching, namely, the Old Testament.

CHAPTER THREE

BURDEN, BARRIER, BLASPHEMY: WEALTH IN MATTHEW 6:33, LUKE 14:33, AND LUKE 16:15

Thomas E. Schmidt

The danger and proper use of wealth is far and away the most common ethical subject in the Synoptic Gospels. The subject accounts for just over 10 percent of the total content of Luke and about 5 percent each of Mark and Matthew. Twenty percent of the parables of Jesus deal directly with the use of wealth. The gospel writers demonstrate thereby a strong interest in preserving this material for application to a late-first-century audience. It had relevance for them beyond the period of Jesus' ministry, beyond the first generation of believers.

The late-twentieth-century audience encounters the hostility of Jesus toward wealth through filters accumulated over several centuries. Most of the standard evangelical interpretations of key passages can be traced historically to Puritan England, where an increase in the general level of prosperity encouraged accommodation of the biblical message to the situation of the audience. The sting of Jesus' teaching was removed by some interpreters either by making it too situation-specific to affect the later audience or by spiritualizing possessions so that they would only "appear" to be retained by the believer: in "reality" they were in God's hands. Wealth as evidence of divine favor was seen as the dominant biblical view, and Jesus provided, at worst, an exception that could be accounted for in one of several inexpensive ways. Today's popular health and wealth gospel may involve only the attachment of a new (designer) label on a well-worn garment. With a higher and more common level of prosperity, and without the checks of Puritan standards of modesty, charity, and personal discipline, the recently evolved form of the justification of wealth is damaging in ways never envisioned by the Puritans.

Political agendas and the tendency toward self-justifying exegesis are not the only challenges for the interpreter of Jesus' teaching about wealth. One of the most insidious barriers to the appreciation of any one passage is the nagging thought that there is some other passage or some other explanation that would, if known, diffuse the tension. The temptation is, therefore, to anticipate and respond to all possible exceptions, opposing texts, and counterarguments. But comprehensiveness is impossible in this context, and I can only warn against the fallacy of interpretation by exception. My approach will be simply to advance arguments for the expression of a negative view of wealth in three texts: Matthew 6:33, Luke 14:33, and Luke 16:15. These three were chosen for two reasons: they are three of the strongest statements of Jesus, and they are three of the most commonly misconstrued passages on the subject. My hope is that by offering insight into the meaning of these texts the reader will encounter them on their own merits and will find an impetus for further research into the biblical view of the nature and use of wealth. I have included a closing section to help the reader to understand how the message of these texts may fit into a larger picture of New Testament ethics.

I. MATTHEW 6:33 – SEQUENCE OR PRIORITY?

Therefore do not be anxious, saying, "What shall we eat?" or "What shall we drink?" or "What shall we wear?" For the Gentiles seek all these things, and your heavenly Father knows that you need them all. *But seek first his kingdom and his righteousness, and all these things shall be yours* as well (Matt. 6:31–33).

The text and its context are familiar. Verse 9 begins a series of strong exhortations whose intent may be clarified by rephrasing. The disciple of Jesus should give away possessions instead of storing them (vv. 19–20). His action in this regard will reveal his inner disposition (v. 21) and will in fact reveal his salvation or damnation (vv. 22–23), because he can retain only one master at a time—God or his possessions (v. 24). If he is obedient to this radical demand, he will naturally become anxious (v. 25), but he should trust that the God who supplies His creation with sufficient sustenance will supply him as well (vv. 26–30).[1]

Despite the apparent simplicity of the conclusion of the section, it contains some knotty problems whose solution will determine the interpretation and application of the entire passage. Does "anxious" (μεριμνάω [vv. 25, 27, 31, 34]) denote internal agitation only or does it involve an active element (synonymous with "seek," ζητέω [vv. 32–33]) as well? Does the activity implied by the word "seek" involve prayer only or other works as well? Does "his righteousness" in verse 33 mean godly conduct or the establishment of God's justice? Is the passage aimed at people who are potentially anxious due to the natural uncertainties of life or due to the unusual demands implied by Jesus in the Sermon? Finally, what of "first" (πρῶτον)? Does it denote sequence or priority? And if it denotes priority, is it a priority that excludes other priorities? Another way to articulate these questions is to diagram interpretive alternatives for verse 33:

a		Itinerant disciples			
b	All	disciples			
c			should	pray for	
d			should	work for	
e					obedience
f					the eschaton,
g	then they				
h	in order that they				
i			may pray for	material provision.
j			may work for	material provision.
k			might receive	material provision.

I will argue that the most promising combinations, in order of the likely intent of the Gospel, are:

$$b + c + f + h + k$$
$$b + d + f + h + k$$
$$b + c + e + h + k$$

A. Verses 25–34 as Inference

Before moving sequentially through the verse, it is necessary to address the question posed above about the connection of the verse to its context; and more particularly, we must consider the connection between verses 24 and 25. Verses 25–34, commonly labeled the "Trust or Anxiety" teaching, are in Matthew introduced by διὰ τοῦτο as an inference from the preceding material.[2] This connection is usually ignored, with the result that the Trust or Anxiety passage is considered as an independent unit or as the continuation of a series of related sayings. As an independent passage, it is easy to see it as a response to the normal exigencies of (especially peasant) life in first-century Palestine. But when verses 19–24 are made subordinate to verses 24–34 by διὰ τοῦτο, the passage takes on a different character. The sequence of thought is unclear unless some statement implied by the context is inserted between verses 24 and 25, since it makes little sense to infer "Do not be anxious" from "Do not accumulate wealth." Indeed, we would expect the opposite inference! The most natural statement to supply, therefore, is "Obedience to this [vv. 19–24] will make you dependent on God's provision for your survival." This implied statement is logically parallel to the latter part of verse 32, which *follows* the repetition of the command not to be anxious with reassurance that God knows (and will provide for) the needs of His children. This consolation is not a response to the human condition, then, but to the peculiar condition of those who have put into action verses 19–24.

B. The Relation Between "Anxious" and "Seek"

In order to gain a clearer picture of the meaning of ζητέω in verse 33, it is necessary to understand μεριμνάω, which is employed three times in the passage (vv. 25, 31, 34). Are the two verbs interchangeable? The movement of thought from verse 31 to verse 33 would seem to suggest so. There the contrast is between "you" who are not to be *anxious* and "the Gentiles" who *seek* "all these things." Verse 33 begins with a positive restatement of verse 31, using ζητέω, and verse 34 restates the thought again in negative form, using μεριμνάω. It appears that the texts could be rewritten, "Do not seek what to eat[3] . . . for the Gentiles are anxious about all these things. . . . Be anxious first for the kingdom. . . . Do not seek for tomorrow. . . ." The existing word choice may be due to the generally negative connotation of μεριμνάω[4] coupled with the neutral or even positive[5] connotation of ζητέω. The Hebrew word ראג probably lies behind μεριμνάω. Among the important parallels are Hillel's warning, "The more possessions, the more anxiety" (ראג—*m. 'Abot* 2:7) and Ezekiel's pronunciation of judgment, "Son of man, eat your bread with trembling, and drink your water with quivering and anxiety" (Ezek. 12:18).[6]

The latter text presents an interesting possibility for speculation: is Jesus' repeated warning against anxiety over food and drink an allusion to Ezekiel's curse? If the similarity of vocabulary is intentional, a further step might be taken to suggest that anxiety accrues from transgression (Ezek. 2:3), specifically here with respect to possessions: disciples who will not trust in God for sustenance when they renounce possessions are punished by agitation. It may be significant that in Ezekiel, by contrast, the obedient prophet receives satisfaction when he *eats* the scroll on which God's words are written (Ezek. 2:8–3:2). The kingdom gives complete satisfaction.

Two other parallels increase the likelihood that Matthew 6:25–34 alludes to specific Old Testament passages about trust in God for material provision. They are Exodus 15:24, "And the people murmured against Moses, saying, 'What shall we drink?'" and Leviticus 25:20, "What shall we eat in the seventh year, if we may not sow or gather in our crop?"[7] Both of these texts employ an interrogative form to express the anxiety resulting in lack of trust, and the response in both cases is, significantly, miraculous material provision. Together with the explicit references to anxiety (ראג) cited above, these texts suggest that the anxious person is one who fails to trust God for his material provision in a crisis.

The texts cited above are joined by Matthew 10:19, the only Matthean occurrence of μεριμνάω outside 6:25–34, to suggest that internal agitation is the most likely meaning of μεριμνάω in this context. There are other occurrences of μεριμνάω with a more active connotation,[8] but they are not close to this context. The metaphors in verses 26–30 imply a lack of labor, not a lack of internal agitation,[9] but these are grounds for the command not to be anxious (οὖν–v. 31), not restatements of the command. Thus the metaphors are logically parallel to verses 9–24: they describe the person who is obedient to the requirement of dependence on God for material provision. The anxious person is one who has either obeyed or considers obeying but, lacking complete trust, is agitated about the implications of such radical obedience.

How does this conclusion affect the interchangeability of μεριμνάω and ζητέω and the meaning of the latter in verse 33? It is possible to substitute "be preoccupied" for both words without doing injustice to either. In 5:6, significantly, the metaphors "hunger and thirst" are used to express a strong desire for righteousness. In 7:7, ζητέω is used for prayer. In the Lord's Prayer itself, strong desire is expressed for His kingdom ("Thy kingdom come") and His righteousness ("Thy will be done"). These factors combine to suggest that in this context, at least for the believer, fulfillment of the command to seek involves primarily internal desire and the activity of prayer. This is not to suggest that activity will end with the experience of desire and the expression of that desire in prayer. The implication of subsequent or concomitant activity is strong enough that we might grant it expression as a legitimate "minority view." But the stronger position is that ζητέω in verse 33 is intended to denote primarily, if not strictly, internal activity, and more specifically, prayer. This conclusion will have important implications later as we consider the overall argument of the verse.

C. Righteousness as Conduct or Vindication

There is some validity to the argument that the phrase "and his righteousness" refers to God's future vindication rather than to godly conduct on the part of believers, as it is usually understood. The Beatitudes, generally speaking, offer promises for the future kingdom rather than for the present period of persecution. They also tend to offer rewards that correspond (usually ironically) to a prescribed behavior or attitude. References to God's righteousness in the Old Testament often occur in the context of promises of the vindication of His elect, and the word in some cases is virtually synonymous with the provision of justice, or salvation.[10] Applying these observations to Matthew 5:6, it appears that the righteousness for which one is to hunger and thirst is not moral rectitude in daily life but vindication in the kingdom; accordingly, the satisfaction offered is not existential but eschatological. This idea might be strengthened by reference to 6:10, where the believer prays ("hungers and thirsts") that "Thy will be done on earth as it is in heaven." This may be understood as a request not that the believer be empowered now for obedience (like that which occurs now in heaven) but that God might "expand his active jurisdiction" from heaven to earth. The petition is then a natural parallel to "Thy kingdom come," not a change in subject matter.[11]

Applying all of this to 6:33, the command to "seek . . . the kingdom and his righteousness" looks very much like the twofold petition in the Lord's Prayer; and even if the similarity is coincidental, the pronoun αὐτοῦ makes a reference here to human conduct doubtful. Although it is grammatically possible that the genitive αὐτοῦ is qualitative ("seek godly righteousness"), the contrasting use of ὑμῶν with δικαιοσύνη in 5:20 and 6:1 constitutes a compelling argument for a subjective genitive in this instance ("seek for God to be righteous").[12] The καί between "kingdom" and "righteousness" is then explicative rather than continuative. In other words, the terms define one another: "Seek the kingdom: that is to say, seek his righteousness." This is consistent with the images of Paul (Phil. 3:12–14) and the writer to the Hebrews (Heb. 12:1–2) in which runners focus on the end of the race (rather than the road or their own feet). The disciple must keep his eyes on the prize.

The connotation of δικαιοσύνη in 6:33, then, is primarily eschatological. This is of course not to deny the ethical dimension of the *command*: to seek the eschaton is indeed a *righteous* thing to do. Furthermore, the strictly ethical connotation of δικαιοσύνη elsewhere in the sermon (5:10; 5:20; 6:1) requires that we allow for some measure of overlap in this instance between the ethical and eschatological dimensions of the word. Referring again to the diagram of preferred interpretations offered above, the ethical interpretation of δικαιοσύνη receives status as a serious second choice.

D. "First": Sequence or Primacy?

The key word for the interpretation of Matthew 6:33 is the adverb πρῶτον. Precisely what does it mean to seek *first*? If it indicates sequence, must we rewrite 6:24: "Serve God, then serve Mammon"?

In twenty-three of the twenty-four other uses in Matthew, πρῶτον should be understood in its primary sense as an indicator of sequence. If that sense applies in 6:33, it will be proper for the disciple to give time to the work of the kingdom before giving time to the work of material provision. In terms of chronology, this may mean that a period of each day should be given to God. This would correspond somewhat to the "day" language of the Lord's Prayer and of 6:34. Alternately, a disciple might give a period or recurrent periods of his life to God. This would correspond somewhat to the apparent return of the disciples of Jesus to the fishing trade (John 21:3) or to Paul's self-supporting business. Furthermore, there is a neat correspondence between the sequence of the petitions of the Lord's Prayer and 6:33: the petition for daily bread follows the petition for the eschaton. These factors have given rise to the traditional view of sequence or the higher critical view that Matthew "softens" Q material here. But chronological sequence is not the only possible nuance of πρῶτον, and another Matthean passage parallel in structure to this passage offers ground to consider an alternative sense.[13]

In Matthew 23:26, Jesus exhorts the Pharisees, "First cleanse the inside of the cup and of the plate, that the outside may also be clean." Here the "first" action is in fact the only action, or the means to the end in view. The similarity in content and structure to 6:33 suggests that primacy, not sequence, is intended. In Gundry's words, "the adverb is emphatic rather than permissive."[14]

The question follows: is this primacy or priority exclusive? That is, can the disciple put aside even for a moment the work of the kingdom in order to labor to put food on the table? If this is the case, we must surely define the word *disciple* in such a way as to exclude almost everyone, including Paul and perhaps some of the Twelve.

The conclusion drawn earlier that to seek means primarily to desire becomes important at this juncture. If to seek is to work, and to work *first* is to work to the exclusion of other activities, there are serious practical objections to the demand, whichever nuance one chooses for ζητέω. If we take it in the ethical sense, one must apparently not lift a finger to earn one's bread. If we take it in the eschatological sense, we produce the unnatural implication that disciples bring about the end by their deeds, which are still left undefined. If, on the other hand, to seek is to be preoccupied (and to express this in prayer), the constituents of the verse begin to fit together. If the kingdom is the disciple's exclusive inward activity, he may engage in it whatever his outward activity. His outward activity will not matter: whether or not he labors for material sustenance, or however long he labors, God will provide sufficient sustenance. This is consistent with the stress on inward righteousness in the sermon, with Paul's pattern of making labor subservient to ministry and with the various New Testament vocational models ranging from dependent itinerants to independent village artisans (1 Thess. 4:11).

Taking into consideration the secondary implication granted earlier—that some measure of activity is implied in ζητέω—the connection to the Lord's Prayer (and to 7:11) is more clear. Just as the petition to see the eschaton will necessarily find expression in consonant actions, so the petition for daily bread will be accompanied by consonant actions. But it must be stressed both that the request is for *daily bread* and not for *financial security* and that the consonant actions do not necessarily involve steady employment. The promise is clear, that the disciple whose obsession is with the kingdom will not be bothered by want. He may or may not labor for bread. If he does not because he is doing the work of the kingdom, his minimal needs will be met by God through others. Alternately, labor for sustenance may be a recurrent but not full-time activity for him, as it is for the birds. In either case, his attitude is carefree. While others are anxious and troubled about many things, he recognizes that only one thing is necessary.

Since the command does not exclude labor for material provision, the inevitable challenge in practice will be to distinguish kingdom-preoccupation from pietistic justification of security-preoccupation. The check on the tendency to the latter provided by the passage is the connection to verses 19–24: 6:33 *presupposes* radical conduct with regard to possessions. Obedience in this regard, then, is not altogether unobservable: the position of the treasure indicates the position of the heart, not vice versa (6:21).

II. LUKE 14:33: HAS THE COST ALREADY BEEN COUNTED?

For which of you, desiring to build a tower, does not first sit down and count the cost, whether he has enough to complete it? Otherwise, when he has laid a foundation, and is not able to finish, all who see it begin to mock him, saying, "This man began to build, and was not able to finish." Or what king, going to encounter another king in war, will not sit down first and take counsel whether he is able with ten thousand to meet him who comes against him with twenty thousand? And if not, while the other is yet a great way off, he sends an embassy and asks terms of peace. *So therefore, whoever of you does not renounce all that he has cannot be my disciple* (Luke 14:28–33).

This section, often entitled "Counting the Cost" or "The Cost of Discipleship," is part of Luke's central section (chaps. 9–19), nearly half of which deals with the nature and use of wealth. The parable of the great banquet dominates chapter 14, and it presents some interesting questions about the continuity of the chapter. If the "excuse makers" and the "disenfranchised" of the parable represent simply those who reject and those who accept Jesus, respectively, the ethical instruction given to banqueters in verses 7–14 appears out of place. In verses 7–11, banquet-goers are instructed take humble places. In verses 12–14, banquet-givers are instructed to invite guests of humble station. Why follow this with a parable in which wealth and poverty are mere literary devices for rejection and acceptance of Jesus? The answer is that ethical and soteriological questions were not distinct. Activity at banquets was expressive of one's eternal destination, and the decision to reject or accept the invitation to the kingdom was quite consistent with social position. Thus when we conclude that the unifying theme of 24 is that a person ought to "humble" himself, the word must be understood in terms of both inward orientation and outward manifestation. There is good reason to include the remainder of the chapter under this heading in spite of the change in setting from a banquet to a general outdoor address. The demand for personal sacrifice in order to achieve a reward from God is clearly common to both sections; and more specifically, the sacrifice in both sections will result in voluntary association with (if not actual identity as) the poor. Beyond this, there is even a formal similarity. In verses 8–12 and in the parables of verses 28–32, the demand to humble oneself is followed by a warning (introduced by μήποτε in vv. 8, 12, and 29) of public shame, expressed in discourse. Verse 11 (perhaps restated in the last part of

v. 26 and v. 17) is the key command; the rest of the chapter is specification and supporting argument. Interestingly, the same structure of two parables on the theme of possessions with a central command occurs in chapter 12 (v. 21 as "center") and in chapter 16 (v. 9 as "center"). This may be expressive of Luke's "orderly" (ἀκριβῶς–1:3) accounting. In any case, the structure serves here to draw attention to verses 7–24 as important for the understanding of verses 5–33.

At first glance, verse 33 appears to be an overly specific inference from the parables of verses 28–32. The explanation for this is found in the connection to verses 25–27. Just before the parables, Luke quotes the double-tradition (Matt. 10:37) demand to put loyalty to Jesus ahead of loyalty to family and the triple-tradition demand to take up one's cross and follow Jesus (Mark 8:34; Matt. 10:38; Luke 9:23–25). All of the demands are expressed in formulaic fashion: "Whoever does not do X cannot be my disciple." Verse 27 is the general command and verses 6 and 33 are its specifications: necessary practical implementations of verse 27. These specifics are common enough in the Gospels, and they are joined in 18:29. The pattern in this section is B-A-B, with the parables intervening between the last two. This structure may seem odd to the modern reader, but it is the only structure that will allow for both a central position of the general command and a single inferential command following the parables. The logical relation to the parables is confirmed grammatically by the γάρ connecting the parables as the ground of verse 27 and the οὖν connecting verse 33 as inference from the parables.

These contextual considerations help to establish the general import of 14:33, but they leave several important questions. The parables themselves appear to present the rather odd notion that an individual calculates in advance whether or not he has "what it takes" to become a follower of Jesus. If this standard explanation is correct, it is very difficult to see a connection to the commands in verses 26–27 and 33. Do the parables argue that personal resources are prerequisite or a barrier to discipleship? The vocabulary of verse 33 itself introduces a series of questions. Does "renounce" require physical separation or only mental detachment (including "readiness" to renounce)? Does "all that he has" mean material possessions or earthly attachments in general? Does "disciple" denote anyone who will enter the kingdom or only those (like the Twelve) with a particular vocation? The options can be charted as follows:

a   Adequate resources are necessary; therefore
b   Adequate resources are unavailable; therefore
c   leave behind
d   practice mental detachment from
e   all material possessions
f   all earthly attachments
g   in order to enter the kingdom
h   in order to fulfill a special calling

I will argue more narrowly here than in the case of Matthew 6:33, contending that the first alternative in each pair is the only viable option: a + c + e + g.

A. Counting the Cost (Verses 28–32)

The familiar explanation of the parables is that one should deliberate concerning one's resources before embarking on the road of discipleship. In the words of Jeremias, "Do not act without mature consideration, for a thing half done is worse than a thing never begun."[15] There are two objections to this explanation. First, it presents an exception to the normal call to discipleship, which is characterized elsewhere by decisive, nondeliberative action. Secondly, it makes the parables virtually irrelevant to the supplied conclusion. We should expect a consonant summary, such as, "Therefore, you must choose from the beginning to endure to the end." Instead, we find a resumption of the "humble yourself" theme. Do the conclusions—verses 26–27, 33—match the parables?

Jülicher came nearer to an acceptable understanding of the passage when he argued that both parables stress complete sacrifice as necessary to accomplish an important task.[16] The weakness of this understanding was noted by Wellhausen, who pointed out that verse 33 requires the opposite: instead of committing all of one's resources to the task, one must abandon one's resources.[17] Jülicher's explanation meets this objection if the parables' conclusion is meant to be ironic, but this is probably overly subtle.

It is possible to understand the parables in a new way by stressing their linguistic connection to the conclusion rather than the phrase "count the cost." The key is the idea of *ability*. In verses 26, 27, and 33, one is or is not able (δύναται) to be a disciple. In verse 31 the king must be able (εἰ δυνατός; cf. εἰ ἕξει in verse 28) to meet the opposing army. The implication in both parables is that the subjects do not have sufficient resources and that they will be mocked if they begin the task. Here the formal similarity to verse 8 (cf. v. 12) becomes important. In verse 8 the one who acts on the assumption of the adequacy of his resources (takes the place of honor) will be mocked (told to sit in a lower place). If, however, he begins by renouncing his resources (taking the lower place), he will be a disciple (moved to a place of honor). The connection between the parables of verses 8–32 and their conclusions is more clear if we state the conclusions in converse form: "Reliance on one's own inadequate resources precludes discipleship." The theme is hardly strange to Luke's gospel: in 17:28–33, ties to family and possessions preclude readiness for the judgment day, and in 12:16–34 and 16:9–12, disciples are urged to get rid of possessions which pose an encumbrance in the present crisis. The οὕτως with which verse 33 begins, then, refers not to the beginnings of the parables, which depict cost-counting, but to their endings, which depict humiliation and failure. As tower-building or war-making with inadequate resources are doomed, so discipleship with the encumbrances of family and possessions is doomed. Humble yourself and you will be exalted: renounce tower- and war-making and you will escape ridicule; renounce family and possessions and you will be rewarded.

B. The Nature of Renunciation

The verb ἀποτάσσομαι is used only here in the New Testament teachings about wealth. When not employing figurative language, the passages employ the formulaic "sell and give."[18] In narrative passages, disciples "leave" (ἀφίημι) possessions.[19] ἀποτάσσομαι is employed in several synoptic passages to denote physical separation from persons or things.[20] Its use in earlier and contemporary literature sheds light on its meaning here. In Philo the word is employed several times, including two passages that express hostility to wealth:

> . . . [N]ot only does [Moses] *renounce* the whole belly, but with it scours away the feet, that is, the supports of pleasure. . . . We must not fail to notice that Moses, when he refuses the entire belly, that is the filling of the stomach, he practically renounces the other passions too [*Leg. All.*, 3.142–45].

> Have you won the Olympic crown of victory over all wealth, and so risen superior to all that wealth involves, that you accept nothing of what it brings for your use and enjoyment?. . . Will you see all the treasuries of wealth, one after the other, full to the brim, yet turn aside from them and avert your eyes? . . . For (a celestial and heavenly soul) taking its fill of the vision of incorruptible and genuine goods, *bids farewell* to the transient and spurious [*Deus*, 147–51].[21]

The consistent sense of ἀποτάσσομαι in the literature of the period, together with the connotation of physical separation in 14:26 (cf. 9:61 and 18:28–29), requires the translation "give up" (NIV, NASB, JB) or "part with" (NEB, Modern Language). "Leave behind" is better yet because it conveys the sense of the word while suggesting a connection to the relevant narrative passages.

The notion that mere readiness is allowed by the use of the present tense[22] is grammatically groundless and contextually meaningless: narrative and didactic material make it clear that readiness must be demonstrated by action. Applying the "readiness" notion to other positive New Testament commands (evangelism, hospitality, unity, etc.) shows its inadequacy as a principle of behavioral expectation. To define action as readiness, or worse, to define inaction as potential action, is to mock the process of sanctification: "Not that I have reached the goal or even that I press on toward it, but I remain perpetually willing to do so if it ever becomes necessary."

C. The Identity of Possessions

"All that he has" (πᾶσιν τοῖς ἑαυτοῦ ὑπάρχουσιν) has been generalized to include

> . . . not merely money and material things, but also his dear ones and everything that his heart clings to, yea, even his own life, his own desires, plans, ideals and interests.[23]

The exegetical error here is the failure to recognize verse 13 as a specification of the general command of verse 27. This requires that verse 33 summarize the whole section, and it can only do so if ὑπάρχοντα is spiritualized in this way. The more insidious result of this error is that ὑπάρχοντα is generalized into vagueness, and so the command becomes virtually impossible to obey. It can then be conveniently classed with commands like "Be perfect" (Matt. 5:48) and ignored, at least in the sense of a requirement for specific behavior. If anything, material possessions become a subset of the general command, and they tend to move far down the list of items to give up. In practice, the list quoted above is usually reversed.

The argument against spiritualization of ὑπάρχοντα is not dependent on the context, however. The consistent use of the word to denote material possessions requires that sense here. Delling is succinct:

> No other understanding of ὑπάρχοντα seems to be possible. The expression always (14 times) denotes earthly goods in the New Testament. In the many LXX references (15 in Genesis) it bears the same sense for a whole series of Hebrew equivalents; it is thus presupposed to be a fixed term.[24]

Luke employs the term in numerous passages on the same theme: 8:3; 12:15;12:33; 19:8; and Acts 4:32. These references are especially significant in that they show signs of Lukan redaction. The adjective πᾶς, which Luke inserts elsewhere to intensify similar passages (5:11, 28; 6:30; 18:22), strengthens the material sense of 14:33. The general notion of renunciation of "self" is excluded by such specific terminology. Possessions in Luke 14:33 are property: things that can be sold, given away, or abandoned.

D. Recipients of the Demand

The passage portrays Jesus as giving conditions to a large group for entrance into the special status of "disciple" (μαθητής). Was he calling for followers from the general population or for an elite corps from among the larger group of followers? Verse 25 tells us that he is addressing here the "multitude" (ὄχλοι), which in Luke always refers to the noncommitted audiences of his preaching. In fact, in four places (6:17; 7:11; 9:18; 12:1) a distinction is made between μαθητής and ὄχλος. Although μαθητής is in some instances apparently synonymous with the Twelve (9:18; 12:1), this is the case only when there is no indication of the presence of other believers. Luke distinguishes between μαθητάς and the "apostles" (ἀποστόλους) in 6:13, and elsewhere he employs μαθητής to designate large groups of believers (6:17; 19:37). He uses the term over twenty times in Acts to indicate believers. These factors combine to create a compelling argument for the general meaning of μαθητής in 14:26–33: a disciple is synonymous with a "believer" or a "follower" of Jesus. The passage is not a summons for a subgroup with special responsibilities.

To read Luke 14:33 as Luke intended it to be read is to question the retention of possessions by any believer, to take in its most literal sense Bonhoeffer's rejection of *cheap* grace. By redefining "give up" as "be perpetually willing to give up," by redefining "material possessions" as "one's whole life," or by redefining "disciple" as "those few [others] called to radical obedience," interpreters have effectively reduced the verse to a harmless platitude. Perhaps the church has indeed counted the cost—and has found it too high.

III. LUKE 16:15: WHAT DO MEN EXALT?

He who is faithful in a very little is faithful also in much; and he who is dishonest in a very little is dishonest also in much. If then you have not been faithful in the unrighteous mammon, who will entrust to you the true riches?

And if you have not been faithful in that which is another's, who will give you that which is your own? No servant can serve two masters; for either he will hate the one and love the other, or he will be devoted to the one and despise the other. You cannot serve God and mammon.

The Pharisees, who were lovers of money, heard all this, and they scoffed at him. But he said to them, "You are those who justify yourselves before men, but God knows your hearts; *for what is exalted among men is an abomination in the sight of God*" (Luke 16:10–15).

This passage follows the parable of the unjust steward, which is applied in one of the most cryptic commands of the New Testament: "And I tell you, make friends for yourselves by means of unrighteous mammon, so that when it fails they may receive you into the eternal habitations" (16:9). The message of the verse and of most of the chapter is this: conduct with regard to material possessions indicates one's eternal destination. These middle verses of the chapter are often overlooked because of the great interest in the parable of the unjust steward and the story of the rich man and Lazarus (vv. 19–31).

A careful analysis suggests that, on the contrary, the verses summarize the didactic material of verses 1–13. Indeed, verse 15 contains what is arguably the strongest statement about wealth in the Bible.

The antitheses of verses 10–12 portray material possessions as "very little, unrighteous," and "that which is another's," respectively. The third contrast (v. 12) may in fact imply that wealth is satanic. Luke 4:6 certainly suggests that this is the claim of Satan himself, and the claim is never contradicted. The immediate context adds weight to the argument. It would be odd for "another" to refer to that which belongs to God when it has been described in the previous antitheses as "very little" and "unrighteous." Verse 13, furthermore, in personifying mammon as the alternative master to God, makes the connection to Adversary even stronger.

The connection between verses 1–13 and verses 14–15 relies on more than the reference to the Pharisees as "lovers of money" (φιλάργυροι–14). It is common for teaching passages to end with an account of the crowd reaction.[25] Luke is explicit that the "heard all this, and they scoffed." The reference can only be to verses 1–13 and more immediately to the negative implications regarding wealth in verses 10–12. We know little about the attitude of the Pharisees toward wealth,[26] but, given their apocalyptic expectations, it is reasonable to think that they associated wealth with divine favor in the eschaton— and by extension, with divine favor to pious Jews in the present age. The line between this biblically based (if somewhat untempered) view and simple greed or luxuriance is easily crossed. If this attitude underlies the label "lovers of money," the charge of self-justification is fitting. What better justification of extravagance than attribution to God Himself? These factors suggest a strong connection between the teaching about wealth elsewhere in Luke (especially in chap. 16) and verses 4–15.

As a summary of verses 1–15, and even on its own merits, the closing statement of verse 15 is very important. There is no need here to chart the alternatives, which can be expressed very simply: does Jesus in 16:15 condemn pride or wealth? The consensus of commentators is that the passage is one of many in the Gospels that condemn the Pharisees for their pride.[27] The pride of the Pharisees is implicit throughout Luke's gospel, and the interpretation finds a precedent in Proverbs 16:5, "Every one who is arrogant is an abomination to the Lord." There are, however, several reasons to reject this interpretation and to accept the alternative.

Even if we consider the statement apart from its context, as a "floating saying," the identification of "what is exalted" (τὸ . . . ὑψηλόν) with pride is nonsensical. People do not exalt pride itself but the things that produce pride. By the simple change of "who" to "what" (τό), the audience is deprived of its spiritualizing defenses. In this manner, Jesus intensifies, or "materializes," the proverbial tradition. Typically, he does this in a way that reverses commonly held values and stresses the radical nature of obedience. Every proud person will agree that pride is bad and convince himself that he is humble. It is much more difficult for the rich man to convince himself that he is poor. By indicating that some exalted *things* are an abomination, Jesus forces the audience to take stock not only of their attitudes but also of the behavior expressive of those attitudes.

The argument for identification of "what is exalted" with wealth grows in strength as attention is paid to the context. In verse 14, reference is made to the Pharisees as money-lovers. This is the closest reference to any object that could be exalted.

The connection to verses 10–13 makes a compelling case for wealth as the "abomination." Wealth is at least demeaned, if not condemned as satanic, in verses 10–12. Then, in verse 13, the implication is that service of mammon is idolatrous: it is the alternative to service of God. The use of βδέλυγμα in the latter part of verse 15 completes this idea. The word is used consistently in the LXX in the context of idolatry.[28] A striking parallel to this verse in the intertestamental *Testaments of the Twelve Patriarchs* confirms the connection. In *T. Judah* 18:2, 6, the readers are warned to "guard yourselves . . . against the love of money [φιλαργυρίας]," because, for the one who serves it, "two passions contrary to God's commands enslave [δουλεύων] him, so that he is unable to obey God." The writer goes on to warn that "love of money leads to idolatry, because once they are led astray by money, they designate as gods those who are not gods" (19:1).

The identification of τὸ . . . ὑψηλόν with wealth finds support in the proverbial style of Jesus, in the vocabulary of the immediate and general context of Luke's gospel, and in contemporary wisdom literature. Wealth was exalted among men of that time, and Jesus used the strongest expression at the disposal of a first-century Jew to reject what was probably the equivalent of today's health and wealth gospel.

IV. CONCLUSION

The tendency of interpreters of the three passages considered here has been to spiritualize their message. Ironically, this is most common among those who are most vociferous about the need to "take the Bible literally." This is not surprising: those who take the Scriptures most seriously have the greatest need to find a fit between biblical demands and modern practice. There are many ways to do this, as we observed above, and the net result of each is, conveniently, pious affluence. When luxuriant levels of living are confronted by strong and recurrent opposition in the teaching of Jesus (these are of course only three of many gospel passages), something has to give. That something is usually the teaching of Jesus. For those who want to lay claim to a biblical justification for affluence, the Pharisaic (mis)interpretation of Moses or Solomon will suffice. This may be supplemented in the New Testament by arguments from silence or by reference to apparent exceptions to or mitigations of the harshness of gospel demands. But whatever may be said by the modern Western church to explain its affluence, it must acknowledge that these things were said by its Founder:

> All disciples should give their attention exclusively to the kingdom, and the necessary material provision will be supplied by God.

> A person must leave behind all material possessions in order to enter the kingdom.

> Wealth is exalted by men, but it is an abomination to God.

What does it mean to take these statements seriously? It is not enough to consider them only as a correction to the current health and wealth gospel. That approach usually leads to the conclusion that obedience lies somewhere between the extremes of unquestioning accumulation and voluntary poverty: in most cases, conveniently enough, at just about the economic level of the interpreter of the passages.

It may be helpful to consider an approach toward obedience that stresses the dynamic relationship between God's requirements and God's mercy in the life of each believer. There are merciful, kind, or generous deeds that we perform in a radical manner occasionally and to an increasing degree gradually as a part of our "pushing toward the mark" (Phil. 3:12–14). We do not reach the mark, of course, but by the power of God we do better as we mature in Christ. Jesus describes these requirements in ways that should make us squirm: we must always forgive, we must be pure in heart, we must rejoice in persecution, we must love our enemies—indeed, we must be perfect. Ten percent is not good enough in these areas, nor is mere inward disposition. And He goes so far as to describe these behaviors as *prerequisites* to kingdom entrance, not just as optional expressions of our gratitude for being let in. We are uncomfortable watering down His requirements or ignoring them "that grace may abound," and we are even more uncomfortable at the prospect that our salvation might be tied up with specific forms of behavior.

The New Testament makes it very clear that God forgives sin completely and also that He requires obedience absolutely. The tension inherent in taking both propositions seriously cries out to be relieved: either by self-righteous and morbid craving for moral perfection; or more recently, and especially among evangelicals, by a functionally libertarian view of God's mercy. The obsessive appetite for a "positive self-concept" that is so closely tied to the current health and wealth gospel is actually fed by this modern evangelical soft-sell of New Testament morality. Vague and unchallenging moral teachings are no match for encouragements toward self-serving behavior without guilt. Nor is a return to old ways a viable alternative. Recent research suggests that the standard prohibitions by which evangelicals once marked out their identity are fast approaching obsolescence, and into the vacuum left by these admittedly pharisaic measures of Christian maturity, no morality of consensus—much less of the New Testament—is evidently being sent.

This may be a sign of hope and not a doomsday prophecy. Perhaps, when all is said and done, when forms fade and movements burn themselves out, substance will remain. And even that substance will probably be visible only to God. For although His requirement and His forgiveness are generally stated in Scripture, they are individually applied. For example, it may require more of God's power for a child abuser to abstain once than for a great evangelist to conduct one more crusade. A greater amount of movement toward perfection may in fact occur in the former case. For each individual, then, God's forgiveness covers the distance between the place that person has arrived and the place of perfection. But to refuse to move, even in one area, in the name of God's mercy, is to demand what a sinner is in no place to demand. A believer must be equally and continually serious—indeed, passionate—both about the dire need for transformation and about the incredible gift of forgiveness. It is truly a narrow road between the two, but to relax in either direction is to leave the Way.

Thus it is that the current generation of believers should be urged to consider afresh the possibility that as Paul meant just what he said about grace, so Jesus meant just what He said about obedience—about purity, about meekness, about forgiveness, and about possessions. To stand still because the end is so far away is to miss the point of discipleship as a journey. Most of us could travel a considerable distance on that road before anyone suspected us of extreme obedience.

Because our response in this area holds such potential for a prophetic voice in today's world, because the model of obedience provided in the Gospels is the most common and detailed among several that might be observed in the Scriptures, and because the teaching comes from Jesus Himself, evangelicalism must move it from the periphery to centrality in its ethical constructs. The New Testament makes Jesus central theologically *and ethically*; as John puts it: "he who says he abides in him ought to walk in the same way in which he walked" (1 John 2:6). The words are simple, clear, and therefore frightening. It is a matter of steps, of movement along a dangerous path. Our desire for an easier way may distract us from His path, especially when we can find biblical warrant for another way. But it is possible to understand diverse biblical models in this area as subservient rather than contradictory to the Gospels. With this understanding, we can commend as biblical and righteous any steps taken in the direction of obedience, while we are quick to acknowledge that these are steps and not the destination itself.

CHAPTER FOUR

DIVINE HEALING
IN THE HEALTH AND WEALTH GOSPEL

Douglas J. Moo

The health and wealth gospel differs from evangelical Christianity generally in its emphasis on the physical blessings that believers can—and *should*—experience in this life. Salvation is for the whole person. Yet traditional Christianity has short-changed this truth by focusing almost exclusively on the soul and on spiritual blessings. So argue prominent health and wealth gospellers such as Kenneth Hagin and Kenneth and Gloria Copeland. And they are determined to right this imbalance by making Christians aware that God has provided in Christ for their material and physical well-being—if only they will reach out and claim these blessings in faith. Most of the proponents of this movement do not seek to downplay the significance of spiritual salvation. What they believe about the basic doctrines of the faith is well within the parameters of orthodoxy. If, indeed, theirs is "another gospel," it is so not because any basic doctrines have been subtracted but because certain questionable doctrines have been added.

As the popular name for this growing but amorphous movement suggests, the promises of financial prosperity and physical health are the two pillars of this "gospel." And, whatever Hagin, the Copelands, and others in the movement may say about their ministries in their more guarded statements, these promises of material well-being loom large in their literature and broadcasts. Other chapters in this book are taking a critical look at the "wealth" side of the movement; in this chapter, we will examine the "health" component.

The focus on physical well-being and healing in the health and wealth gospel—hereafter HWG—has its roots in a century-and-a-half-old tradition. Key figures in this tradition were the "Irvingites" in early nineteenth-century Scotland, the Blumhardts in Germany, and A. J. Gordon and A. B. Simpson (founder of what came to be the Christian and Missionary Alliance) at the end of the century in America. Divine healing was prominent in Pentecostal circles and in those stepchildren of the Pentecostals, the charismatics. Oral Roberts is perhaps the best known representative of the charismatic healing movement.[1] More recently, the Vineyard movement, associated with John Wimber, has highlighted divine healing as one of those "signs" that should accompany and witness to the present-day manifestation of the kingdom of God in the church.[2]

While having in common with these movements and individuals the conviction that God does heal miraculously at the present time, advocates of the HWG

57

differ from most of them in their claim that good health should characterize *every* believer. Ken Blue, for instance, a representative of the Vineyard movement, thinks that it is God's will to heal all believers. Yet, because of the continuing opposition of Satan to the rule of Christ during this period of human history, God's will to heal will not always be accomplished.[3] The health and wealth evangelists, on the other hand, make it clear that a failure to be healed can be ascribed only to ignorance or lack of faith. The provision is there for every believer—but we must step out in faith and claim it. Faith means that we should not add "if it be thy will" when we pray for healing—while very pious-sounding, this only indicates doubt in the promise of God. And, after praying, it is important that a "positive confession" be made: thanking God for the healing that has taken place, even if the physical symptoms remain. For faith must rise above the physical evidence, resting secure in the promises of God in His Word.[4]

The teaching about divine healing in the HWG rests, then, on two main contentions: that God has promised physical well-being in this life to every believer and that only ignorance or lack of faith can prevent this promise from being realized. The former is shared with many other advocates of divine healing, but the latter—while not unique to the HWG—is what gives to the movement its distinctive and extremist flavor. Several key scriptural and theological arguments are used to support these two key contentions, and we examine these in what follows. Our focus will be on the HWG, but the similarities in teaching about divine healing between the HWG and other movements means that our analysis will inevitably touch on these other movements also. Many authors cited in the notes, then, are not in agreement with all the tenets of the HWG.

I. JESUS' HEALINGS AND OURS

The Evangelists narrate thirty-three miracles of Jesus. Of these, seventeen are healings and four are exorcisms that involve healing. In one of several similar summaries of Jesus' ministry, Matthew tells us that "Jesus went about all the cities and villages, teaching in their synagogues and preaching the gospel of the kingdom, and *healing every disease and every infirmity* [emphasis mine]" (9:35). The healing of people who were sick, incapacitated, or handicapped was characteristic of Jesus' ministry; and nowhere is Jesus seen turning away a person who sincerely wishes to be healed. It is only unbelief that prevents Jesus from healing (Mark 6:5–6). If, then, Jesus is "the same yesterday, today, and forever" (Heb. 13:8), He must be willing and ready to heal all now who come to Christ, through the church, in faith.[5]

But we have more than this (somewhat dubious) *a priori* argument to go by: for Jesus passes on to His followers the power and responsibility to continue His own ministry of healing. The charges to both the Twelve (Matt. 10:1=Luke 9:1; cf. Matt. 10:8) and the Seventy (Luke 10:9) include the command to "heal the sick," a charge that is renewed by the resurrected Christ, who commands the disciples to "lay their hands on the sick" with the promise that "they will recover" (Mark 16:18). And Luke records the fulfillment of this command and promise: Peter heals the lame man at the temple (Acts 3:1–10), Aeneas in Lydda (Acts 9:32–35), and even brings a woman back to life (Acts 10:36–43). Paul, not to be outdone, also heals a lame man in Lystra (Acts 14:8–10), the father of

Publius on Malta (Acts 28:7–8), and restores Eutychus to life at Troas (Acts 20:9–12—although it is not entirely clear whether Eutychus was dead). Both Peter and Paul heal indirectly (Acts 5:15; 19:11–12). Luke, in fact, is at pains to show that "signs and wonders" accompanied the preaching of the early Christians (Acts 5:12) and were no small reason for the success of their evangelism.

Should not the church today be characterized by the same "signs and wonders"? As disciples of Jesus Christ are we not recipients of the scriptural privilege—nay, command—to "heal the sick"? Does not Jesus Himself promise that we will accomplish "greater works" than even He (John 14:12)? And, since both Jesus and the early Christians (cf. Acts 5:16) healed all who came to them, should not a biblically faithful church today have a similar track record?

This argument for divine healing is repeated again and again in the literature and in the teaching of the HWG. One could, of course, quibble about details—Mark 16:15 is almost certainly not part of inspired Scripture;[6] the charges to the Twelve and to the Seventy cannot without careful qualification be made applicable to the church at large; and John 14:12 is probably not promising that disciples will perform greater miracles than Jesus but that the coming of the Spirit will enable them to enroll people from the entire world on the lists of those members of the kingdom of God[7]—but the argument as to the situation in the early church is sound enough. The question, of course, is the significance of this situation in the early church for the church today.

Suspicious of Roman Catholic claims that *their* miracles accredited *their* doctrines and *their* church, the Reformers argued that these "signs and wonders" were strictly confined to the apostolic age.[8] They were used by God to accredit the bearers of revelation; that revelation being closed after the death of the apostles, no more such miracles can be expected. We should point out, by the way, that this view in no way dismisses the supernatural from playing a role in the life of the church, including physical healing: the question, rather, is whether God supernaturally heals through the "suspension" of the "laws of nature," e.g., miraculously. The position of the Reformers is argued cogently and with skeptical analysis of many reported phenomena to the contrary by B. B. Warfield in *Counterfeit Miracles*.[9] And this view resembles in important ways the "cessationist" view espoused by many dispensationalists.[10] Its advocates can make a pretty good case. The relevant promises of Jesus are all made to the apostles or to those who could be regarded as acting in the capacity of apostles (e.g., the "seventy"). All those who perform miracles in the book of Acts are apostles. Moreover, standard hermeneutical procedure dictates that Christian doctrine and practice should be based primarily on teaching passages—and the epistles have very little to say about healings.

The Reformers are right to raise questions about a willy-nilly application to the contemporary church of what was true for the apostolic church. As the plan of God unfolds in time, different periods are characterized by different elements and emphases, and what God chooses to do in one period or epoch cannot necessarily be assumed to be what He will do in another. We would, in fact, expect that there would be features unique to the apostolic age. Most Protestants would agree, for instance, that the mediation of divine inscripturated revelation is confined to this period of time—and associated particularly with the apostles themselves. Similarly, the apostles play a unique role in salvation history as the "foundation" for the church (Eph. 2:20; cf. Matt. 16:18). These differences between the apostles and *any* Christian in our day and, therefore, between the apostolic age and our's, cannot be glossed over. And this means that it is simplistic to argue that because Jesus and the apostles performed miracles of healing, the church in our day can. Particularly is this so if we view the miracles as having the purpose of accrediting individuals. For if anyone is capable of wielding miraculous powers, the miracles cease to have any value in marking off individuals as in any way distinctive. Warfield puts the point this way: "If miracles came to be common, everyday occurrences, normal and not extraordinary, they cease to attract attention, and lose their very reason for existence."[11]

Evangelists for the HWG, as well as many other advocates of miraculous healing, frequently fail to take seriously enough the discontinuities that are the product of salvation history. We cannot imitate everything Jesus did; there were features unique to the apostolic age; Peter, Paul, and the other apostles had an authority and position not held by anyone since their day. Moreover, Luke does appear to attach the working of miracles closely to the persons of the apostles: "Many signs and wonders were done among the people *by the hands of the apostles* [emphasis mine]" (Acts 5:12); when Tabitha dies, the local Christians do not bring her back to life but send for Peter (9:38); again, in Ephesus, Luke affirms that it was "by the hands of Paul" that "extraordinary miracles" were performed. Luke's presentation of miracles in Acts is debated, but a good case can be made for thinking that he views "signs and wonders" as having particular relevance in the accrediting of the apostles. And note also 2 Corinthians 12:12: "the signs of *a true apostle* were performed among you in all patience, with signs and wonders and mighty works [emphasis mine]." All this lends plausibility to the argument that we should not expect miracles to be as pervasive in the church in our day as it was in the days of Jesus or the apostles.

We are not, however, convinced that the Reformers are right to deny the possibility of miraculous healing after the apostolic age. First, while the evidential value of miracles cannot be gainsaid—and the HWG is to be faulted for downplaying or ignoring this—the miracles of Jesus and the apostles have a significance beyond the evidential (see the following section). This being so, there is no reason to think that miracles could be done only by Jesus or the apostles. Second, the possibility that God will heal miraculously in the continuing life of the church appears to be implied by James 5:14–16. Here, it is not the apostles but "the elders of the church" who pray and anoint with oil with the purpose of bringing physical healing. This makes Calvin's view (see *Institutes* 4.19.18) that this power to heal was confined to the apostolic age untenable. Warfield, on the other hand, finds "nothing miraculous" in the circumstances of the healing.[12] But the simple assertions that the prayer of faith will "save"—e.g., heal—the one who is sick, and that "the Lord will raise him up," point to a healing that occurs outside the sphere of natural physical healing or medical therapy. Third, there is no reason to think that the "gift of healing" mentioned by Paul in 1 Corinthians 12:9 and 28 has been withdrawn from the church.

Other points will arise in the course of this discussion that follows, but it suffices for now to say that we find no reason to rule out the possibility of miraculous healing after the age of the apostles and some reason to expect that such healings would continue to occur. While critical of the hermeneutical naiveté by which their conclusions are reached, we agree, then, with the HWG that miracles of divine healing can still occur. Indeed, the openness in this movement to the possibility of miraculous interventions of God may be more "biblical" than the skepticism that too many of us unwittingly share with our materialistic culture. When, however, the HWG argues that the healings of Jesus or the apostolic church give reason to think that all Christians should be healed, they have gone far beyond the evidence. To be sure, Jesus and the apostles are never seen to have "turned away" a person who came to them for healing, but neither are they said to have healed all the sick they came into contact with. A "multitude" of sick people lay by the Pool of Bethzatha; Jesus, as far as we are told, healed only one (John 5:1–9). One could argue, of course, that it was only this individual who had the faith to be healed, but we are then importing an element that is not mentioned in the text. The point is that the actual healing practices of Jesus and the apostles provide us no evidence at all about how widespread we should expect miraculous healing to be in our day.

II. SIGNS OF THE KINGDOM

The miracles of Jesus and the apostles had evidential value—that is, they were, as John calls them, "signs" of something else, pointers to the truth that Jesus was, indeed, the Son of God and the apostles His accredited representatives. Nevertheless, as recent scholarship has particularly—and in some cases in too one-sided a fashion—emphasized, the miracles had other purposes than this. When Jesus is asked by John the Baptist whether He is the "one to come" or not, He sends back the reply: "Go and tell John what you hear and see: the blind receive their sight and the lame walk, lepers are cleansed and the deaf hear, and the dead are raised up, and the poor have good news preached them" (Matt. 11:4–5). Jesus' point is that He is accomplishing those things that the prophets predicted would occur at the coming of the kingdom, in the messianic age (His language reflects several texts from Isaiah: see 29:18; 35:5–6; 42:18). Similarly, Jesus claims that His exorcisms indicate the presence of the kingdom (Matt. 12:28). Jesus' miracles do not just prove who He is but reveal the presence of the kingdom. Their evidential value lies not in their being pointers *to* the kingdom but in being signs *of* the kingdom. The miracles of Jesus are not "external" signs but "internal" signs, part of the reality to which they point. When the reign of God is established, Satan is vanquished, the dead are raised, illness is no more. Jesus' exorcisms, raisings of the dead, and healings give evidence that the kingdom of God is at work in His ministry.

The implications of this for divine healing in our day can be formulated in a simple syllogism: where the kingdom of God is present, the healing of diseases is present; the kingdom of God is present in and through the church in our day; therefore the healing of diseases must be present in and through the church in our day. To be sure, one could quarrel with either of the premises. The second, for instance, is denied by advocates of the "postponed kingdom" theory: that Jesus offered the kingdom to the Jews, only to have it rejected, and so "postponed" until His second coming. On this view, held by many dispensationalists, we should not necessarily expect divine healing in our day because the kingdom is not, in fact, present. But this view of the kingdom appears to be losing ground, and a pretty good consensus of evangelicals from various theological persuasions holds to some form of "inaugurated" eschatology, whereby it is held that the kingdom of God has been inaugurated through Jesus' first coming but will be "climaxed" or fulfilled only at this second. On this view, the kingdom is indeed present in our day, and we should expect to see signs of that kingdom.

But there is more reason to question the first premise. Granted that the miraculous healing of diseases was part of the kingdom's power in Jesus' day, can we say that it is a *necessary* part of the kingdom? That wherever the kingdom is, the miraculous healing of diseases must be taking place? This is not clear. Nowhere does the New Testament make this equation, and the paucity of references to healing as part of the life of the church in the epistles suggests that the insistence on such an equation is not in keeping with the biblical emphasis and perspective. What can be said, it seems to us, is that the presence of the reign of God in and through the church makes miracles of healing *possible* but not *necessary*. Biblical balance is best preserved if Christians remain open to the exercise of miraculous healings but do not insist on them. While the evidence is notoriously difficult to evaluate—and many in the divine healing movement have been far too quick to identify "miraculous" healings—there does seem to be reason to think that God has bestowed miracles on one time and place and withheld them from others. Error on each side is perilously easy: to expect miracles so eagerly that natural or at best ambiguous circumstances are labeled miracles and to be so closed to the possibility that unbelief stifles miracles or prevents them from being recognized when they do occur. Scripture and history suggest that God bestows miracles in sovereign freedom and we would do well not to force the evidence one way or the other.

But the understanding of physical well-being as a sign of the kingdom has another important implication for the HWG. As we have seen, proponents of the movement proclaim that God's will is to heal all believers *in this life*. But such a view buys into what many scholars have labeled "over-realized eschatology"—the mistake, probably the root of the problem at Corinth, of thinking that God's kingdom has already arrived in its full and final state. If this were so, we would indeed expect healing to be available for everyone; indeed, we would expect there to be no need for healing, because there would be no disease or physical incapacity of any kind—we would all enjoy transformed bodies. But God has not chosen to bring the kingdom into existence in its final state at this point in time. As the parables of Matthew 13 and other passages teach, the kingdom, which was inaugurated at Jesus' death and resurrection, has not come in its fullness. Jesus will come again to eradicate sin entirely, vanquish Satan, and restore the unchallenged reign of God. The believer in this life lives in the "already-not yet" tension of this salvation-historical framework. And to expect physical well-being and divine healing to characterize every believer is to ignore the "not yet" side of this tension. Only in the final state of the kingdom has God promised to remove all disease and physical incapacity; in Jesus' miracles, in the apostles' miracles, and in those miraculous healings that still take place, God graciously "anticipates" for some individuals this final state. But to expect physical ailments to be eradicated from the church in this age is just as foolish as to expect physical death to be removed, natural disasters to stop occurring, and the power of sin to be destroyed. The HWG is right to proclaim that God has promised to remove all our physical infirmities, but they are wrong to claim that we can expect this to take place in this life. As Adrio König puts it, "If the prosperity gospel is an accurate reflection of the gospel, one might ask whether we still need a new earth?"[13]

Finally, without denying that miracles can be used of God to point people to Jesus Christ and to the message of the Gospel, we should not lose sight of Paul's teaching that God's strength is often made known in "weakness" (see 2 Cor. 10–13). It is not always the spectacular, or the comfortable, or the triumphant that manifests the kingdom; often it is the quiet, the suffering, and (apparent) defeat.

III. SUFFERING, SICKNESS, AND DIVINE SOVEREIGNTY

Is it ever God's will for a Christian to experience illness or physical incapacity? No, answer advocates of the HWG; God wants every believer to be healthy and makes health freely available—all we have to do is ask in faith. No, answers Ken Blue of the Vineyard movement; God wants every believer to be healthy, although in addition to this purpose being defeated by ignorance or lack of faith on the part of Christians, Satan also has the power to prevent healing from occurring.

We are not so sure that this answer is correct. The question is a tricky one. The phrase "God's will" conceals a crucial issue: do we mean God's "decretive" will or His "permissive" will? And at some point along the line we run up against the insoluble issue of the relationship between God's sovereignty over all things and the existence of evil. How can God exercise such control of *all the circumstances of life* such that "all things work to our good" (Rom. 8:28) and yet be untainted by evil? This is not the place, nor does this writer have the competence, to deal adequately with these larger issues.[14] But one thing is clear: however we explain it, the Scriptures make clear that God is, in some sense, "behind" all things—even evil things, although He is, of course not responsible for, or the cause of, that evil. Anything less than this makes God less than the God of the Bible, the God who sovereignly disposes *all things* according to His will. God judges His people through the evil of human greed and violence (the Assyrian and Babylonian campaigns against Israel) and through the evil of sickness and death (1 Cor. 5:5; 11:29–30). To argue that Satan inflicts the suffering of physical illness on believers *against* God's "will"—however we finally define it—comes close to an unbiblical dualism.

If this is so, we cannot exempt sickness from the New Testament statements about the purpose and value of suffering. Such a distinction is made by a number of writers who want to avoid the idea that sickness may be a divinely "allowed" "trial" intended to strengthen the faith of the believer.[15] According to these authors, the suffering that Christians can expect in this life and that they are to endure patiently as a faith-refining experience is confined to persecution, "suffering for Christ." But this will not do. To be sure, the word πάσχω ("suffer") and its cognates often refer specifically to persecution in the New Testament (e.g., Phil. 1:29; 1 Thess. 2:14; 2 Thess. 1:5; 1 Peter passim), but the word group is not limited to persecution. "Suffering with Christ" (Rom. 8:17; Phil. 3:10) or "for Christ" is a broad concept that includes all those difficulties and trials that befall a Christian in this age of warfare between God and Satan. Note that "suffering with Christ" in Romans 8:17 is described as the "sufferings of this present age" (τὰ παθήματα τοῦ νῦν καιροῦ) in 8:18—and the context allows no restriction in the scope of those "sufferings" (see v. 35, where trials such as "famine," "nakedness," and "peril" are mentioned). Even more to the present point is 2 Corinthians 1:3–11, where the "sufferings" Paul has endured (v. 6) are narrowed specifically to the "affliction" (θλίψεις) he experienced in Asia (v. 8); and the description of this affliction in verses 9–10 best fits a physical illness.[16] In the same way, the assurances in Romans 5:3–4 that "tribulations" (θλίψις) and in James 1:2–4 that "trials" (πειρασμοί) will have beneficial spiritual results for the believer cannot be confined to the situation of persecution. Neither word is so restricted in the New Testament. θλίψεις refers to mental distress in 1 Corinthians 7:28 and Philippians 1:17, to the various difficulties experienced by Joseph in Egypt in Acts 7:10, and to the physical sufferings resulting from famine in Acts 7:11. And πειρασμός refers specifically to a physical illness of Paul's in Galatians 4:14.

This is probably the place also to look at one of the most debated biblical texts about sickness and divine healing: 2 Corinthians 12:7–9, where Paul describes his "thorn in the flesh." If Paul refers here to a physical illness, we would have conclusive biblical evidence both that God does not always remove sickness from faithful believers and that God has a positive purpose in allowing His servants to suffer illness. Advocates of the HWG, along with most evangelists for "divine healing," deny that the "thorn" is a physical illness. The word translated "thorn," σκόλψ, is used in the LXX to denote adversaries of Israel who oppress and scorn Israel (Num. 33:55; Ezek. 28:24), and this has led many to argue that the word is an idiom for oppression. This is certainly not true: we have far too few occurrences of the word with this connotation to justify calling it an idiom. But the LXX evidence does allow this interpretation, and there is no doubt that Paul has a great deal to say in 2 Corinthians about "false apostles" who are contesting his apostleship and sincerity toward the Corinthians. Moreover, the use of the dative τῇ σαρκί—rather, than, e.g., the prepositional phrase ἐν τῇ σαρκί—may suggest that the "thorn" was not a difficulty in Paul's body but a trial "to" himself (σάρξ in the general sense of "person").[17] Yet three considerations suggest the reference might be to a physical ailment of some kind. First, the style of the text resembles certain Hellenistic literary forms in which *physical* weakness was usually the subject.[18] Second, Paul goes on in the text to correct his "thorn" with "weakness." Yet "weakness" in Paul refers to the incapacities and corruptible aspects of life in this age before the final redemption (Rom. 6:19; 8:26; 1 Cor. 2:3; 15:43; 2 Cor. 11:30; 13:4—in Gal. 4:13 and in 1 Tim. 5:23, it refers to physical illness or incapacity). This fits a reference to physical incapacity much better than a reference to oppressors or opponents of the Gospel. Third, the way in which Paul ascribes his thorn both to God ("it was given") and to Satan ("a messenger of Satan") resembles other texts in which physical incapacities are described (1 Cor. 5:5; cf. Job 2:1–10).[19]

We think that Paul's "thorn" was most likely an unidentifiable physical incapacity.[20] If so, several conclusions result. First, we see that illness is something that can be described both as "given by God" (the implied agent of the passive verb ἐδόθη is God) and as a "messenger of Satan." We could ask for no clearer expression of the tension between the ultimacy of God and the agency of Satan in suffering than this. Second, unless we are prepared to fault Paul for lack of faith, it is clear prayers offered in faith do not always bring physical healing. Third, and the point of most relevance to our present discussion: we have a clear indication that God brings physical suffering on His people with the purpose of improving their spiritual lives. Paul's thorn had the purpose of curbing his pride; and God may both bring and allow to remain physical difficulties in the lives of other believers to accomplish similar spiritual good. Nevertheless, we cannot be certain that Paul is speaking here of a physical malady. and the issue is clouded enough to make it necessary to use this text only with caution in the case we are building. We therefore prefer to use it only to corroborate points based on texts elsewhere rather than to use it as the primary basis for an argument.

What we want to argue in this section is that physical illness cannot be excluded from those sufferings that Christians can expect to experience in this life and from the assurances God gives that such sufferings will be used by God to bring spiritual benefit to the Christian who responds to them in the right way. This is not to say that physical illness is a divine visitation that must always be passively accepted. Nor are we suggesting that sickness is a "blessing," for sickness, whatever God's ultimacy in relation to it, is always an evil, one instance of that tragic disruption in God's creation that has resulted from the Fall. But the texts we have examined do show that sickness can *bring* blessing and that the Christian who has come to accept his or her sickness as a divinely allowed trial that is not going to be removed and who seeks to grow and learn through and because of that sickness is by no means taking an unbiblical position. Indeed, accepting as God's will and living triumphantly under a physical disability may evidence a faith far stronger than a "name and claim it" attitude that demands healing from God.

IV. HEALING AND SALVATION

Partly due to the influx of Eastern modes of thinking in the last decades, the Western world has awakened to the interrelationship of mind and body. In the medical profession, this has brought an increasing emphasis on the psychical and emotional causes of physical disorders. In Christian circles, emphasis has been put on "wholistic healing." To the extent that this approach gives due recognition to the biblical perspective on human beings as integrated wholes and on salvation as affecting the body as well as the soul, this is welcome. Advocates of the HWG and of divine healing generally are justified in criticizing the church in the West for too often unintentionally fostering an unbiblical anthropological dualism by confining God's concerns to the human soul.

Nevertheless, certain distinctions are important. First, we must distinguish the obvious fact that living according to God's guidelines can often foster good health from what the HWG is saying. To the extent that a Christian, following biblical precepts and principles, refrains from excessive consumption of alcohol, the taking of unnecessary drugs, and sexual promiscuity, and maintains a positive mental attitude as a result of the security and joy in knowing Christ, he or she can be expected to avoid illnesses that those who do not refrain from these things will often suffer. On the other hand, the most scrupulous adherence to these biblical guidelines in the world will not keep the believer from getting multiple sclerosis, becoming disabled as a result of an auto accident, or developing a brain tumor. Right living can help us avoid some diseases but not all or even most diseases. The HWG insists that the Christian can avoid disease by "claiming" the promise of perfect health from God by faith. The "wholistic" or "mental" or "spiritual" health movement must, then, be carefully distinguished from the HWG.

Our evaluation of the HWG's teaching on this matter also requires some distinctions. First, while agreeing that the body and the soul cannot ultimately be separated and that God's salvific promises refer to both, we must ask whether there are not distinctions to be made in the *nature* and the *timing* of the salvation God has promised the soul of man on the one hand and the body on the other. That a distinction in timing is necessary is suggested by the salvation-historical "already-not yet" tension we elaborated above. A key element in the "not yet" part of the Christian's salvation is the transformation of the body. Not until death or Christ's return in glory will the bodies of believers be "redeemed" (see Rom. 8:23) through resurrection (for those who have died) and transformation (for those who are alive at Christ's return). Until then, Christians "groan" in limited and sin-prone bodies (Rom. 8:23; 2 Cor. 5:2), "earthen vessels" in which "death is at work" (2 Cor. 4:7–12). Without suggesting that the "already-not yet" tension is equivalent to a "soul-body" distinction—for that is clearly not the case—it remains true that the physical body is clearly said not to have participated fully yet in the salvific benefits of Christ's death. Advocates of the HWG admit, of course, that Christians live in bodies that will die; but can we distinguish between the death of the body and the illnesses that afflict and often bring about the death of the body? Indeed, is not aging itself, with the limitations in physical abilities that it brings, a type of that physical incapacity of which illness is another type? Once again, the HWG has committed the error of "over-realized eschatology" in claiming that the benefits of salvation can be claimed for the *body* in this life the same way in which they can be claimed for the soul.

But a distinction must also be made in the *nature* of the salvation that is experienced by the body on the one hand and the soul on the other. To be sure, to speak this way is in itself rather unbiblical: for it is the *person*—a physico-spiritual unity—who is saved. But what we have in mind is what seems to be a necessary distinction between the immediate and mediate effects of Christ's salvific work. Christ died *"for our sins,"* and when we believe, we are saved from both the penalty and the power of sin. Salvation from sin is the immediate purpose for which Christ died; and this salvation, because it ultimately works to undo all the effects of sin, eventually brings transformation of the body as well. But the latter is a mediate rather than an immediate effect of Christ's death.

This distinction raises questions about the popular belief that there is "healing in the atonement." The classic text to which appeal is made for substantiation of this belief is Matthew 8:17. The Evangelist here claims that Jesus' healing of diseases fulfills Isaiah 53:4: "He took our infirmities and bore our diseases" (αὐτὸς τὰς ἀσθενείας ἡμῶν ἔλαβεν καὶ τὰς νόσους ἐβάστεσεν). This same verse is quoted in 1 Peter 2:24 but with reference to Jesus' vicarious "bearing" of our sins (Peter, like the LXX, describes Christ as bearing our "sins" [ἁμαρτίας] rather than our "diseases"). And later in this same verse, Peter also cites Isaiah 53:5, "by his wounds you have been healed," also with reference to spiritual rather than physical "healing."[21] The argument is then that Jesus atoned for our sicknesses in the same way that He atoned for our sins; and the one, like the other, may be claimed through faith.[22] Even if this were true, it would not lead to the conclusion that God will heal all diseases of all believers in this life; for, as we have seen, the application of Christ's redemptive work takes place over a period of time—and the New Testament makes clear that we cannot expect the transformation of our bodies in this life. But, to ask the prior question, can we claim on the basis of Matthew 8:17 that "there is healing in the atonement"?

The problem is that Matthew says nothing in this context about Jesus' death. Matthew may not, then, have Jesus' death in mind at all as he cites Isaiah 53:4: the verse, in the Hebrew text that he appears to use, may simply have presented itself to him as a useful Old Testament "prooftext" for the healing ministry of Jesus.[23] But we may question whether Matthew would have used this verse without regard for its context. For he, like other New Testament authors, applies Isaiah 53 to the vicarious death of Christ (Matthew uses Isaiah 53 with reference to Jesus' suffering and death in the "passion predictions" [17:22; 20:18; 26:2] and in 20:28 and 26:28). This makes it more likely that Matthew considers Christ's bearing of diseases to have reference to the Cross.[24] This being the case, we are justified in concluding that Matthew 8:17 implies that Jesus' death is the basis for His healing of physical disease. But we should probably refrain from speaking of healing being *"in"* the atonement. For, as Warfield points out, "atonement" has to do with the cancellation of guilt and should be directly applied only to sins.[25] We would prefer, then, to say that physical healing is one *effect* of the atoning death of Christ.

This being the case, and the effects of Christ's death being applied to people through a process of time, it is specious to claim that the believer must have deliverance from sickness in the same way and to the same extent that he or she has deliverance from sin. The atoning death of Christ provides for the healing of all our diseases—but nothing in Matthew or in the New Testament implies that this healing will take place in this life. Indeed, as we have seen, the New Testament gives reason to think that triumph over physical disease, like triumph over physical death, will not come for most believers until the future "redemption of the body."

V. FAITH AND THE PROMISES

In a thought-provoking essay, C. S. Lewis explores the New Testament teaching on petitionary prayer.[26] He finds two apparently conflicting patterns. One, exhibited by Christ in Gethsemane, lacks specificity, leaving things up to God—"let your will be done." Such a pattern suggests an attitude of self-doubt and humble dependence. Not being able to know and discern God's will because of our present "weakness" (Rom. 8:26), we must qualify even our specific requests with an "if it be thy will." The other pattern of prayer, however, is one of bold confidence that God will give us whatever we ask. It is taught in Mark 11:23–24, where Jesus tells His disciples

> Truly, I say to you, whoever says to this mountain, "Be taken up and cast into the sea," and does not doubt in his heart, but believes that what he says will come to pass, it will be done for him. Therefore I tell you, whatever you ask in prayer, believe that you have received it, and it will be yours (RSV).

Lewis himself does not resolve the conflict between these two patterns, but Kenneth Hagin, a prominent exponent of the HWG, argues that the former is to be used only in prayers of "consecration" while the latter is the appropriate pattern for prayers of petition.[27] Indeed, Mark 11:23–24 is a key passage for the HWG, substantiating two of their key tenets: that faith is the means of getting *whatever* God has for us and that a "positive confession"—"believe that you have received it"—is necessary to secure an answer from God.

To be fair to the preachers of the HWG, while they are not always as careful to state the qualification as they might be, they hold that the believer has the right to "name and claim" only those things that the Bible has promised the believer. But once the believer realizes that he or she has been promised what he or she is praying for, qualifying the prayer with an "if it be thy will" is unnecessary. Worse, it is harmful, because it suggests an attitude of doubt toward what God has promised, and a prayer uttered in such doubt is not likely to be answered.

The nub of the issue, then, is whether God has promised healing in this life to every believer. If He has, then bold, unqualified petitions requesting that healing are entirely in place and we may confidently expect God's answer. We have already suggested that God has not, in fact, made such a promise to believers; but we need now to look at a text that appears to suggest the contrary and to analyze further the place of faith in divine healing.

James 5:14–16 is perhaps the most important text in the New Testament on the topic of divine healing, for it is the only prescriptive text that appears to apply to the church at large. It therefore deserves careful consideration here.

> Is any among you sick? Let him call for the elders of the church, and let them pray over him, anointing him with oil in the name of the Lord; and the prayer of faith will save the sick man, and the Lord will raise him up; and if he has committed sins, he will be forgiven. Therefore confess your sins to one another, and pray for one another, that you may be healed. The prayer of a righteous man has great power in its effects (RSV).

A few scholars have claimed that the text is not about physical illness at all that the "weakness" referred to (the word translated "sick" by RSV in v. 14 is ἀσθένεια) is a spiritual problem or an interrelational problem.[28] But this is most unlikely, for the vocabulary of the passage resembles very closely narratives of physical healings in the Gospels. There is also, of course, great controversy over the reference to "anointing with oil." Some take this to be a sacramental action, a means by which God's healing grace is conveyed to the person who is sick.[29] Others insist that the use of oil has purely medicinal purposes. We know that oil was widely used as a medicine in the ancient world (cf. Luke 10:34) and James's choice of the word ἀλείφω rather than χρίω to describe the action of "anointing," or "rubbing," may suggest that he has in mind a physically- rather than a religiously-oriented action. An implication of this view that renders it very attractive is the clear biblical endorsement it would give to the use of medicine and other appropriate medical remedies on the part of believers. To be sure, the HWG is not generally characterized by the extreme position of a Hobart Freeman, who counseled his church members not to use any medical remedies at all. A more typical view in the HWG is that medicine and doctors should be used by anyone who is not absolutely certain of having the faith necessary for healing.[30] Still, this easily leads to abuse, and the interpretation of "anointing with oil" in James 5:14 as a medical remedy would affirm the use of medicine in conjunction with the faith of the believer in divine healing and would therefore severely damage the HWG's case.

Nevertheless, this interpretation is probably not correct. Nothing from the ancient world would lead us to expect that oil would be an appropriate remedy for *any* sickness; yet this is what would seem to be implied on this view. Moreover, it is peculiar that James would make the elders of the church responsible for the administration of medical remedies. The best interpretation is that the anointing with oil is a symbolic action, intended to assure the sick person that he or she is being singled out for special attention from the Lord. Anointing has this significance in both the Old Testament and the New Testament, and James probably uses the word ἀλείφω because the action, though symbolic, is nevertheless, a real, physical action.[31] This does not, of course, mean that James would discourage the sick person from seeking appropriate medical help; indeed, we may surmise that he and other New Testament authors felt about doctors as did the second century B.C. Jew who wrote

> Honor the physician with the honor due him, according to your need of him, for the Lord created him; for healing comes from the Most High, and he will receive a gift from the king. The skill of the physician lifts up his head, and in the presence of great men he is admired. He created medicines from the earth, and a sensible man will not despise them [Sir. 38:1–4].

The element in the text that is directly relevant to our present purpose, however, is the promise of verse 14: "the prayer of faith will save him." James does not qualify this assertion, and it appears to support the HWG in their claim that God will heal everyone who prays for healing in faith. We can avoid this conclusion, of course, by taking the promise to mean simply that God will, *sometime,* heal the person who is sick—although not, perhaps, until heaven. But the promise then becomes a truism, and James appears to be promising more immediate results. Nevertheless, the claims made for this verse by the HWG are not without their difficulties. Two qualifications, one minor, one major, are needed.

The minor qualification is that, since it is the elders whom James counsels to pray in verse 14, the faith that backs up the prayer in verse 15 must also be the faith of the elders'—not the faith of the person who is sick. Technically, then, this verse gives no support at all to the contention that the person who is sick can be healed by his or her faith.

The major qualification has to do with the nature and origin of the faith exercised in the context of this prayer. The HWG advocates assume that faith is a sort of emotion that one can build up by one's own will power. Hence the constant encouragement to have "enough" faith to claim God's promise of healing. Yet this view of faith appears to be less than biblical. Faith is God's gift—and while human beings are responsible to exercise that faith, it cannot be manufactured by a human. We can often stifle faith by closing our minds and our spirits to God's work, but we may question whether we can get faith apart from God's will and work. This being the case, James's addition of the word "of faith" (πίστεως) to the word *prayer* in verse 15 may express not a condition that can be met on man's part but a condition that can ultimately be met only by God. In other words, we may question whether the faith to pray effectively for healing can be present unless it is God's will to heal. As H. van der Loos puts it, ". . . faith, forgiveness and healing are all three in essence dispensations of the grace of God. This implies that the relations between these three are not governed by the law of causality but by the will and intention of God."[32] At times God may grant us the insight to see that it is, indeed, His will to heal, and we can pray in the consciousness that we have the faith to grasp this promise of God. On the other hand, perhaps most occasions—as Romans 8:26–27 suggests—will be characterized by ignorance on our part about God's purpose to heal. We pray sincerely that God would bring healing and with the faith that God *can* heal. But, not knowing the will of God for this specific circumstance, we cannot know whether the faith to tap into God's healing power is present or not.[33]

On the view we are suggesting, then, faith is given the place that James accords it as an instrument in divine healing, but we avoid the implication that is unavoidable with the view of the HWG: that a failure to be healed must be due to people who have failed to exercise faith whether the failure is that of the person who is sick, the "elders" who pray, or the church at large. As Barron puts it, the HWG at this point appears "to be following Job's friends into theological error."[34] On our view, a failure to be healed may be because of unconfessed sin (see v. 15) or because someone stifled the faith that God had made available for the accomplishing of the healing, but it will perhaps more often be because God has not chosen to heal at that time.

This is not to devalue the importance of faith in divine healing. While faith is not always explicitly present when Jesus heals,[35] it is often prominently mentioned—see Jesus' frequent assertion that "your faith has made you well"—and Mark 6:1–6 implies a close relationship between Jesus' healing and belief (and see also Acts 14:13). The issue, rather, is how this faith is conceived and how it is related to the sovereign purposes of God. It is just at this point that the issue raised by Lewis at the beginning of this section comes home. For the issue he raises is ultimately the question of how the prayers of human beings interact with the sovereign purposes of God. No facile answer—and perhaps no logically satisfactory answer at all—can be given to this question. But what does seem clear is that the HWG loses biblical balance on this matter by giving too much place to human faith and too little to the sovereign, and sometimes mysterious, ways of God. As one critic has put it, "When faith becomes a 'condition' rather than the empty hands with which we receive God's gift we are dealing with a man-centered gospel: God is there for the sake of supplying our needs."[36] Praying "conditionally"—"if it be thy will"—is not a sign of doubt or unbelief but of humble recognition of our inability to know the mind of God. And Scripture does not suggest that cases of physical illness will be exempt from these uncertainties.

When properly regarded as a condition rather than as a cause, then, we can agree with the HWG that "faith gains whatever God has promised." The crucial question is: what has God promised? No biblical or theological basis can be found for the HWG contention that God has promised physical well-being to every Christian in this life,[37] and several of the texts we have examined in earlier sections suggest, in fact, the contrary.

Much more could be said about the HWG teaching about physical healing, and far more needs to be said on the larger question of physical healing in general. We close, however, with a final observation. We may—justly—criticize the HWG for its excesses and for its obsession with the things of "this world"— material prosperity and physical well-being. Yet is not the HWG simply a symptom of a much more widespread disease: a preoccupation with personal material well-being? a preoccupation that is eating into Western Christianity like a cancer? The HWG deserves, and requires, criticism. But we should not criticize it without stopping to consider whether we, too, are guilty of similar misconceptions and imbalance. Do we give material things and physical health the place in our prayers, in our work, and in our priorities that corresponds to the biblical worldview? Are we as willing to sacrifice material and physical ease for the sake of bringing others to know Christ as was Paul? Until we answer these questions positively, we must be sure to include in our criticisms of the HWG a healthy dose of self-criticism as well.

CHAPTER FIVE

THE GOSPEL OF GREED VERSUS
THE GOSPEL OF THE GRACE OF GOD

A Sermon Critique by
David L. Larsen

> Then he said to them, "Watch out! Be on your guard against all kinds of greed;
> a man's life does not consist in the abundance of his possessions" (Luke 12:15).

A pernicious and dangerous teaching is stalking our land. It has filtered into evangelical communication and thinking more than we realize. Unfortunately we have exported it to Europe and the Third World where it has brought dissension and even schism. I am referring to what we may call "the gospel of greed." It is the prosperity gospel, health and wealth theology, the grab it and get it, name it and claim it, God is for our gain message that has such widespread currency in our time.

One of the major textbooks of the movement is Mrs. Kenneth Copeland's *God's Will Is Prosperity*. On the far south side of Chicago, Dr. Johnnie Coleman preaches to the largest audiences within the city limits on the topic, "What Is Your Dream? Peace? Health? Prosperity? Love? Your Dreams Can Come True."

A particularly blatant and brash expression of this message has been given by the Reverend Terry in San Diego. In an extended article, *The Wall Street Journal* reports that "The Rev. Terry has a Gospel to Cheer the Me Generation—Affluence Is Your Right—Yuppies Take Notice." "You can have it all now! Being rich and happy doesn't carry with it a burden of guilt. If you are poor, you're irresponsible," she proclaims with gusto. Her parishioners have bumper stickers reading, "Prosperity is your divine right."[1]

The Journal goes on to describe her as bouncy and relentlessly upbeat as she preaches her gospel of "happiness now." "Live fully now and create a heaven on earth. We are the cause of our own unhappiness. Our ministry isn't into sin, guilt, disease, pain or hunger. Truly religious people are happy and light instead of sober and serious." Her emphasis is on success. Attending these services is like a trip. One devotee testifies: "I feel great every time I leave a service." This is "the new Christianity . . . people don't need to change for the better but simply to realize that they are already perfect." She doesn't believe in sin or hell. "Sin is simply self-hatred." Her latest book is entitled *How to Have More in a Have Not World*. Adherents can take advantage of all kinds of seminars and workshops such as "Dressing to Win" (charge is two hundred dollars a day) conducted by a fashion consultant who is also a member of the church board. He says, "My clients and Terry's congregation want the same things . . . a more affluent lifestyle and to live life more fully."

Beyond any question, this is what the apostle Paul would call "another gospel." None of the rudiments of the New Testament Gospel of the grace of our Lord Jesus Christ is in any evidence. This teaching is a pathetic and tragic accommodation to the cultural mores of upwardly mobile American culture and lifestyle. Sadly, it has seeped into our thinking and motivation far more profoundly than we are aware. It is further a cruel hoax. Health and wealth are not promised to the believer in Christ. Many of the godliest Christians who have ever lived have enjoyed neither health nor wealth. G. K. Chesterton wisely said, "If prosperity is the reward of virtue, then prosperity is the mark and symptom of virtue" and that is manifestly not taught in Scripture nor confirmed in experience. Paul asserts concerning our sovereign God that "My God will supply all your need" (Phil. 4:19), not all of our greed.

It is important for us to analyze this message and this mindset, which have become so pervasive in our time. Several very critical components of "the gospel of greed" are seen in the parable our Lord told as He urged His hearers, "Be on your guard against all kinds of greed." The rich fool's delusions are in a sense paradigmatic for us today.

I. THE "GOSPEL OF GREED" IS ROOTED IN SELFISM

The patently and painfully "me-first" obsession of the prosperity gospel is by no means new. The rich fool in the parable of Jesus has serious "I-trouble." He suffers from severe "I-strain." Look at the prominence of the first-personal pronouns: "He thought to himself, 'What shall *I* do? *I* have no place to store *my* crops . . . this is what *I'll* do. *I* will tear down my barns and build bigger ones, and there *I* will store all *my* grain and *my* goods . . . and *I'll* say to myself . . .'" (Luke 12:17–19).

The physicians of our culture have spoken of ours as a narcissistic age. Narcissus was the Greek mythological character who fell in love with his own reflection in a pool. Christopher Lasch, Aaron Stern, and Robert Coles have written with special poignancy about the narcissism of our times. Robert Nisbet has a particularly searching analysis in which he argues that "in the twilight of authority" and its ensuing vacuum, modern man has turned to "obsessive concern with self."[2] Selfism is at the bottom of health and wealth theology.

What we are seeing is the Copernican revolution in reverse. Whereas Copernicus determined that the earth and man are not at the center, we are once again seeing the assertion that man is at the center of the universe. Martin Luther argued that man's problem is that he is *incurvatus in se*—turned in upon himself. God is no longer seen in His infinite majesty and holiness. He is no longer the point of reference, the center. Man wishes to be autonomous. This is the very essence of what sin is.

Sin is the assertion of self to the exclusion of God. Hell is the ultimate and final assertion of self to the ultimate and final exclusion of God. This was at the heart of Satan's primal rebellion against God (Isa. 14:13–15). This was the tempter's appeal in Eden, "You will be like God" (Gen. 3:5). This conceit drove the builders of the tower of Babel in their arrogant project, "Then they said,

'Come, let us build ourselves a city, with a tower that reaches to the heavens, so that we can make a name for ourselves and not be scattered over the face of the whole earth'" (Gen. 11:4). This misguided effort to achieve unity on man's terms shows further the dangers and perils of being self-bound.

Allan Bloom in his epochal *The Closing of the American Mind* argues that no small part of our American problem today stems from an identity crisis which has arisen because we have made "the self the modern substitute for the soul."[3] Eugene Peterson quotes de Tocqueville a century and a half ago saying of America, "Each citizen is habitually engaged in the contemplation of a very puny object, namely himself."[4] He also quotes the eminent Cambridge historian, Herbert Butterfield, to the effect that "Concealed egotism is perhaps a greater cause of political conflict, a greater source of political problems, than anything else on this globe."[5]

Thus this perennial human problem has flowered and borne its malignant fruit as the inspired apostle said it would: "But mark this: there will be terrible times in the last days. People will be lovers of themselves, lovers of money, boastful, proud." (2 Tim. 3:1ff.). What has always characterized our fallen natures will intensify and be exacerbated as history draws toward its climax. The "me-first" penchant has spawned religious progeny—it is the self-fixated "gospel of greed" in which our great God is seen as subordinated to the whim and satisfaction of the sinner's bloated ego.

Walt Whitman long ago wrote his famous "Song of Myself," which begins with the lines, "I celebrate myself." This epitomizes the mood of modernity. We used to sing:

> Oh what a beautiful morning,
> Oh what a beautiful day,
> I've got a wonderful feeling,
> Everything's going my way.

Again, notice the point of reference. Self is at the center. Scripture characterizes our stubborn and willful ways in terms of "All we like sheep have gone astray, we have turned everyone to his own way" (Isa. 53:6). This self-centeredness is our problem.

So John Lennon sang, "I just believe in me, that is reality." The crooner sang, "I did it my way." We now have on the newsstands the periodical *Self*. The best seller of awhile back put it boldly: *Looking Out for Number One*. Other book titles with religious flavoring include *Love Yourself, The Art of Learning to Love Yourself, Celebrate Yourself, You're Better Than You Think, How to Write Your Own Ticket with God*. Consider the arrogance and the depravity of these sentiments.

The old biblical ethic of self-sacrifice has given way to grandiose notions of self-fulfillment, self-realization, self-aggrandizement, as Yankelovich has shown so clearly in his book *Searching for Self-Fulfillment in a World Turned Upside-Down*. Etzioni's powerful *An Immodest Agenda: Rebuilding America Before the Twenty-First Century* cites our ego-centered mentality as the chief villain in our societal morass.[6]

Tina Turner lauds Buddhism as her new religion and has put up a new altar in her home. She gurgles, "What I love about my new religion is that every person decides for him or herself what is right and what is wrong." The West German mountain climber, Reinhold Messner, has scaled the fourteen highest peaks on earth. He refused to plant his nation's flag on any of them, sullenly explaining, "I do things only for myself."[7] That is the spirit that has infected our culture and is now infiltrating our own thought-categories as Christians. This is the root cause of the obviously increasing reluctance of believers to make any long-range commitment to Christian service or involvement.

Aesop said long ago: "It is easy for me to curry favor with myself." Walt Whitman unashamedly and brazenly articulated the spirit of our times: "I find no sweeter fat than clings to my own bones." Max Stirner in *The Ego and His Own* puts it as crassly as anyone: "Nothing is more to me than myself . . . whether what I think and do is Christian, what do I care? Whether it is humane, liberal or inhumane, illiberal—what do I care about that?"

This is a tragic reduction, because man is not the center nor the goal. God is not the means to our ends. "The chief end of man is to know God and glorify him forever." Jesus said, "If any man would come after me, let him deny himself, take up his cross and follow me" (Matt. 16:24). The anthropocentric corrosion of God in the "gospel of greed" is to make the everlasting God our errand boy. GOD WILL BE GOD!

II. THE "GOSPEL OF GREED" REVELS IN MATERIALISM

The appalling consequences of the acutely inflamed ego are to be observed in the rich fool of our Lord's parable. Caught in the flypaper of self-preoccupation, his horizon is limited to his own material enhancement. More crops and bigger barns become the predictable extension of the greedy self. Things and possessions are self-maximizers and thus they are in the saddle. "And I'll say to myself, 'you have plenty of good things laid up for many years'" (Luke 12:19). "Greed is idolatry" (Col. 3:5), and the foolish man is seeking from material substance the satisfaction that only God Himself can give.

Our grave peril in the U.S. is that we do not worship G O D, but the G N P. Affluence has become our religion (and it might be said we are suffering from affluenza). Our consumptive orientation is without parallel in the history of the planet. Our credit-laden economy fosters greed and exposes us to the danger of excess. No people have ever had a higher standard of living than we. We are 7 percent of the world's population who possess 50 percent of the real wealth of the world and annually consume one-third of what is consumed on spaceship earth.

Think of how the Scripture warns us of the danger of riches. "People who want to get rich fall into temptation and a trap and into many foolish and harmful desires that plunge men into ruin and destruction. For the love of money is a root of all kinds of evil. Some people, eager for money, have wandered from the faith and pierced themselves with many griefs" (1 Tim. 6:9–10). Some can remain unruined by wealth and they are good stewards, but money and goods are hazardous generally to spiritual health. In our movement, the days of our material poverty were the days of our spiritual vigor. History shows a correlation. The church in America has become increasingly well-to-do and increasingly

Laodicean in outlook (see Rev. 3:17ff.). The rich young ruler basically floundered "because he had great wealth" (Mark 10:22).

How many of us are hooked like the rich fool? We want more and more and more and then bigger and bigger and bigger. Impaled on the "Imelda Marcos syndrome," we are never satisfied. The "gospel of greed" goes hand in glove with this prevailing ethos of our time. "All this and heaven too!" President Eisenhower confessed: "I believe in the American way of life." The secularization and privatization of faith effectively cut the lordship of Jesus Christ out of our lives.

The rising tide of materialism among us is shown in a recent study made by the Cooperative Research Program. It found young people in America to be "overwhelmingly materialistic; interested more than ever primarily in making money."[8] The objective of developing a meaningful philosophy of life as an essential or very important reason for going to college used to rank high. It is now the lowest in ranking that it has ever been in the twenty-year history of the annual survey. To be "well off financially" is now at the top of the list. In this study of 290,000 college freshmen in more than five hundred colleges, 75.6 percent indicated they were interested primarily in financial success. In 1966, 83 percent said "developing a meaningful philosophy of life" was at the top of the list. There is clearly a shift in student values. The study concludes that recent trends show an unprecedented concern for money, power, and status.

The burgeoning of materialism in the upcoming generation is overtly the legacy of the older generation. Ivan Boesky, the Wall Street swindler, articulated the implicit premise of many when he announced to an investor's group before he was indicted: "I think greed is healthy. I think you can be greedy and still feel good about yourself." He was given a standing ovation. Contrast that wisdom of this world with the words of our divine Savior, "Be on your guard against all kinds of greed; a man's life does not consist in the abundance of his possessions" (Luke 12:15).

Many of us who would take strong exception to the dialectical materialism of Marx and Lenin seem unaware of the degree to which we have been victimized by an equally vicious materialism in our society. We seem numbed by the greed factor. But greed is the engine that drives much that we do. I am convinced that opulent lifestyle and the acquisitive urge were the beginning of the end for several of our preachers and their families. Owning five cars and five houses and luxuriating in what they called "the blessing of God" was in fact capitulation to greed and theft. "Watch out!" Jesus says. Both those who have much and those who have little can alike be ravished by the compulsion to shop until they drop.

And it isn't only money and possessions that may consume us. Our twitching, convulsive egos can be stroked by the lure of name and fame. John Dean of Watergate notoriety admits in his book, *Blind Ambition,* that "All my life I wanted to be in the oval office, at the right hand of the President of the United States." As kids we loved to play "king of the mountain." Who can get to the top and keep throwing the others down? *Pleonexia* or the striving after power is a familiar game to us in the church. We want bigger congregations and bigger buildings and bigger staffs and bigger budgets. Is it very clear as to just why church leaders and pastors want ever bigger and bigger domains? I have found that the pulpit is a dangerous place for a son of Adam such as myself. My pride loves adulation and applause. I can strut sitting down.

Our sensate age fosters an appetite for the things that are seen. Jesus warned about the "days of Noah" when citizens were absorbed in eating and drinking and marriage—fine things, but they easily preempt the more important spiritual priorities of ministry and service for Christ. The grab for power and possessions is so unlike the Lord Jesus. The servant heart of the Master is in such contrast to the overbearing conceit and self-interest prevalent all about us. We used to want to keep up with the Joneses. Now we are intent on being the Joneses with whom everyone seeks to keep up.

The irony for those who put their eggs in this basket is pointed out by Jeremy Rifkin in *The Emerging Order*. In point of fact we are beginning to see the end of unlimited growth and wealth. Jacques Ellul reminds us of the trap of the technological society—the illusion that technology will solve the problems. The unparalleled abundance of our time has not addressed the deep and claimant issues in our society as our cities decay, the permanent underclass festers, drugs and substance abuse proliferate, and every significant index of the health of our culture points to dissolution and disintegration.

Jesus unequivocally asserts the eternal bankruptcy of the person who "stores up things for himself" (Luke 12:21). Do we really believe him? Health and wealth theology mistakenly puts its emphasis on "things for self" but is not "rich toward God."

III. THE "GOSPEL OF GREED" RESULTS IN HEDONISM

Engrossed with self-advantage, employed in the accumulation of what this world offers, the enthusiast for prosperity is relentlessly and inescapably bound and chained to an outcome. What is it all for? What is the bottom line? The rich fool drew the inevitable conclusion: "Take life easy; eat, drink and be merry" (Luke 12:19). The outcome is hyperhedonism. Have a good time. Maximize the present moment and its potential enjoyment and good feeling.

The apostle Paul spoke of the pitfall of being "lovers of pleasure rather than lovers of God" (2 Tim. 3:4). We seem to live in our country in one enormous Atlantic City in which fun and pleasure and indulgence are the highest priority. We see these values invading the church. We sense a rash of "upbeat Christianity," in which the Gospel is seen as a giant cornucopia overflowing with good things. "God wants us to be happy" is the ruling principle.

What prosperity theology has forgotten is that God does not exist to make us happy. Our righteous God has no truck with the rising tide of appetite that brooks no restraint nor with our increasing unwillingness to defer gratification. The reality of God's being with which we must come to terms is set forth in Holy Scripture:

> You are worthy, our Lord and God,
> to receive glory and honor and power,
> for you created all things,
> and for your pleasure they are and were created (Rev. 4:11).

God is more concerned to make us holy than He is to make us happy. "Without holiness no one will see the Lord" (Heb. 12:14). Something very heretical has lodged among us to the effect that a person can be a Christian and not follow Jesus. So Mickey Cohen talked about being a Christian gangster and Larry Flynt argued that there was such a thing as pornography for Jesus. The hedonistic agenda of the world cannot be the agenda for God's people. Rather, "Since we have these promises, dear friends, let us purify ourselves from everything that contaminates body and spirit, perfecting holiness out of reverence for God" (2 Cor. 7:1).

Ours is an era of soft living. Think of the bumper sticker: "Are we having fun yet?" There is the be-all and end-all. Or the T-shirt inscribed: "The one who dies with the most toys wins." The bumper sticker to top them all in capturing the temper of our times must be "Jesus—open 24 hours to serve you."

The summum bonum seems to be, as the Rev. Terry's congregant put it, "I feel great every time I leave a service." It is surely not "the comfort of the Scriptures" that this spiritual epicure seeks. Did people leave the ministry of Jeremiah or Elijah "feeling great"? Did those who attended the ministry of John the Baptist by the Jordan exit in euphoric bliss? "I don't feel like it" is sufficient grounds today. Where is the sense of duty and the dedication to truth? "It can't be wrong when it feels so right," we hear it said. An unrepentant criminal and acknowledged pervert was so pleased with his minister because, as he said, "My minister helps me feel so good about myself." Is that our high calling in the Christian ministry?

The paramountcy of pleasure with its primary pursuits of fun and pleasure (even in the church) will ultimately incarcerate us in the sarcophagus of self. Joseph Sittler used to tell of a woman at a church where he was the interim pastor. She worked at a hospital in Chicago. She often testified: "Every morning on my way to work, I pray to Jesus that he will find me a parking space. As you know, pastor, he always does." Sittler says that he kept asking himself what kind of God-relationship could be built on this parking-space-finding Jesus that could sustain this woman in profound deprivation and tragedy.

He asked the woman, "What if there was another woman driving to the hospital to take a sick child to the emergency room, and you drove right into the parking space that Jesus found for you, and this woman who is frantic with a sick child cannot find a space. How about her?" The woman retorted, "She didn't pray hard enough."

Something here is very distorted and very wrong. But this is precisely the hole into which "grab it and get it" has fallen most miserably. It reminds me of a hotel at Lourdes in France, called the Gethsemane. The twinkling lights say it all: GETHSEMANE: WITH ALL MODERN COMFORTS. Where is discipleship? Where are the examples of self-sacrifice? A psychologist recently lamented in an interview over TV the results of a survey: of 287 college youth she found that all wanted greatness or satisfaction in life but few understood that there was any connection between being great and serving others. "They are a generation accustomed to being served," concluded the psychologist, "not to serving."

God said to the rich fool, "This very night your very life will be demanded from you. Then who will get what you have prepared for yourself?" (Luke 12:20). The hedonistic lifestyle of the fool was a tragedy. Many today say it,

> When we live, let's live in clover,
> For when we die, we die all over.

The studies show that the greatest crisis right now is not the church in the world but the world in the church.[9] We Christians are lapping up our culture and demonstrating a conformity to this age, which is rapidly enveloping us in the labyrinths of modernity.

There is no cross of Christ in the prosperity gospel. Even those of us who would glory in the cross are squeamish. We will go to the cross, but we don't want to get on the cross. Jesus dying for us is all right, but we are not too willing to die with Jesus. At this point, it seems to me, we must be countercultural with a vengeance. A dear young missionary said: "I have been invited to say good-bye to myself" as she left things and family to go into the jungles of southern Mexico.

George Mueller spoke of a truth we cannot find in the "gospel of greed." "There was a day when I died," he said, almost touching the floor. "Died to George Mueller, his opinions, preferences, tastes, and will; died to the world, its approval or censure; died to the approval or blame even of my friends or brethren."

The greatest problem we have is the unsurrendered self. Our problem is pride. We do not want to acknowledge, "Vile and full of sin am I." It is not flattering. It is not popular. The Pelagianism of the "gospel of greed" makes man big and God small. It caters to our conceit. When I was a boy I read about *The Little Engine That Could*. The heroic little train chugged and puffed up the steep grade, "I think I can, I think I can." The reality is: Thinking you can just ain't enough! This typical American symbol, like Jonathan Livingston Seagull later on, embodies our vain and futile insistence that we are sufficient.

So a thoughtful interpreter of Jonathan Edwards insightfully analyzed the reason for Edwards's influence: "While others preached self-reliance and sang the song of the self, Edwards drove nearer the truth—that nothing can be saved without confronting its own damnation, that the way to gain one's life is to lose it." The "gospel of greed" is truly another gospel. Let our loyalty and our fidelity ever be to the everlasting Gospel of our Lord Jesus Christ.

DEFENDING THE GOSPEL

CHAPTER SIX

RELIGIOUS PLURALISM AND TRUTH

Harold A. Netland

We live in a religiously pluralistic world. In recent decades we have been made aware as never before of the tremendous diversity among religious traditions. And with increased awareness of religious pluralism has come a greater emphasis on questions dealing with the relation between various religious traditions. Such questions lead naturally to what is often regarded as the scandal of religious pluralism—the problem of conflicting truth-claims. The problem arises from the fact that adherents of the major religions seem to be saying quite different and even incompatible things about the nature of the religious ultimate and of humanity's relation to this ultimate. For example, evangelical Christians believe in an infinite Creator who has definitively revealed Himself in the incarnation in Jesus of Nazareth. Muslims, while acknowledging God as the omniscient, omnipotent creator of the universe, reject as blasphemous any suggestion that Jesus was God incarnate. Theravada Buddhists, on the other hand, do not regard the universe as the product of an ontologically distinct creator but rather as the product of the creative efficacy of karmic effect. And even within a single religious tradition significant differences emerge: in considering the soteriology of Mahayana Buddhism, for example, we see that followers of Jodo-Shinshu Buddhism maintain that salvation/enlightenment is attainable simply by exercising faith in the Amida Buddha and the recitation of the *nembutsu,* whereas adherents of Zen, who reject as illusory any worldview that implies dualism, hold that *satori* (namely, enlightenment, commonly regarded as the direct, unmediated apprehension of the ultimate nature of reality, transcending all distinctions) is to be attained only through rigorous self-discipline.

Until relatively recently it was widely assumed that since incompatible truth-claims[1] are being made not all of the claims made by the various religions can be true. At least some must be false. Thus, it has traditionally been held that the Muslim and the evangelical Christian cannot both be correct in their beliefs about the identity of Jesus. For the sake of convenience let us call this the "exclusivist" view of the relation between religious traditions. On the exclusivist view, if the major religions make at least some claims that are incompatible with each other, and where two or more such claims contradict each other, they cannot both be true—at least one must be false.[2] It is clear that the exclusivist position has been presupposed by most people involved in Christian missions up until fairly recently. Indeed one could argue that the exclusivist position, combined with the conviction that the claims of Christianity are true, has been the driving force behind the modern missionary movement.

However, the exclusivist view has come under sharp attack in recent years and is rejected by many theologians and even missionaries as naive, arrogant, bigoted, and a vestige of an immoral religious imperialism. A number of pervasive assumptions seem to be responsible for this. For example, it is often assumed that there is something arrogant and insensitive about claiming that only one religious tradition is true. Why should just one religion be granted such privileged status? Or it is held that exclusivism must be rejected since it produces reprehensible effects upon interaction between adherents of different religions. Closely related to this is the assumption that since we are a global village dependent upon each other for survival we must at all costs strive for peaceful coexistence and harmony, and that accusing other religions of embracing false beliefs is somehow incompatible with this. A strong reaction against the perceived evils of the exclusivist position has resulted in a preoccupation with searching out areas of agreement among religions and a pursuit of mutual understanding at the expense of consideration of questions of truth. To be sure, all of us ought to be working toward greater understanding and respect for adherents of other religious traditions. But this hardly entails ignoring the issue of truth. Veteran missiologist Arthur Glasser is right in lamenting the fact that the truth question is virtually ignored in contemporary discussions of religious pluralism and interreligious dialogue.[3]

Careful reflection shows each of the above assumptions to be gratuitous. The first simply misunderstands the exclusive nature of truth. Of course, one can be arrogant and insensitive in claiming the truth of one's own view, and it is to be regretted that such religious triumphalism has all too often been manifest in Christian missions. But there is nothing in the exclusivist position itself that demands such arrogance. Truth is by definition exclusive: if a given statement is true it necessarily excludes its contradictory as false. But there need not be anything arrogant about this (is one necessarily arrogant in claiming that "the earth is round" is true and its contradictory false?). The central issue here is whether the claims of a given religion are true or false; if they are true, their contradictories must be false.[4] Similarly, while we can readily admit that the history of religion gives ample evidence that exclusivists have acted in barbarous ways to adherents of other religions, we should note that there is no necessary connection between holding a given group's religious beliefs to be false and the radical mistreatment of members of that group.[5] Certainly one can consider the beliefs of another to be false and yet treat that individual with respect and dignity. And finally, the third assumption seems to presume that we can only cooperate and live harmoniously with those we happen to agree with. But surely this is nonsense. On the contrary, is it not a mark of maturity to be able to live peaceably with those with whom we may profoundly disagree?

In this chapter I wish to refocus attention upon the issue of truth in religious pluralism, with special reference to the problem of conflicting truth-claims, by examining critically two positions that have been proposed as alternatives to the exclusivist view. By criticizing the views of Wilfred Cantwell Smith of Harvard and John H. Hick of Claremont, I will be defending the thesis that it is indeed legitimate to apply the categories of truth and falsity to major religious traditions and that it is reasonable to hold that if the central beliefs of one tradition are true then at least some of the conflicting beliefs from other traditions will be false. It may be of interest to know that I write as an evangelical Christian whose formal training has been primarily in analytic philosophy of religion and who has encountered religious pluralism in a dramatic way while living in Kyoto, Japan.

I. WILFRED CANTWELL SMITH

Wilfred Cantwell Smith is well known as a distinguished historian of religion and interpreter of Islam. Our concern, however, is not with his contributions to these fields but with an influential thesis advanced in a number of his writings on religious faith. He argues that it is a serious error to speak of religions or religious belief as being true or false in themselves, as these adjectives are generally understood. Rather, he claims, religions and religious beliefs can be regarded as true or false only in a fresh "personalistic" understanding of truth. Since the personalistic view of truth is offered as an alternative to the exclusivist view it will be helpful to spend some time looking at what is meant by personalistic truth.

Cantwell Smith suggests that the concept of a religion as a distinct entity that can be true or false irrespective of considerations of the personal faith of its adherents is a modern distortion of the actual nature of religion.

> It is a surprisingly modern aberration for anyone to think that Christianity is true or that Islam is—since the Enlightenment basically, when Europe began to postulate religions as intellectualistic systems, patterns of doctrines, so that they could for the first time be labelled "Christianity" and "Buddhism," and could be called true or false.[6]

> Further, I would contend that man's religious life is liberated, not devastated, when it is recognized that "a religion" cannot in itself be true or false. The notion that a given religion may be true, or even more, that it may not be true, has caused untold mischief. Or again, that one religion is true while another is false; or equally misleading, that all religions are equally true (which is, of course, nonsense). We must learn that this is not where religious truth and falsity lie. Religions, either simply or together, cannot be true or false—as one rejoices to recognize once one is emancipated from supposing that there are such things in our universe.[7]

> It is dangerous and impious to suppose that Christianity is true, as an abstract system, something "out there" impersonally subsisting, with which we can take comfort in being linked—its effortless truth justifying us and giving us status. Christianity, I would suggest, is not true absolutely, impersonally, statically; rather, it can *become* true, if and as you or I appropriate it to ourselves and interiorize it, insofar as we live it out from day to day. It becomes true as we take it off the shelf and personalize it, in actual existence.[8]

The exclusivist view mentioned earlier presupposes that religions and particular religious beliefs can be regarded as either true or false, that there is an important sense in which we can speak of religions and religious beliefs as true or false.[9] This assumption is rejected by Cantwell Smith. In his classic *The Meaning and End of Religion* he presents an elaborate historical argument defending the suggestion that the concept of a religion as a distinct entity that can be true or false is a relatively modern one and is the product of an illicit reification. Rather than concentrate upon separate religions as such, we should be concerned with the personal faith of religious individuals. Faith is defined as "that quality of or available to humankind by which we are characterized as transcending, or are enabled to transcend, the natural order."[10] Discussion of Cantwell Smith's understanding of religious faith is beyond the scope of this paper. However, two brief comments are in order. First, although one may well wish to question his historical argument at several points, even if it were sound and the notion of Christianity or Buddhism as distinct religions that are true or false were a relatively modern one, what follows from this? Simply because it is a modern concept it does not follow that it is somehow mistaken or illegitimate (surely history provides evidence of at least some progress in knowledge?). Something more than merely an historical argument is needed to show that such a concept is inappropriate. (Cantwell Smith does indeed provide such an argument, which will be examined below.) Second, even if we grant that the notion of a religion as a distinct entity is somehow misguided, the question of truth (and that of conflicting truth-claims) remains: we would still have individuals who accept and propagate certain beliefs, dogmas, teachings, etc., and presumably these are either true or false.[11] We would still have, for example, St. Augustine believing that an omnipotent God exists who created the universe and Vasubandhu maintaining that it is simply the product of karmic effect.

It is important to recognize that Cantwell Smith is not suggesting that the adjective *true* cannot be applied to religion at all; he is simply claiming that it cannot be applied in the same sense in which it is generally used. The heart of his attack upon the exclusivist view consists in his argument that when applied to religion or religious belief "true" cannot be understood as the adjective of "propositional truth" but of "personalistic truth." He correctly notes that truth is generally understood in a propositional sense[12]—namely, truth is held to be a property of propositions such that a proposition is true if, and only if, the state of affairs to which it refers obtains; otherwise it is false. That is, a proposition is true only if reality is as it asserts it to be. The notion of propositional truth, widely accepted by contemporary philosophers, reflects the most basic sense of "true" as this adjective is used in ordinary discourse. But according to Cantwell Smith propositional truth is inappropriate in religion.

> Truth and falsity are often felt in modern times to be properties or functions of statements or propositions; whereas the present proposal is that much is to be gained by seeing them rather, or anyway by seeing them also, and primarily, as properties or functions of persons. . . . The very suggestion that truth is not an inert and impersonal observable but that truth means truth for me, for you, is challenging. . . . I particularly wish to query the vision that it is legitimate or helpful to regard truth, and falsity, as pertaining to statements considered apart from the person who makes them or about whom they are made.[13]

And in place of propositional truth Cantwell Smith proposes what he calls "personalistic truth." A clear definition of personalistic truth is never given, but what he has in mind seems to be this: the locus of truth is not propositions but persons and, in a derivative sense, also religions.[14] Personalistic truth does not reflect correspondence with reality so much as it signifies integrity and faithfulness in a person, or authenticity in one's life.

> Human Behavior, in word or deed, is the nexus between man's inner life and the surrounding world. Truth at the personalistic level is that quality by which both halves of that relationship are chaste and appropriate: are true.[15]

There is a strong moral element in personalistic truth. "There is no room here for that kind of truth that leaves unaffected the moral character and private behavior of those who know it."[16] Further, personalistic truth is not something abstract or detached from one's personal life; it demands existential appropriation. "No statement might be accepted as true that had not been inwardly appropriated by its author."[17] There is nothing static or unchanging about personalistic truth; beliefs and even religions can become true or might be true for me but false for you.

> Christianity, I would suggest, is not true absolutely, impersonally, statically; rather, it can *become* true, if and as you or I appropriate it to ourselves and interiorize it, insofar as we live it out from day to day.[18]

Acceptance of the notion of personalistic truth has far-reaching implications for the exclusivist view of the relation among religious traditions. Instead of regarding truth and falsity as properties of beliefs (namely, of propositions expressing beliefs) or of religions in themselves, we will see truth as a dynamic, changing product of the faith of individuals. No longer will it make sense to speak of the truth of, say, the doctrine of the Incarnation without also making reference to the response of faith to the doctrine; the doctrine of the Incarnation can only be said to be true *for someone*, and it will only be true to the extent that someone "existentially appropriates" the belief in the doctrine. Since the problem of conflicting truth-claims presupposes the notion of propositional truth, Cantwell Smith is convinced that acceptance of the concept of personalistic truth will do away with the problem of conflicting truth-claims.

What are we to make of this proposal? It is possible that Cantwell Smith intends his theory of personalistic truth simply to emphasize the point that in religious matters mere intellectual assent to certain propositions is not enough—one must appropriate such beliefs so that one's character and conduct are significantly altered (we are to be doers of the Word and not hearers only). If so, this is certainly a necessary reminder, even if it is somewhat misleadingly presented as a theory of truth. But I suspect that much more is intended than simply this healthy exhortation. For throughout his writings the personalistic view of truth is presented as an alternative to the concept of propositional truth. Unfortunately, the precise relationship between the personalistic and the propositional notions of truth is never clarified.[19] There is a pervasive ambiguity in his discussion that allows for at least three possible interpretations:

a. Personalistic truth can legitimately be applied to religion whereas propositional truth cannot.

b. Both personalistic and propositional truth can be applied to religion, but personalistic truth is somehow more basic and fundamental than propositional truth.

c. Both personalistic and propositional truth can be applied to religion, but propositional truth is more basic than personalistic truth.

I will argue that only (c) is defensible and that on such an interpretation the problem of conflicting truth-claims in religion is still with us.

The major difficulty with both (a) and (b) above is that the logically most basic or fundamental notion of truth in any realm whatsoever is that of propositional truth. Now we can readily admit that "true" has a wide variety of uses and meanings (e.g., "a true Swede," "a true friend," "the purse is true alligator, not imitation," "he was true to his word," etc.) and it may even be that something like the concept of personalistic truth is indispensable to understanding religion (although in that case one would hope that a less misleading locution for the concept would be utilized!). But what Cantwell Smith fails to recognize is that there is an important sense in which propositional truth is logically basic and is presupposed by all other meanings of "true." This can be illustrated by considering the following statement:

(S_1) The propositional theory of truth is misleading when applied to religion and should be rejected.

It is crucial to see that if S_1 is offered as something that should be accepted as true, then it is itself dependent upon the notion of propositional truth. For S_1 expresses a proposition that makes a claim about reality: it asserts that reality is such that the notion of propositional truth is somehow misleading when applied to religion and thus should be rejected. Presumably someone uttering S_1 intends to be saying something true (if not, of course, we need not bother taking his statement seriously). But if so, then he presupposes that the proposition expressed by S_1 is true, and this is precisely what is meant by presupposing the propositional notion of truth. This can be further illustrated in reference to Cantwell Smith's concept of personalistic truth. Let us use "S_2" to stand for the statement of his theory of personalistic truth:

(S_2) In religion, truth is to be understood primarily as personalistic, that is, as having its locus in persons who satisfactorily appropriate beliefs.

Now if Cantwell Smith intends us to accept S_2 as true (and surely he does) then he is presupposing propositional truth in articulating his theory. For S_2 expresses a proposition he takes to be true and would like us to accept as true as well. We should note that the sense in which S_2 is said to be true is not that of personalistic truth but rather propositional truth. For if S_2 were said to be true only in a personalistic sense then it would be "true" only in so far as you or I appropriate it, or allow it to have significant impact on our lives. Indeed, S_2 might then become true for you or might be true for me but false for you, etc. But this is clearly not what Cantwell Smith has in mind when he argues for his theory. He is claiming that S_2 is true in the logically more basic sense of propositional truth.

A related difficulty emerges when we consider Cantwell Smith's suggestion that religions or religious beliefs can become true in a personalistic sense. Again, it seems, what is presupposed in the discussion is the notion of propositional truth. Certain beliefs (e.g., beliefs in the deity of Jesus or Nazareth, or in reincarnation, or that Allah is a righteous and holy judge, etc.) are said to be true in a personalistic sense only in so far as they are somehow appropriated by adherents of the respective traditions. But one will only appropriate such beliefs if one already accepts them as true in a nonpersonalistic, or propositional, sense. That is, the belief that Allah is a righteous judge will only "become true" in a personalistic sense if the adherent of Islam first accepts the proposition expressed by "Allah is a righteous judge" to be true. Similarly, religions such as Islam or Buddhism can only "become true" in a personalistic sense if certain relevant beliefs are accepted by the respective adherents as true in a propositional sense. The key point in all of this is simply that the coherent articulation and affirmation of any belief or view whatsoever presupposes the notion of propositional truth.

Finally, we should note that Cantwell Smith's theory fails to recognize that propositions are inseparable from religious beliefs.[20] To be sure, "belief" and "proposition" are not synonymous, and there is more to believing than simply giving mental assent to a proposition. But in believing one always believes *something*, and *what* one believes is a proposition. Believing may include more than simple assent to propositions, but it does not involve less than that. The fact is that adherents of the various religious traditions believe certain propositions about the religious ultimate, humanity, and the nature of the universe to be true. And where these beliefs conflict (as they often do) we have the problem of conflicting truth-claims. In sum, we have seen that, contrary to the suggestion of Cantwell Smith, the concept of propositional truth is logically basic and thus cannot be eliminated from religious beliefs, and that in so far as various religions embrace conflicting beliefs we have the problem of conflicting truth-claims.

II. JOHN HICK

If we accept propositional truth as basic and admit that the major religions do make at least some claims that seem to be incompatible with each other, should we not conclude that at least some of the claims of some of the religions are false? Not so, according to John Hick, the influential philosopher of religion and theologian. Hick accepts both the priority of propositional truth and the fact that there are significant conflicts between some of the claims being made by the various religions.[21] He recognizes that it follows from this that questions about the truth or falsity of basic claims made by religious traditions cannot be avoided. But he rejects the suggestion that this entails that at least some of the claims of some of the religions must be false.

Hick proposes a comprehensive theory that allegedly portrays the distinctive nature of each religious tradition, recognizes significant differences in claims being made by each religion, and yet does not necessitate our concluding that at least some of these claims must be false. His theory calls for nothing less than a revolution in the way in which we think about the relation between religions. The traditional "Ptolemaic" view that regards one's own religion as exclusively true and others that conflict with it as false is said to be no longer acceptable. What is needed is a "Copernican revolution" in our thinking about religions that acknowledges that ". . . it is God who is at the center and that all the religions of mankind, including our own, serve and revolve around Him."[22] Hick's suggestion is that ". . . the great religions are all, at their experiential roots, in contact with the same ultimate divine reality. . . ."[23] God (or as Hick prefers, the Eternal One, or the Real) is said to be the center of religious awareness, with the various conceptions of the divine in the many religions all being reflective of the one divine reality. Hick's thesis is essentially a restatement of a familiar Advaitin theme, but it is unique in that it is formulated by a major Western thinker who is trained in analytic philosophy and thus has an informed concern for epistemological issues.

But if the various religious traditions all reflect the same divine reality, then why the bewildering diversity in their claims about the divine reality? Why are there what clearly seem to be incompatible religious beliefs? Hick has a twofold answer that brings us to the heart of his theory. First, the various religious beliefs expressed in the major traditions reflect various culturally conditioned human responses to the one divine reality.

> The basic hypothesis which suggests itself is that the different streams of religious experience represent diverse awarenesses of the same transcendent reality, which is perceived in characteristically different ways by different human mentalities, formed by and forming different cultural histories. . . . One then sees the great world religions as different human responses to the one divine Reality, embodying different perceptions which have been formed in different historical and cultural circumstances. . . . The divine presence is the presence of the Eternal One to our finite human consciousness, and the human projections are the culturally conditioned images and symbols in terms of which we concretize the basic concept of deity.[24]

It is helpful in understanding Hick's theory to realize that he regards religious experience as basic to religious epistemology, and that there is a strong element of interpretation in all religious experience.[25] Religious beliefs, then, are at least partially the product of the interpretative element in religious experience and are influenced by various historical and cultural factors. The precise extent of such interpretative, historical, and cultural influence is left unclear, but presumably religious belief cannot be totally reduced to such factors; presumably religious belief does to some extent also reflect the "projective" element of the self-revelation of the divine reality.

The second part of Hick's answer to the above questions lies in his distinction between the divine reality as it is in itself and the divine reality as it is experienced by culturally and historically conditioned persons.

> To develop this hypothesis we must, I think, distinguish between the Eternal One in itself, in its eternal self-existent being, beyond relationship to a creation, and the Eternal One in relation to mankind and as perceived from within our different human cultural situations. . . . Thus, the many gods are not separate distinct divine beings, but rather different *personae* formed in the interaction of divine presence and human projection.[26]

Immanuel Kant's famous distinction between *noumenon* and *phenomenon* is adapted (and used in a most non-Kantian manner!) to clarify this thesis.

> Summarizing this hypothesis in philosophical terms made possible by the work of Immanuel Kant we may distinguish between, on the one hand, the single divine noumenon, the Eternal One in itself, transcending the scope of human thought and language, and, on the other hand, the plurality of the divine phenomena, the divine *personae* of the theistic religions and the concretizations of the concept of the Absolute in the nontheistic religions. . . . The Eternal One is thus the divine noumenon which is experienced and thought within different religious traditions as the range of divine phenomena witnessed to by the religious history of mankind. The philosophical framework here is Kantian, but with the proviso that the phenomenal world *is* the noumenal world as humanly experienced. The result is the distinctively non-Kantian thesis that the divine is experienced (rather than postulated, as Kant believed), but is experienced within the limitations of our human cognitive apparatus in ways analogous to that in which he argued that we experience our physical environment.[27]

In making this distinction Hick claims to be able to maintain consistently both that the conceptions of the divine in various religions are indeed different and even conflicting and that these various conceptions are human responses to and are reflective of the same single divine reality. If these can be maintained consistently then the problem of conflicting truth-claims can be disposed of without concluding that the beliefs of any particular religion are false. For all religious traditions would then be partial reflections of the same divine reality.

Will Hick's proposal release us from the problem of conflicting truth-claims inherent in the exclusivist position? I think not. It seems that the adequacy of his theory will be the function of at least two factors: (a) the accuracy with which the theory reflects and the ease with which it can accommodate distinctives of the various religious traditions and (b) the internal consistency and plausibility of the theory itself. I have argued elsewhere[28] that Hick's theory seriously distorts certain basic beliefs of traditions such as orthodox Christianity, Islam, and Zen Buddhism, and that to the extent that this is done it counts against his theory. This particular criticism will not be pursued here. Instead, I will concentrate upon a major epistemological difficulty with Hick's theory, a difficulty which, incidentally, brings into graphic relief the problem of conflicting truth-claims.

The Eternal One in itself is said to be the divine noumenon and the various conceptions of the divine in the many religions are said to be the divine phenomena or *personae,* that is, manifestations of the Eternal One. Thus, Yahweh, Allah, Krishna, Shiva, Brahman, Nirvana, Sunyatta, etc., are all divine *personae* through which the Eternal One is manifested. Now the distinction between the divine reality in itself and the divine reality as experienced by finite humans has a long and distinguished history; within the Christian tradition alone variations on this distinction can be found in Augustine, Aquinas, Calvin, Luther, Barth, and many others. But Hick's distinction is considerably more ambitious than that found in these theologians. For he is claiming that when the great religious figures have experiences of, say, Yahweh, or Amida Buddha, or Sunyatta, they are actually experiencing the Eternal One, although always in terms of a culturally conditioned divine image or *personae*.[29] The relation between the Eternal One and the *personae,* then, is this: the *personae* are the manifestations of the Eternal One to culturally conditioned humans. They are the culturally conditioned images of the Eternal One.

If the *personae* are indeed accurate reflections of the Eternal One there must be significant continuity between these images and the divine reality they supposedly reflect. This can be expressed in another way by saying that the set of true propositions about a given image (e.g., Allah, Amida Buddha) must form a subset of the set of all true propositions about the Eternal One as it is in itself. For if this were not the case, it is hard to see how the *personae* could be regarded as at all informative of the Eternal One or even why they should be considered to be images of the divine reality in the first place.

But it is precisely the great diversity among the images of the divine in the various religions that presents the greatest difficulty for Hick's thesis. He correctly notes that such images can be placed into two broad categories—those that conceive of the divine reality as personal (e.g., Yahweh, Allah) and those that conceive of it largely in nonpersonal categories (Nirvana, Sunyatta).[30] Now it is crucial to Hick's theory that the Eternal One (which is said to be a neutral designation encompassing both personal and nonpersonal connotations) can be accurately conceived of in both personal and nonpersonal categories. Ultimately, there can be no contradiction between statements describing the Eternal One in personal categories and those describing the divine in nonpersonal categories.

> The divine nature is infinite, exceeding the scope of all human concepts, and is capable of being experienced both as personal Lord and as nonpersonal ground or depth of being.[31]

On Hick's theory it is not simply that the Eternal One can be experienced as both personal and nonpersonal; if his theory is to reflect accurately the actual beliefs of the respective traditions, the ontological status of the Eternal One must be such that it can be correctly described as both personal and nonpersonal as these categories are understood in the traditions. That is, if Hick's thesis is sound, it should be possible to speak correctly of the divine reality as Yahweh, Jesus Christ, Allah, Nirguna Brahman, Sunyatta, the Amida Buddha, and Nothingness, as these designations are understood in the respective traditions. Such terms as "Yahweh," "Allah," "Shiva," "Nirguna Brahman," etc., should all ultimately have the same referent. To be sure, in one sense the terms do have different meanings: they do not all share the same connotations and they can be paraphrased in different ways. Perhaps a distinction should be made here between what we might call the direct, or penultimate, referent of a term and the ultimate referent of a term. Thus, we could say that the direct referent of "Allah" is not the same as that of "Sunyatta"—they refer to different manifestations of the Eternal One, as Hick would put it. But if indeed such images are manifestations of the same single divine reality, then it seems clear that they must have the same ultimate referent; they must denote the same divine reality.

Is this plausible? Does it make any sense to speak of a single divine reality in both personal and nonpersonal terms as these terms are understood in the respective religious traditions? Careful consideration of the meanings of the personal and nonpersonal images of the divine reveals that several of them seem to have clearly incompatible entailments. It is difficult, for example, to avoid the conclusion that the ontological implications of the Judeo-Christian image of the divine as Yahweh, the ontologically distinct, independent, personal, creator and sustainer of the world, are incompatible with the ontological monism of the image of the Nirguna Brahman or with the ontologically ultimate concept of Nothingness in Zen Buddhism. John Hick's intriguing proposal does not seem to be capable of producing the desired effect. The problem of conflicting truth-claims remains.

III. CONCLUSION

The views of two prominent thinkers who challenge the exclusivist view of the relation between major religious traditions have been examined and found to be deficient. The exclusivist view still seems to be the best way in which to understand the relation between various religious traditions. If we are to take seriously the concepts and beliefs of the various religions and portray them accurately and also have a view that is internally consistent and plausible, I do not see how we can avoid something very much like the traditional exclusivist position. Careful investigation of the actual claims advanced by adherents of the major religions makes it clear that at least some incompatible claims are being made. For example comparison of the ontological implications of the Judeo-Christian concept of God with that of the concept of Nirguna Brahman in Advaita Vedanta shows the two concepts to be incompatible. Further incompatibilities emerge if we compare fundamental beliefs about humankind and its relation to the religious ultimate. We do the religious traditions an injustice if we distort or reinterpret basic beliefs so as to minimize differences. Further, given the fact of incompatible truth-claims, although it is theoretically possible that none of the claims is true (that all are false) it is clear that not all of them can be true. At least some must be false.

I suggest that the most significant question we can ask of any religious tradition is whether its fundamental claims are true. Certainly religions can be appreciated and evaluated on a variety of other grounds—we might evaluate them on the basis of their historical contributions toward promoting literacy, health care, education, and so on, or on the basis of their providing social stability and cohesion. But the most important question is not what a religion does for a society but whether what it affirms about the nature of reality is in fact true.

As a Christian I believe that the central claims of the Christian faith are true and that those claims made by other traditions that are incompatible with them are false. This does not, however, entail that *none* of the claims made by other religions are true. Indeed, if we as Christians take seriously Romans 1 and the doctrines of general revelation and the *imago Dei* it seems that we must conclude that at least some of the beliefs of adherents of other religions will very likely be true. What must be denied is that where beliefs of other traditions are incompatible with those derived from Scripture the former can be true. Further, we should note that the exclusivist position does not boast of exhaustive knowledge of God. Certainly there is a vast sum of knowledge about God and the world that is unavailable to us. To maintain that one apprehends particular truths is a very different thing from claiming to have exhaustive or comprehensive knowledge about something. And finally, there is no room in the exclusivist position, properly construed, for an arrogant triumphalism. We are all of us no more than sinners saved by grace. Nor should we forget that adherents of other religions are, like us, created in God's image and the objects of God's unfathomable love. Humility and genuine respect should mark our interactions with those of other faiths. But it is a serious error to presume that such humility and respect demand glossing over the problem of conflicting truth-claims.

CHAPTER SEVEN

REFLECTIONS ON
MEANING IN LIFE WITHOUT GOD

J. P. Moreland

Rumor has it that Woody Allen was engaged in a philosophical discussion one evening at a dinner party when he was asked his opinion about the meaning of life. His response was equal to the occasion: "You ask me about the meaning of life? Good Lord, I don't even know my way around Chinatown!" Questions about the meaning of life can appear to be so broad, and so difficult, that one may be tempted to adopt an attitude toward them like that of Harvard philosopher W. V. Quine: "Why the world began, or why life began . . . I think are pseudo questions, because I can't imagine what an answer would look like."[1]

On the other hand, questions about the meaning of life simply will not go away. Everyone, at one time or another, wonders whether or not life has any real point to it. In *The Myth of Sisyphus*, Albert Camus expresses the urgency of the question in this way: "There is but one truly serious philosophical problem, and that is suicide. Judging whether life is or is not worth living amounts to answering the fundamental question of philosophy."[2]

It seems to me that Camus is right. Questions about the meaning of life can and must be asked, even if the answers we give cannot achieve apodictic certainty. But once we grant the appropriateness of these questions, it is natural to discuss issues about the existence and knowability of God in connection with them. In fact, in more popular versions of Christian apologetics, one frequently encounters the following sort of dilemma: either we accept the existence of a personal God, such as the Christian God, or we deny the existence of such a being. In the former case, we have a ground for the objective meaningfulness of life. In the latter case, there is no such ground whatever, and one must settle for some sort of nihilism or some naive type of optimistic humanism wherein we identify the meaning of life with the pursuit and attainment of subjective satisfaction, leaving the definition of such an end of each individual.[3]

Prima facie, this dilemma seems reasonable enough. But in point of fact, the horns presented are not exhaustive. There are those who believe that a case can be made for life to be objectively meaningful, in a sense to be defined later, without the need to postulate a God to make such meaning possible. Let us call this position the Immanent Purpose view. For those of us who do believe that God is relevant to, and in some sense the best explanation for, the possibility of objective meaning in life, it is important to understand the Immanent Purpose view and its strengths and weaknesses.

In order to facilitate such an understanding, I will first try to clarify what is involved in asking questions about the meaning of life. Then we will look at how the Immanent Purpose view answers these questions, and in the process, we will consider objections that can be raised against the Immanent Purpose view. We could approach these objections by considering only one of two of them in detail. But I think it would be more profitable to sketch several problems with the Immanent Purpose view, even if that means that we will not look at any particular area of debate in depth. The advantage of this latter approach is that it gives one a better feel for the texture of the Immanent Purpose view by suggesting the different kinds of problems relevant to its evaluation.

I. WHAT IS THE QUESTION OF THE MEANING OF LIFE?

What does the question "What is the meaning of life?" mean? What are we getting at when we ask for an answer to our queries about the meaning of life? There are, I think, at least four facets to this question which, if clarified, will shed light on the question(s) of the meaning of life as we are using it.

First, the question is not asking whether or not people find life subjectively satisfying and of personal significance. Meaning in this sense would be involved in the statements "I get a lot of meaning (satisfaction) out of golf" or "The World Series means a lot to me" (I find that it interests me). In general, this understanding of meaning could be spelled out as follows:

x is meaningful if and only if x satisfies desire y

This understanding of meaning is intended to be a denial of the existence of objective moral properties and values. There are no desires that are intrinsically valuable from a moral point of view; there are only desires that we, in fact, have and that we want satisfied. This understanding of meaning is involved in the following statement by A. J. Ayer:[4]

> But without the help of such a myth [religion] can life be seen as having any meaning? The simple answer is that it can have just as much meaning as one is able to put into it. There is, indeed, no ground for thinking that human life in general serves any ulterior purpose but this is no bar to a man's finding satisfaction in many of the activities which make up his life, or to his attaching value to the ends which he pursues, including some that he himself will not live to see realized.

This sentiment is echoed by Paul Hurtz:[5]

> The humanist maintains as his first principle that life is worth living, at least that it can be found to have worth. . . . The universe is neutral, indifferent to man's existential yearnings. But we instinctively discover life, experience its throb, its excitement, its attraction. Life is here to be lived, enjoyed, suffered, and endured.

Both Ayer and Kurtz deny nonnaturalism (moral statements are indicative statements that ascribe irreducibly moral properties to persons, things, and acts) as a metaethical theory. Kurtz embraces some form of imperativalism (moral statements are mere commands) and Ayer holds to either emotivism (moral statements merely *express* feelings) or private subjectivism (moral statements merely *describe* feelings).

But the subjective satisfaction of desire is not the same thing as objective meaning. For example, one could find subjective satisfaction by giving his life to pushing a boulder up Mt. Everest, to being the best male prostitute in California, or in killing Jews in order to promote Hitler's vision of Germany. Further, one could do something that had objective value, say give his life in order to save his family but fail to find any "throb, excitement, or attraction" in such an act. It may turn out that there is no objective point to life and there may be no objective values. But when Ayer and Kurtz talk about subjective satisfaction, they have changed the subject. This is not what most people are wondering about when they raise questions about the meaning of life. After all, who could seriously puzzle over whether or not people found subjective satisfaction in different ways?

Second, the question of the meaning of life can be raised with different scopes in mind. For example, one can ask:

1. Why (for what purpose) does the universe exist? Why is there something rather than nothing?
2. Why (for what purpose) do human beings in general exist?
3. Why (for what purpose) do I exist?

Although these are different questions, one's answer to one of these questions can affect his answer to the others. It would be possible to hold that the universe as a whole, including history as a whole, is without meaning but that objective values exist as a brute fact and the meaning of my life consists in my relationship to those values. Similarly, one could hold that the cosmos as a whole has meaning, perhaps by holding to a Hegelian-type view that it is evolving into God, but that humans are of little or no significance to that meaning.

On the other hand, it is possible (and I think reasonable) to hold that one's answers to the first question will have a bearing on one's answers to the second and third questions. For example, nihilists hold that there is no purpose in the cosmos and, therefore, there is no purpose for humans in general or my life in particular. Christians hold that God has a purpose for the cosmos and this purpose informs the purpose of human life in general and each individual life in particular.

Third, the question of the meaning of life involves the notions of value and purpose. Do values exist objectively and if so, what is the nature of those values? Are moral properties reducible to natural, scientific ones, or are they irreducible? How does one know what values are the right ones? Is there any point to life, is there any end or goal that is objectively and intrinsically valuable and toward which the cosmos, human beings, and my life should move?

Fourth, a position about the meaning of life will also include an answer to the question of why one should be moral. Unfortunately, this question itself is somewhat vague and stands in need of clarification. Three points should help to clarify the question "Why should I be moral?"[6]

For one thing, one can distinguish specific moral acts (an act of kindness, an act of self-sacrifice) from what philosophers call the moral point of view. The question "Why should I be moral?" is really asking "Why should I adopt the moral point of view?" so it is important to understand what the moral point of view is. If one adopts the moral point of view, then one does the following: one subscribes to normative judgments about actions, things (e.g., persons, environment), and motives; one is willing to universalize one's judgments; one seeks to form one's moral views in a free, unbiased, enlightened way; one seeks to promote the good. In others words, if one adopts the moral point of view, one submits to and seeks to promote the dictates of normative, universalizable morality in a mature, unbiased, impartial way. One embraces the dictates of morality and seeks to live in light of the moral point of view. Such a viewpoint governs one's life and priorities. So understood, the question "Why should I be moral?" becomes the question "Why should I adopt the moral point of view as a guiding force over my life?"

Further, one can distinguish between motives and reasons for adopting the moral point of view. Regarding the former, the question is asking what motivates one to adopt the moral point of view. But motives do not need to be rational factors. For example, one could say, "I was motivated to adopt the moral point of view because it gave me approval with my parents and society." Regarding reasons, the question is asking what rational justification can be given for adopting the moral point of view. The question is usually framed in terms of reasons, but both reasons and motives are relevant to a full discussion of why one adopts the moral point of view.

Finally it is not clear what kind of justification the question is seeking. What kind of "should" is involved in "Why should I be moral?" If it is a moral "should," then the question is asking for a moral justification for adopting the moral point of view. If a moral "should" is used in the question, then some philosophers think that the question involves a pointless self-contradiction. For one is then asking for a moral reason for accepting moral reasons. In other words, if one is using a moral "should" in the question, then one is already reasoning from *within* the moral point of view, since one is already willing to acknowledge a moral answer to a moral question. But if one has already adopted the moral point of view, then there is not much point in asking for a moral reason for doing so. About the only answer one could give to the question would be that it is just morally right to adopt the moral point of view. But if one is willing to adopt the moral point of view because such an act is morally right, then one has already adopted the moral point of view without knowing it. So the question "Why should I be moral?" is not really using a moral sense of "should," and if it is, the only answer is that such an act is just the morally right thing to do.

But there is a different notion of "should" which is better suited as a part of the question. This is a rational sense of "should." According to this sense of "should," one is not asking the question "'Why should I be moral?' from within the moral point of view but from outside the moral point of view altogether. In others words, one is asking the question "What rational justification and motives can be given to me as to why it would be reasonable for me to adopt the moral point of view rather than some other point of view (say, an egoistic self-interested point of view where I govern my life for my own best interests without regard for the moral point of view at all)." As I seek to formulate a rational life plan for myself—a well thought-out, reasonable approach to the way I will live my life so as to be a rational person—why should the moral point of view be a part of that rational life plan?

In sum, the question "Why should I be moral?" is asking for the motives but more importantly the reasons why someone should adopt the moral point of view as a part of a rational plan of life.

With the above distinctions in mind, the question of the meaning of life as we are using it is this: *Are there any objective values that provide significance for the universe as a whole, human life in general, or my life in particular; that provide a goal or purpose for the universe, human life, or my life; and that rationally justify me in adopting the moral point of view as a part of my rational life plan?* Let us now turn to the Immanent Purpose view to see how it answers this question and to assess its adequacy.

II. THE IMMANENT PURPOSE VIEW

A. The View

The Immanent Purpose view holds that God does not exist, that there is no reason why something rather than nothing exists, that there is no overarching purpose for human history, that there is no life after death, and that humans are, as one proponent puts it, modified monkeys, that is, the result of a blind process of evolution.[7] But while there may be no reason to believe that there is any objective meaning or purpose outside human life that gives it meaning, this does not mean that life is not objectively meaningful. Life has objective meaning because objective values can be found within life.

According to the philosophy of Immanent Purpose, objective values and moral properties exist and are part of the furniture of the universe. Values are there as brute givens. They are like Platonic forms (according to one reading of Plato); they are ultimate entities that do not need to come from anywhere, including God, to exist. Moral properties supervene upon certain natural properties of things and events. So, according to the Immanent Purpose view, values exist as irreducible, moral entities, and they attach to various things within life—to the pursuit of truth, to persons, and so on. As Karl Britton says, "The relationships between persons matter in themselves and many are of value in themselves."[8]

Why should I be moral? According to the Immanent Purpose view, my motives may be varied, but some of them can be the desire to love persons, to do what is right, and to be a virtuous person. It is simply morally right to be moral. Further, it is rational to adopt the moral point of view in my life plan because that point of view allows my life to have objective meaning. Life becomes objectively meaningful, as opposed to merely subjectively satisfying, when I pursue the realization of objective values that exist. When I seek to promote the good, moral values are realized within my life and my life becomes virtuous. This provides meaning in life, but this meaning does not come from God or some overarching meaning to the cosmos. Rather it comes from objective values that are immanently realized in life itself.

Some examples may help to clarify the Immanent Purpose view. In a widely used introductory textbook in philosophy, William H. Halverson presents the Immanent Purpose view as including four theses relevant to our present discussion.[9] First, values are discovered, not invented. They "certify themselves"; they thrust themselves upon us as we respond to the depths of human life and existence. To live, says Halverson, is to encounter values that cry out for our allegiance. Meaning in life is found within life itself as we live for the values that exist and impress us as worthy of our efforts. Second, the values that do, in fact, exist are the ones that most people of good will embrace, e.g., the intrinsic values of truth, beauty, goodness, honesty, the intrinsic worth of persons, justice, freedom, and so on. Third, scientific naturalism and physicalism are inadequate worldviews. In its place, says Halverson, the worldview of Transcendentalism should be substituted. According to Transcendentalism, in addition to the spatio-temporal universe of physical things, there exists a transcendent dimension of reality wherein values exist. These values emerge and impinge upon the depth of human existence in a variety of ways. These values are the source and ground of the meaning of life. Finally, Halverson holds that moral intuitionism is the view of moral knowledge most consistent with the Immanent Purpose view: the mind has an ability to intuit (be directly aware of) nonempirical qualities such as moral and aesthetic qualities.

Although he ultimately rejects the view, J. L. Mackie has presented one of the most succinct statements of the Immanent Purpose view in recent years.[10] According to Mackie, this view includes the following notions. First, values are objective and moral properties supervene upon things (e.g., persons) and actions (e.g., an act of kindness). Some state of affairs A supervenes upon some state of affairs B when the presence of A is sufficient to guarantee B. For example, wetness supervenes over a cluster of water molecules when certain features obtain in the world— a cluster of H_2O molecules group together within a certain range of temperature and pressure. Similarly, moral properties supervene upon a certain configuration of matter that constitutes the physical nature of a person.

Second, the existence of moral properties and the nature of their supervenience in the world are brute facts that have no explanation and that in and of themselves constitute reasons for acting morally. While Mackie does not specifically address the question of the meaning of life, it should be clear that the meaning of life would come from within life as one lives consistently with the moral values that have emerged in the universe. Finally, Mackie argues that such a view implicitly includes moral intuitionism—the moral thinker responds to the value-laden atmosphere that surrounds him in the actual world by intuiting the moral facts which exist.[11]

In order to understand the moral implications of the Immanent Purpose view, we need first to grasp the difference between offering a moral justification for a moral action and offering a metaphysical justification for the existence and nature of morality itself. The former involves an appeal to some moral principle or rule that serves as a court of appeal in deciding some moral course of action. For example, one could appeal to the rule "one ought to tell the truth and not deceive others" in trying to decide whether or not a patient ought to be told what is going to be done in an operation or medical experiment. Here the issue is one of trying to decide what is the morally permissible or obligatory course of action, and the issue is settled by appealing to one or more moral rules relevant to the situation. These moral rules can, in turn, be given moral justification by broader ethical theories, e.g., deontological theories or utilitarian theories.

The task of giving a metaphysical justification of the nature and existence of morality is not really a *moral* task but a broader philosophical and metaphysical task. It involves, among other things, asking whether or not moral values exist, what they are (e.g., do they refer to natural or nonnatural properties or something else), how they could emerge in the universe, and so on.

Now the Immanent Purpose view holds to an absolutist view of morality, that is, moral values and moral properties are objectively real, they can be rationally apprehended, and they are truly independent of human beliefs about them. Thus, a Christian vision of morality and the vision of morality contained in the Immanent Purpose view overlap when it comes to a denial of relativism and a concomitant acceptance of absolutism. There can also be agreement over the specific moral values held to be absolute.[12] But where a Christian view of morality differs most from the Immanent Purpose view is over the question of the metaphysical justification of the existence of morality itself. Christians believe that moral values are more at home in a universe created by a personal God while the Immanent Purpose view is content to leave the existence and nature of values as a brute given in the universe. More will be said about this difference momentarily.

The distinction between a moral justification of a moral action and a metaphysical justification for morality itself is important for several reasons, not the least of which is the need to understand how a believer can bring his or her Christian theism into bioethical discussions in a pluralistic society. In the last decade, the rise of bioethics committees, in both acute and long-term care, has been staggering. An entire literature has surrounded this phenomenon, and educational seminars are being held all over the country in an attempt to train people how to function on bioethics committees. I myself have served on a bioethics committee for a group of nursing homes for three years. Not all but most of the people involved in bioethics committees—doctors, nurses, laypeople, pastors, lawyers, theologians, philosophers—are deontological in their ethical orientation and not utilitarian. Further, most people agree that a certain set of ethical rules are true and morally binding, although there is more difference of opinion as to how to weigh the principles in general and in specific ethical areas.

Some examples of these ethical principles are these:

1. The Principle of Autonomy: A competent person has a right to decide his or her own course of medical action in accordance with a plan he or she has freely chosen.
2. The Principle of Beneficence: One should act in order to further the welfare and benefit of another.
3. The Principle of Nonmaleficence: One should refrain from inflicting harm on another.
4. The Principle of Justice: One ought to be treated fairly and receive the benefits and burdens due one.

I have found that my non-Christian colleagues will often decide that a case should be handled in the same way I decide it should be handled. And they often appeal to some of the same reasons I utilize: the various principles cited above, the fact that people have intrinsic value and ought to be treated as ends in themselves, and so on. On the other hand, where my Christian faith becomes most relevant is not in the adherence to the above principles, but in the world view-type justification I can give for how it could be the case that values exist in the first place and how it could be that persons are, in fact, ends in themselves. It is precisely at this point that the Immanent Purpose view is weakest, and this will be brought out when we look at some criticisms of the Immanent Purpose view.

In sum, the Immanent Purpose view seeks to give real, objective meaning to life, not mere subjective satisfaction, and it does so by postulating the existence of an absolute, objective moral law and real moral properties that can be known through moral intuition (in most cases). But the meaningfulness of life does not depend on the existence of God or on some external purpose outside human life. Values realized within human life can give it real meaning.

B. Objections to the Immanent Purpose View

In this section, I want to raise five objections against the Immanent Purpose view. As mentioned earlier, our purpose is to suggest relevant lines of approach in assessing this view point that, I hope, will sketch a better picture of just what the view is asserting and how it differs from a classic Christian view of the meaning of life.

For one thing, the Immanent Purpose view cannot adequately account for at least three features of the moral life as we really experience it. First, moral responsibility seems to presuppose a robust form of free will incompatible with determinism. I do not want to argue this point, except to suggest that it makes little sense to say one "ought" to do something if someone has no ability whatever to choose to do it. If someone is caused to act in such a way as to bypass the actor as an agent with causal powers, then notions of "ought" and "responsibility" must be readjusted away from our common sense notions of them. This will be the case regardless of whether the factors that causally determine someone to "act" are external or internal to the person. As Robert Nozick has observed, when it comes to moral responsibility it is no better to be a marionette than to be a hand puppet.

But if humans are merely the result of a blind process of evolution, then it is hard to resist some form of mind/body physicalism or epiphenomenalism, since it is hard to see where mind could come from in this scenario. And, in any case, an emergent mind would still be an epiphenomenon, given that the physical is closed as far as causation is concerned. Full-blown freedom seems to make more sense if one presupposes some form of substance dualism to support an agent view of action. And as I have argued elsewhere, substance dualism makes sense if God exists so as to create the mind.[13]

If this admittedly brief and inadequate sketch is correct, then the Immanent Purpose view must either deny free will (which undercuts the possibility of morality) or postulate substance dualism as an unexplained fact about the world. Either move is possible but neither is without serious difficulties. In any case, the above dilemma points out how one would need to fill out the Immanent Purpose view to make it more intelligible.

Another feature of the moral life is the feeling of moral guilt or shame at moral failure. H. P. Owen has argued that it is often rational to have guilt feelings in the face of moral failure even when no human is present toward whom one feels shame. Or, if someone is present, one's sense of shame may go beyond what would be appropriate if only another human were involved.[14] Owen goes on to argue that guilt *feelings* do not make sense if abstract moral principles are all there is to moral failure. Guilt feelings make sense if one feels shame in the presence of a Person. So if the depth and presence of guilt feelings is to be rational, there must be a Person toward whom one feels moral shame; and the Immanent Purpose view allows for no such Person.

A third feature of the moral life is the fact that we often believe in retributive punishment, that is, punishment of a crime which is not merely for the purpose of rehabilitation, protection of society, or deterrence. In such cases, we are not merely trying to communicate to the person or show him or her how wrong his or her action was.[15] We sometimes simply feel that certain actions "deserve" punishment. But as Joel Feinberg, H. L. A. Hart, and others have pointed out, such an understanding of retributive punishment makes sense only if we think that in such cases we are balancing the moral universe, setting the moral record straight by balancing the good and evil in the universe by paying the moral universe back for the evil.

But if such talk is to make sense, especially in cases where there is no clear victim of the crime present, then there must be some being that we have in mind when we "pay the moral universe back." Perhaps an impersonal law could conceivably be balanced by retributive punishment, but the feeling of owing the moral universe such a balance or paying it back makes more sense if God exists. For He is the victim of every crime, and His justice demands retribution.

These three features of the moral life—free will, rational guilt feelings, and retribution without a human victim—are far less adequately explained in the Immanent Purpose view than in Christian theism. The Immanent Purpose view requires us either to revise our basic intuitions about these matters or to postulate these features as brute givens. The former move may be too high a price to pay, and the latter move has an *ad hoc* feel about it.

Let us now turn to the second objection to the Immanent Purpose view. The existence of moral values and properties as an ultimate, brute given in an impersonal universe is counterintuitive and puzzling.[16] We usually think of a command involving a commander. Further, propositions or principles usually come from or exist in minds, so absolute moral propositions—ones that existed before humans evolved—would seem to come from or exist in an objective Mind.

So either we take moral claims to be self-evident modes of impersonal existence or we explain them in terms of an ultimate Person. The latter makes their existence less puzzling than the former. This type of argument is one of the reasons the late J. L. Mackie adopted subjectivism as a moral theory. He argued:[17]

> Besides, we might well argue . . . that objective intrinsically prescriptive features, supervenient upon natural ones, constitute so odd a cluster of qualities

and relations that they are most unlikely to have arisen in the ordinary course of events, without an all-powerful god to create them.

This point can be strengthened by the following consideration. Suppose I claim to see a table in front of me. I am *prima facie* justified in this claim in the absence of defeaters of that claim. In other words, I am entitled to my knowledge claim unless there is some overriding reason to suspect that I am wrong. One source of defeaters, one source of information for suspecting my knowledge claim, is background information about the way the world is in general. For example, suppose I have background knowledge that when people seem to see water on a highway when it is hot outside, they are really seeing heat waves. The experience is a mirage. If I seem to see water in front of my car while driving in the desert under hot, dry conditions, I would not be justified in believing that water is really there.

Now consider the claim of the Immanent Purpose view advocate who says that he or she knows that moral values exist. If he or she also accepts current evolutionary theory (and, by definition, denies the existence of God), then this further belief would constitute background information that goes against the claim that moral values exist and can be known. According to that theory, the entire physical cosmos came from a blind explosion and life arose by random mutation and competition for reproductive advantage. Morality is merely the result of this struggle, for men discovered that life was safer when they banded together in communities.[18] Moral rules are not reflections of an objectively existing moral universe. They are social conventions grounded in the human instinct to survive. Further, no moral faculty of perception evolved to aid one in knowing moral properties and values.

Now one could argue that the evolutionary account of morality (and my use of it as a defeater against the Immanent Purpose view) commits the genetic fallacy—it confuses how morality came about with what morality is and what justifies it. There is a point in this rejoinder. Taken by itself, the evolutionary account of morality is an example of the genetic fallacy. But there are some cases where a genetic argument is not really a fallacy at all. These are cases where the causal account of the origin of an idea serves to discredit that idea in some way. In a trial, if the testimony of a witness comes from someone with bad motives, then one can rule out his testimony because of where it came from. His testimony could still be true, but it is unlikely. In the case of the mirage, one can rule out the veridicality of this experience by citing what caused it (hot air waves), even though it *could* still be an accurate experience.

If evolutionary theory is all there is to the development of the cosmos from the big bang to man, then any view which postulates the brute existence of morals would seem to do so in an *ad hoc* way. The general background theory would count against the veridicality of the claim to know that morals exist by providing another account for morality that serves as a defeater to that claim, even though it would still be logically possible for objective morals to exist and be knowable by some intuitive moral faculty.

If theism is entertained as a background hypothesis, then one's background theory explains the existence of human morality and helps justify moral knowledge claims. But if one denies God and accepts evolution, then it would seem more reasonable to go along with Mackie and accept an evolutionary, subjectivist account of morality. The existence of objective values and an intuitive moral faculty would still be possible, but it would be unlikely and *ad hoc,* given this background theory. The background theory of theism supports such claims and makes them *prima facie* justified for, among other things, it removes the background theory that is the defeater. So objective morality is problematic for the Immanent Purpose view.

A third objection to this view is this: even if we grant that moral values and properties are part of the ultimate furniture of the universe, it is hard to see why they would have anything whatever to do with human beings. Given that moral values are brute entities that simply exist, why would those entities refer to a small, short-lived species on a little planet circling around a modest star called the sun? Further, given the evolutionary process, *homo sapiens* are merely an instrumental cause of future forms of life. That is, we stand to future life as amoebas stand to us.

Scientists John Barrow and Frank Tipler have argued that humans are just one stage in evolutionary development, which is moving toward higher and higher forms.[19] All intermediate stages from amoebas to humans only have instrumental value insofar as they contribute to later stages. Earlier stages do not have intrinsic value. In fact, Barrow and Tipler argue that humans do not have intrinsic value, but the DNA program in humans is what has value. We exist in order to perfect that program for life that will exist in the future.

It is easy to see why humans would have value if Christian theism is true, but it is hard to see on the Immanent Purpose view how morality and value ever came to be related to humans and their activities at all, if these latter are regarded as ends in themselves. It would seem to be just a happy coincidence.

A fourth problem with the Immanent Purpose view is that it would seem to be inconsistent to allow that moral values can exist and be known and not allow that God exists and can be known. According to the Immanent Purpose view, some of the reasons for atheism count against their own moral views as well. They cut both ways.

For example, it is sometimes said that science has explained features of the world and made God unnecessary; but the same claim can be made for evolutionary ethics as applied to the Immanent Purpose view. Sometimes it is claimed that God, heaven, and the world are unclear, odd concepts that seem out of place in a scientific world where scientific concepts (allegedly) are clear, can be quantified, and so forth. But the same has been said about the existence and nature of moral values.[20]

Again, it is sometimes said that religious experience is not good evidence for God because the notion of spiritual intuition by which God is directly experienced or perceived is problematic. But spiritual intuition is similar to moral intuition. Ethical experience is very similar to religious experience.

Finally, the Immanent Purpose view does not have an adequate answer for why I should be moral when doing so goes against my own interests or for why it is rationally justifiable to perform what are called supererogatory acts. These are acts of heroism that are not morally obligatory—no one would be immoral for failing to do them—but they are morally praiseworthy if they are done. For example, the act of throwing one's body on a bomb in order to save others in the room would be a supererogatory act. It is not morally obligatory but it is praiseworthy if done.

Are such acts rational? Why is it ever rational to do such acts, or why is it ever rational to do a morally obligatory act (e.g., turning myself in for murder) if it is not in my own best interests to do so? The answer cannot be merely that such acts are right. The question is why I would be rational in such cases to do what is right. On the Immanent Purpose view, the best answer I can think of would be that such acts give objective purpose to life and such purpose is desirable. This may be a sufficient answer, but if such acts cause me to lose my life, it is hard to see how I can be rational in paying this price for a short period of objective meaning.

This point can be expressed somewhat differently in the language of virtue ethics.[21] An ethics of virtue can be utilized in areas of moral discussion beyond those of normal duty. Thus, supererogatory acts are those acts done by moral saints and heroes who have adopted an ethics of virtue transcending the normal ethics of duty. Now it seems that such an ethic is possible and that moral saints and heroes who adopt such an ethic are paradigms of praise and rationality. But from within the Immanent Purpose view, it is difficult to see how such an ethic could ever be rationally adopted. From a Christian point of view, such an ethic is adopted in light of a higher calling by God. But such a vantage point is unavailable to a proponent of the Immanent Purpose view.

III. CONCLUSION

I have tried to shed light on issues which surround theism and the meaning of life by discussing these issues in the context of a popular and not altogether unreasonable dilemma: either God exists and, therefore, life has meaning, or God does not exist and life has no meaning. My purpose has been to show that this dilemma does not exhaust the options available and, thus, to advance the discussion about God and the meaning of life beyond the well-known horns stated above.

Such an advance involved us with a clarification and definition of the question of the meaning of life itself. And we have investigated a major alternative— the Immanent Purpose view—which attempts to split the horns of the dilemma by holding that life has objective meaning without God. The criticisms I have raised against the Immanent Purpose view are only suggestive. Much more could and should be said about each point. But I hope enough has been said to indicate the types of considerations relevant to an assessment of how the Immanent Purpose view compares with Christian theism on the question of the meaning of life.

The Immanent Purpose view has a fairly consistent response to most of the criticisms we have raised against it. It merely postulates the relevant feature of the universe as brute givens in need of no explanation—the existence of objective values and nonnatural properties, the intersection of those values with homo sapiens, the presence of an intuitive faculty adequate to give insight into the nature of morality, and (perhaps) substance dualism. The advocate of the

Immanent Purpose view wants to take God out of his conceptual framework but leave the universe just as the Christian theist finds it to be—populated with pretty much the same type of moral universe Christianity embraces. But the Christian finds these features of the universe troublesome and in need of an explanation, and the growth of naturalism only intensifies this need. The Christian takes it to be the case that the existence of objective morality and objective meaning in life is more at home in a universe where a personal God is there and has not been silent.

CHAPTER EIGHT

UNIVERSALISM AND THE THREAT OF HELL

Paul Helm

T hose who have held that all men will finally be saved have often believed that this follows logically from the character of God. They have held that since God is essentially and omnipotently loving it follows that he could not allow any human being to suffer an eternity of torments in hell. For such Christians there is a serious stumbling block, namely those sayings of Jesus recorded in the Gospels that unequivocally speak of an eternal separation between the saved and the damned. How often the sayings of Jesus say or imply this is open to dispute, but that some of them do (e.g., Matt. 25:41, 46) is beyond question.

Faced with this evidence the universalist may deny its authenticity, regarding it, for example, as a later interpolation of the church. Alternatively he may claim that Jesus had not fully fought free of the teaching of the Judaism of his day. I shall not comment on the merits of these and several other approaches but instead look at one particular suggestion that claims that in such sayings Jesus must be taken to be *preaching* rather than *theologizing*, endeavoring in an "existential" situation to turn his hearers from their evil ways by issuing threats or warnings.

One recent example of this approach can be found in the writings of John Hick. Although he thinks that there may be reason to doubt the authenticity of such sayings, he supposes for the sake of the argument that Jesus threatened eternal punishment.[1] But he claims that such warnings or threats occurred in the context of personal admonition and exhortation.

> Jesus was neither propounding a theological theory nor defining theological doctrines. He was preaching to contemporary men and women, warning and challenging them with vivid parables and images. He was standing with them in the flow of human life at a certain moment in time, trying to get them to wrench themselves round in the direction of their lives and open their hearts to one another as fellow children of the heavenly Father. In this situation he was in effect saying: If you go on like this, heedless of your neighbour, you will come to absolute disaster: for this way of living ends in spiritual self-destruction.[2]

Professor Hick supports this by saying there is nothing incompatible about the statements "If you will not repent you will be eternally damned" and "You will not be eternally damned"; and this seems to be correct. But contrary to what Professor Hick appears to think, in order for them to be logically consistent it is certainly not necessary that the first occur in a different context, and fulfill a different function, from the second. The question of context and purpose, of whether Jesus is preaching or theologizing, is irrelevant to the question of consistency. The conditional does not have to be a threat; it could be a prediction. There is nothing necessarily "existential" about the statement, "If you eat unripe apples you will get stomachache"; and nevertheless it is perfectly consistent with the statement "No one will get stomachache."

So on the question of consistency Professor Hick seems to be correct. However, there are other objections to his view that he does not consider and that raise serious difficulties for a universalist. For although the sentences "If you do not repent you will go to hell" and "No one will go to hell" are formally consistent, the first could not be uttered as a threat if the second were also uttered or if its truth were in some way *known* to the one to whom the first was uttered. So our question is, on universalistic assumptions, could Jesus *threaten* or warn against eternal hell?

In order to formulate objections clearly it is necessary to distinguish between two kinds of universalism. Let us call universalism that asserts, on whatever grounds, that no people *can be* finally lost "hard" universalism. And let us call universalism that asserts that no people *will in fact* be lost "soft" universalism.

There is a corresponding distinction to be drawn between "hard" and "soft" particularism.[3] For the particularist who argues that some but not all men will be saved, the salvation of such men is due either to the will of God or to the will of men. But the parallelism between universalism and particularism is incomplete in that *hard* particularism is not entailed by the will of God—at least, I have been unable to find such a case in the literature. To find discussions of such questions it is almost essential to consult seventeenth-century writers. Not even the most ardent supralapsarian, or the strongest believer in particular redemption, would argue that it is inconceivable, given the character of God, that all men should finally be saved. For instance, the supralapsarian William Twisse, the prolocutor of the Westminster Assembly, argued that the salvation of the elect did not require an atonement, for God could have freely pardoned them without it. *A fortiori* (presumably) God could have pardoned all men without an atonement.

Twisse could have argued both that God could have saved anyone without an atonement and that He could only save a limited number; but in fact he appears to argue that God could have saved all men (*Nos nihil dubitamus quin omnium hominum salutem facile procurare posset deus* ["We do not doubt at all that God could easily procure the salvation of all men"]).[4] John Owen, at one time Vice-Chancellor of the University of Oxford under Cromwell, though disagreeing with Twisse on the question of the necessity of the atonement, likewise argued that the decree to create the universe was an act of God's freedom and the decree to save some was also an act of God's freedom. Hence (presumably) God was free to save more (or fewer) than He did and free to save all.[5] Neither of these writers makes the point explicitly; it has to be dragged out of them by inference. B. B. Warfield is a little more explicit: "So far as the principles of sovereignty and particularism are concerned there is no reason why a Calvinist might not be a universalist in the most express meaning of that term, holding that each and every human soul shall be saved."[6] Those who argue that the salvation of any is due to their free will must be soft universalists.

Which version of universalism does Professor Hick espouse? It is not clear. As he presents the matter he notes that on one traditional view universalism follows from the divine attributes.[7] If he accepts this argument consistently he is a hard universalist, for such attributes are necessary properties of God; and what they are alleged to entail, the final salvation of all men, is likewise going to be necessary; and therefore no one *could* finally be lost. On the other hand Professor Hick recognizes the problem that certain views of human freedom present for such a version of universalism, and this seems to take his position in the direction of "soft" universalism; for he appears to hold that the threats could be ignored but in fact will not be.

Whether we take Hick's view about the threats to be a contribution to a *hard* or a *soft* universalism it can be argued that both have damaging objections to them if they intend to take seriously the idea that Jesus' words are *threats*. An attempt will now be made to show this.

I.

First, I shall assess Professor Hick's views considered as a form of soft universalism. The assumption of soft universalism, the view that all men will in fact be saved, although it allows us to treat the language of Jesus as genuinely threatening, does nothing to protect or defend the moral character of Jesus. An argument for soft universalism might be expressed as follows:

1. God desires the salvation of all men.
2. Those not saved by other means are threatened by God in order to be saved.
3. All those threatened will finally heed the threats.
4. Therefore all men will finally be saved.

Let us begin an examination of this argument by considering the notion of a threat.

For what a person says to another person to count as a threat, for a person to be *threatened*, certain conditions are necessary. A chief one of these conditions is that the person threatened must believe that what is being said to him constitutes a threat, that is, that there is a real possibility that the unpleasantness being threatened will actually come about. Of course a person may mistakenly believe this and take something to be a threat that is not intended as such. But this kind of case cannot be what Professor Hick has in mind, since the point about this interpretation of Jesus' words is that Jesus *intends* to threaten, not merely that His hearers mistakenly take His words to constitute a threat or a warning. So what Professor Hick is maintaining is that these words of Jesus are intended by Jesus as a threat which Jesus hopes and believes that His hearers will pay attention to and so avoid what is threatened.

But if Jesus *intended* to threaten and did not merely wish to be taken to be threatening, then His words must be accompanied by the intention to carry out what is threatened should no one pay attention to them. If Jesus really and seriously threatened eternal hell for the impenitent in order to warn them of their impending fate, then it must follow that He would recognize the consistency of sending the impenitent to hell should they remain impenitent. A threat that the threatener is unwilling to carry out is hollow and not a threat.

If the reply to this is that Jesus did not really threaten, nor really intend to threaten, but that He merely gave the impression to His hearers that He was threatening, then this leaves the difficulty that it would make Jesus guilty of intentionally misleading His hearers. In any case it would substantially change the interpretation of what Jesus was doing according to Professor Hick.

The point can be put in terms of the notion of a deterrent. On Professor Hick's view, Jesus' words ought to be considered as a deterrent to His hard-hearted hearers, having the intention of turning them away from their impenitent course of action. But to be intended as a deterrent an action must be genuinely threatening. If the possession of a nuclear bomb is to act as a deterrent then at least the would-be aggressor must believe that in the event of his aggression, or his aggression under certain specific circumstances, the bomb would be used. Otherwise possession of the bomb can have no genuinely deterrent effect, for the aggressor knows that should he attack the bomb would not be used in self-defense. If, in a legal system, punishing Mr. Smith is meant to have a deterrent effect upon the behavior of Mr. Jones, deterring him from certain illegal courses of action, then Mr. Jones must believe that if he does behave illegally he will be punished. If he has good reason to think that he will not be punished then the punishment of Mr. Smith cannot be a deterrent.

To say that if the threat of punishment is genuine then there is a real possibility of it being carried out is equivalent to saying that there is a possible world in which it is carried out, a possible set of circumstances in which a person remains impenitent and suffers for it. If one is saying that there is no possible world in which this happens then in effect one is saying that the threat could not be carried out and so is no threat. So for someone seriously to threaten another the threatener must be willing to carry out the threat under the appropriate circumstances. According to Professor Hick this is precisely the case in Jesus' words about hell.

When Jesus threatened hell what precisely was He threatening? One necessary condition of something's being hell is that it involves a state of unrelieved and inescapable suffering. It is suffering without termination, unjustified by the achieving of some purified or restored state for which the suffering is a necessary condition. If it is an adverse reflection upon God's moral character (and inconsistent with His purposes) that some people should suffer in hell then it is an adverse reflection on God's moral character that He, or His spokesmen, or His Son, should seriously threaten men with hell.

What is the difference, so far as the character of the threatener is concerned, between a successful and an unsuccessful threat? Any difference between the two situations is solely due to the way the impenitent chooses to respond to the threat. If he chooses to respond in penitence, then this is logically sufficient for the threat's being successful. If he chooses to respond by a continued act or disposition of impenitence then this is logically sufficient for the threat's being unsuccessful. There is nothing Jesus can do to guarantee that any threat has a successful outcome in dissuading a person from a course of impenitence. If there is, then to that extent the threat is not a serious one. So whether the threat of hell succeeds or not depends solely upon the character and disposition of the one threatened, upon whether he chooses to cooperate or not.

If it is no adverse reflection upon God's moral character that men freely chose evil then it is no additional adverse reflection upon Jesus' character that men choose to remain impenitent and go to hell in accordance with His threats. Jesus' moral character as regards the final state of the impenitent remains precisely the same irrespective of whether his serious threatenings succeed or not, just as God's moral character remains unblemished irrespective of the fact that there is moral evil freely willed by men.

If this is so then there is nothing to be gained, in terms of the moral character of Jesus, in insisting upon soft universalism, provided it is allowed that He seriously threatened hell. Jesus is not morally better if He threatens and as a matter of fact all men heed His threats and avoid hell than if only some men heed and avoid hell, or indeed if no men heed and avoid hell. There would be a moral difference in the two situations if the threatener also had it in his power to make the threat effective in changing the state of the impenitent, for then the question would arise as to why in one case the threat was made effective while in the other case it was not. But in a situation in which the free exercise of the human will is a necessary and sufficient condition for making the threat effective, the effectiveness or otherwise of the threat is clearly irrelevant to the moral character of the threatener.

As we have seen, Professor Hick claims that the texts in the Synoptic Gospels that predict hell can be taken to be conditionals, as threats, and so can be taken to be consistent with there being no possibility of hell; but it can now be seen that the serious threat of hell entails the possibility of hell, and the possibility of hell is inconsistent with there being no possibility of hell. Professor Hick has therefore failed to establish, by interpreting the synoptic sayings of Jesus as he does, that there is no possibility of hell according to the teaching of Jesus.

Let us now consider several objections to this argument. The first could be put as follows: in considering the moral character of Jesus in the light of His serious threat of hell to His hearers, no account has been taken of His *motive* in threatening, and this is relevant to the assessment of His moral character. For He threatens, it might be said, with the motive or desire of seeing the impenitent change their ways. This objection can, in a sense, be granted. No account *has* been taken of Jesus' motives. Nevertheless it is irrelevant to the point at issue, for what is at issue is the moral character of the one prepared to threaten eternal hell to the impenitent (for whatever motive) as against the moral character of someone prepared actually to subject the impenitent to hell. And given Hick's views about free will, there is nothing to choose between them. Indeed the positions are strictly parallel despite the impression that this objection gives, in that it is perfectly consistent with consigning the impenitent to hell that the consigner should feel regret at so doing. Morally praiseworthy motives or feelings can be present in both situations. Therefore the introduction of the consideration about motives is irrelevant.

It might be objected, secondly, that it is preposterous to suppose that a situation in which a threat is made and not carried out, and an identical situation in which a threat is made and is carried out, are morally equivalent. The consequences of such situations are manifestly different. But the claim that is being made is not that the two situations are morally equivalent in all respects but only in respect of the moral character of the threatener.

The third objection has to do with Jesus' foreknowledge. It might be said that what makes Jesus' situation unique is that He threatens the impenitent with hell knowing that all those threatened will in fact change their ways, that his threat will be successful. This objection sits rather uneasily with some of the things that theologians often want to say about the restrictedness of Jesus' knowledge of the future, but we can let that pass. Three points need to be made about this objection. The first is that knowing that the threat will succeed does not take away the genuineness of the threat as made. It is on the basis of a genuine threat that Jesus foreknows the threat will succeed in turning the minds of the impenitent. Secondly, granted that it is a genuine threat, it follows that in the mind of the threatener hell is a possibility, though a possibility that, given his perfect knowledge of the future, he knows hell will not actually be fulfilled. And thirdly, if it is granted that the foreknowledge of the outcome of the threat does not take away from its genuineness then it is irrelevant to the question of the morality of the threatener. To say that Jesus foreknows that the threat will in fact be effective and that in fact no one will go to hell is quite compatible with its being possible that there should be people who go to hell, and it is the possibility of there being such people that is at issue.

A fourth objection might be that the hearers of Jesus took His sayings to be threats because they were ignorant of the outcome of the future, including their own future decisions. Let us suppose that they were ignorant in this way. Nevertheless, this fact would have no bearing upon the issue. For either it is relevant to the genuineness or otherwise of the threats, or it is not. If it is, and the threats are not genuine, then once again the interpretation of Professor Hick is being seriously modified. If on the other hand the threats are genuine then whether or not those threatened are ignorant, whatever is threatened remains a real possibility for them. Otherwise the threats are not genuine threats.

Fifthly, it might be argued that the whole point about the threats is that the conditional propositions expressing the threats are neither true nor false. It might be argued that the "seriousness" of hell is not tied up with its being a real possibility but that it is a necessary condition of choosing salvation that the one who chooses it believes that there is a hell. Therefore in His sayings what Jesus was doing was getting His hearers to choose, and for them to do this it is not necessary that there be the possibility of hell in the future, only that the hearers believe that there is this possibility. This objection would not be one that Professor Hick would himself make, for as we saw earlier he is emphatic that the statement "If you do not repent you will go to hell" is consistent with "No one will go to hell," and in order for two propositions such as these to be consistent both must have a truth-value; whereas according to the view we are now considering neither of the above expressions has a truth value, and hence the question of their consistency or otherwise cannot arise. But such a view can be found in J. A. T. Robinson's book *In The End, God . . .*:

> The two myths [of universal salvation and of the final separate of men into the saved and the lost] represent two different standpoints. They are not to be

understood as parallel "objective" statements of the final outcome of the universe. In this case, of course, one must be true and the other false. To take them as such alternative predictions and then to try and hold them together is necessarily to invite the theological errors discussed in the last chapter. The two myths represent, rather, the two sides of the truth which is in Jesus. The one says: "Christ is all in all, and always will be"; the other says: "Christ has to be chosen, and always must be." Though both are the truth, one is the truth as it is for God and as it is for faith the other side of decision; the other is the truth as it must be to the subject facing decision.[8]

What can we make of this? Robinson appears to state that everyone must say, "If I do not choose Christ, I will go to hell." But it is also true, so Robinson tells us, that no one can go to hell, because hell is an impossibility. But then if this is true it follows that I am entitled to believe it. It follows in turn that I am entitled to believe the conjunction "If I do not choose Christ I will go to hell, and it is impossible that I will go to hell." But this is in effect to say that it is both possible and impossible that I shall go to hell, and this is nonsense. No doubt Robinson will say that to think of his words in this way is to become entrapped by "objective logic," but it is hard to see how else they can be taken. It follows that if sense cannot be made of what he says it cannot be treated as a serious objection to the earlier argument.

So I conclude that Hick's argument about the threatening character of Jesus' words does not, in the context of soft universalism, do anything to preserve the moral character of Jesus. This is not to say that what Jesus says is in any way immoral but only that there is no significant moral difference between justly threatening punishment and being placed in the position of actually having to carry out the punishment.

II.

Let us now consider, more briefly, Professor Hick's thesis interpreted as a case of hard universalism. As we have noted, there are elements in what Professor Hick says that make it plausible to suppose that he is sympathetic toward hard universalism. He says that God has made man for Himself such that "the inherent gravitation of our being is toward him"[9]—that is, there is a divine structuring of human nature such that all men will finally be saved.

But if it is inconceivable that any human being should finally be lost, then however the language of Jesus is to be interpreted it cannot be regarded as genuinely threatening since as we noted earlier for a threat to be genuinely *threatening* there must be the possibility of the threat being carried out. But according to hard universalism there is no possibility of the threat being carried out, no possibility of anyone actually suffering an eternity of hell torments. If a given event such as the final salvation of all men is necessary then there is no possibility of its not occurring. If there is no possibility of its not occurring then the "threat" that it will not occur is idle.

Furthermore, if Jesus' words are taken in the context of hard universalism then it follows that the "threats" of Jesus are not so much threats as guides driving and guiding people along the path of inevitable universal salvation. And if the words are guides they cannot be genuine threats.

Are there any other arguments that might be deployed? It might be claimed that the notion of a threat can be *general*, not intended for any one person or group of people in particular but for any one who fits a certain description. So it might be said of Jesus' threat, that being general in this sense, the question of whether or not it is genuine with respect to some group of people cannot be raised, because it is not that group as such that is threatened but anyone who fits a certain description, e.g., that of remaining impenitent. But it is hard to see how the notion of a general threat avoids the dilemma that either a threat is genuine or it is not.

So I conclude that, on the assumption of "hard" universalism, Hick's interpretation of Jesus' words is not plausible.

III.

In this chapter I have attempted to argue two things:

1. On the assumption of soft universalism, if it is immoral to punish the impenitent in hell then it is immoral genuinely to threaten such punishment. (I have not argued that it *is* immoral to punish the finally impenitent in hell.) So on this argument soft universalism does not require or support the interpretation of Jesus' language given by Professor Hick.

2. If on the other hand hard universalism is assumed then the so-called threats of Jesus cannot be genuine threats since to be a genuine threat there must be the possibility of the threat actually being carried out.

So if the doctrines of "hard" and "soft" universalism are exhaustive of universalism as such (as they appear to be) then the Christian universalist interpretation of the words of Jesus as constituting a threat is impaled on the horns of a dilemma. If such a universalist opts for "soft" universalism, Jesus' moral character is on exactly the same footing as a threatener of hell as it would be as a consigner of the impenitent to hell. If he opts for "hard" universalism Jesus' threats cannot be considered to be genuine.[10]

CHAPTER NINE

ARE THEISTIC ARGUMENTS RELIGIOUSLY USELESS? A PASCALIAN OBJECTION EXAMINED

Douglas Groothuis

As a part of his multidimensional attack on natural theology, Blaise Pascal claims that the kind of argumentation required for theistic proofs is unacceptable for engendering true religious devotion. Rather than enlisting the services of natural theology to convince unbelievers, Pascal argues that the venture, however nobly conceived, goes wrong because it fails to do justice to the subject matter to which it attends so earnestly. Hence, instead of accepting any theistic arguments as a service to faith, Pascal rejects them as wrongheaded in principle because traditional theistic arguments are too opaque to be religiously helpful. In his words, they are too "remote from reasoning" and so have "little impact."

Pascal was, of course, a Christian theist and a defender of Christianity; however, he argues that natural theology, given its very nature, is ill-suited to the Christian cause. He is not alone in this contention. On similar grounds, John Baille, in the fideistic tradition, states that "the knowledge of God of which the New Testament speaks is a knowledge for which the best argument were but a sorry substitute and to which it were but a superfluous addition."[1] For Baille, Pascal, Kierkegaard, and other theists suspicious of natural theology, the classical arguments for God's existence miss the point entirely and should therefore be avoided. This claim is worthy of attention since it appears in various forms throughout the Christian tradition. Moreover, Pascal's particular kind of complaint voices the concerns of many theists that the philosophical enterprise is a poor handmaiden to religious faith.

I. THOMISTIC ARGUMENTATION

In order to understand the nature of Pascal's complaint and assess its force, we should note that he is rejecting the standard Thomistic approach to theistic proofs (and, *mutatis mutandis,* rejecting any other relevantly similar natural theology); but neither Thomas nor other natural theologians consider themselves to be in the peril Pascal suspects, as we will see. Thomas argues from nature to deity through the use of natural reason. His argumentation comprises the preambles of faith. The Five Ways claim to demonstrate, in order of Thomas's exposition, an Unmoved Mover, a First Cause, a Necessary Being, a Perfect Being, and a Designer. And these, he claims, all people call God.

This Being can be known through the proper operations of reason; the existence of God need not be an article of faith, though those who do not have the time or the facility for such proofs may believe in God's existence by faith in lieu of reason's demonstrations. Thomas acknowledges that natural theology lacks certain uniquely and indispensably Christian features such as the *ex nihilo* creation of the universe, the Trinity, and the Incarnation. Thomas takes these divine truths to be "above reason" and knowable only by faith (not by unaided reason) in the authority of revelation. But since "grace does not destroy nature but perfects it,"[2] this reliance on faith, he thinks, poses no epistemic or moral threat to his philosophical project or theological integrity. Neither is the process of argumentative proof ill-suited for God as its object because, for Thomas, philosophy is the handmaiden of theology.

II. CONTEMPORARY APOLOGETIC THEORY

Some contemporary evangelical apologists stand essentially in the Thomistic tradition, but as a whole they are divided over apologetic methodology and the place of theistic arguments in the defense of the Christian worldview. Although they unite in eschewing fideistic refusals to marshal rational support for Christianity, evangelical apologists disagree on such matters as the logical starting point for apologetics, the nature of common ground between believers and unbelievers, the tests for truth, the role of faith, and the basis for Christian faith.[3] To limit the field to the issue addressed in this paper, I will survey several schools of evangelical apologetics that give different orientations toward the traditional project of natural theology.

Those generally identifying with the Thomistic apologetic orientation (although not Roman Catholic in other respects) of arguing from an element or elements of the creation to the Creator believe that some of the classical theistic arguments for the existence of God—such as the cosmological, design, or moral—are both biblically permissible and epistemically credible and are, therefore, apologetically potent. In the forefront of this kind of defense are apologists such as J. P. Moreland[4] and W. L. Craig.[5] They find intellectual strengths in natural theology but refine the argumentation through the rigors of analytical philosophy. They tend to present the various arguments for Christian theism as part of a cumulative case argument; that is, various kinds of arguments are proffered that converge on the Christian perspective, although the conclusion is reached with less than deductive certainty.[6]

Other apologists in the presuppositional tradition believe that one must start from the truth of Christianity in order effectively to dismantle the unbeliever's worldview and make room for Christian faith. The late G. Clark[7] and his student C. F. H. Henry[8] expend considerable intellectual effort criticizing non-Christian philosophies and defending the rational coherence of the Christian position. Yet both deem natural theology as unnecessary and ill-equipped to lead unbelievers to the God of the Scripture, who is far more than First Cause or Designer. Similarly, the late C. Van Til[9] and his disciples such as J. Frame[10] and the late G. Bahnsen,[11] give little sympathy to traditional theistic arguments and instead emphasize the illogic of non-Christian systems. The Van Tillians differ from the Clarkians in that the latter view Aristotelian logic as how God's mind operates and therefore necessary for apologetic endeavors while (some)

Van Tillians seem to view logic as a useful tool but not as an absolute truth binding on God himself.

Another group of evangelical philosophers of religion, represented by A. Plantinga and N. Wolterstorff, articulate what has become known as Reformed epistemology: the notion that empirical or inductive evidence is not necessary for belief in God because this belief can be "properly basic"—a fundamental belief that is rational although not evidentially based on other beliefs.[12] These analytic philosophers also criticize non-Christian worldviews as rationally defective but do not esteem traditional natural theology as epistemologically crucial for the rationality of Christian faith.[13]

Differing from the approach of modern natural theologians, presuppositionalists, and Reformed epistemologists is the apologetic method of E. J. Carnell[14] and his followers, such as G. R. Lewis.[15] Carnell developed a model of apologetics that was influenced by Clark's deductive rationalism but considered the Christian worldview as a hypothesis to be verified through various spheres of evidence rather than as an *a priori* presupposition. Carnell put little stock in natural theology, classically understood, but left room for corroborating empirical and moral evidence for the Christian hypothesis.

This abbreviated tour through modern evangelical apologetics theory reveals a variety of responses to the kind of theistic arguments that Pascal rejected. However, none of them, it seems, captures exactly the heart of Pascal's concern. To this we now turn.

III. PROOFS AS REMOTE FROM REASONING

Pascal objects to Thomistic and any other natural theology as the wrong approach entirely. Even if some recondite argument could be constructed that would prove God's existence, the conclusion of the argument would not have the kind of psychological staying power worthy of the subject matter. He says:

> The metaphysical proofs for the existence of God are so remote from human reasoning and so involved that they make little impact, and even if they did help some people, it would only be for the moment during which they watched the demonstration, because an hour later they would be afraid they had made a mistake.[16]

In this objection, Pascal is not concerned so much that the *object of the proof* is not the living God of scriptural tradition but that the *process of argumentation* used in the proofs is somehow inappropriate or imprudent. We can fill out Pascal's objection by stating his argument like this:

1. Metaphysical proofs for God's existence are remote from reasoning in that they are involved or complex.
2. What is remote from reasoning has "little impact" existentially because of its complexity and tentativeness; one would be afraid of being mistaken in reasoning.
3. Therefore, metaphysical proofs have little existential impact.

4. True knowledge of God (that is, religiously relevant understanding) cannot be remote from reason and have little existential impact (implied).
5. Therefore, metaphysical proofs cannot deliver any true knowledge of God.

Premise 2 is only intimated in the above quotation by Pascal, but it is borne out by Pascal's celebrated distinction between the "God of the philosophers" (supposedly proved through abstruse reasoning) and the "God of Abraham, Isaac, and Jacob." Pascal draws this distinction dramatically in an account of a gripping religious experience recorded in "the memorial."[11] The philosophers' God makes "little impact" religiously while the God of religion is the deity whom Pascal believed was the source of his religious experience. By referring to the "God of the philosophers," Pascal not only refers, I think, to the nature of this deity but also to the God of *philosophizing;* that is, the philosophical approach to the issue of God's existence, involving complicated proofs.

We need to inquire more deeply into just what bothers Pascal about these "metaphysical proofs." He is concerned that they are "so remote from human reasoning and so involved that they make little impact." By "little impact" Pascal appears to mean that the proofs lack existential effect on one's conduct. That is, the proofs are not earth-shaking or deeply engaging. If I learn the exact age of my neighbor this belief will likely have "little impact." On the other hand, if I am an African-American and I learn that my neighbor is a member of the Ku Klux Klan, the impact increases.

My account of what Pascal means by "little impact" is something of an educated reconstruction because he does not explicitly or at length explain just what he means by this locution (besides his worries that the proofs will be moot because of their complexity and tentativeness). I suggest he may have also had in mind the notion that the proofs have little existential impact in that they do not positively affect one's religious conduct by engendering spiritual sanctity. If the proofs are so tentative they could not hope to ground a solid faith.

I believe this construal is Pascalian in spirit, if not in letter. Whatever the case, I will use this enriched notion of "little impact" in my assessment of Pascal's criticism of philosophical reasoning used in service of religious faith. Even if Pascal did not have precisely this latter notion in mind in the above quotation, it nonetheless seems worthwhile to include this idea as part of an antiproof argument because this understanding of "little impact," if defensible, would only strengthen Pascal's overall case against natural theology.

IV. SIMPLE PROOFS AND REMOTENESS FROM REASONING

Our investigation will begin with premise 1: *Metaphysical proofs for God's existence are remote from reasoning.* Pascal does not identify just what proofs he is addressing. He may intend to distinguish metaphysical proofs from moral proofs or from religious experience arguments. Whatever the case may be, Pascal's assertion lacks substantiation: not all proofs are esoteric and hence "remote from reasoning" or "so involved." Thomas's Five Ways, whatever their ultimate cogency may be, are not opaque to human reasoning—particularly the arguments for a First Cause or a Designer as stated in the *Summa Theologica.*

Certain simplified versions of these kinds of arguments are used even by non-specialists. Consider this argument, which involves only two premises and a *modus ponens* form of argument:

1. If anything intricate and beautiful evinces design then it implies a designer.
2. The world is intricate and beautiful and evinces design.
3. Therefore: the world implies a designer.

This gives the rudiments of an argument from design. To be sure, it is elementary or embryonic to the point of being almost crude. But arguments like this open up the kind of considerations needed to discuss theistic proofs intelligently. They can be understood without esoteric philosophical or theological training.[18] Attentive undergraduates can understand more sophisticated versions of these arguments when they are clearly presented. These arguments in their more developed form may be remote from conversation at most collegiate social events (excepting the Philosophy Club), but they need not be remote from reasoning *per se*.

Most theists do not come to believe in God through these arguments, but the fact that they are used in conversation shows that theists deem them intelligible and worthy of discussion. These examples of simple theistic arguments are only meant to show that some nonphilosophical theists adduce these mini-arguments and show some understanding of them. This being the case, the germ of Thomas's arguments cannot be considered so "remote from human reasoning." In fact, the more rigorous statement of the arguments in Thomas's *Summa Theologica* takes up only a few pages and is not highly arcane (though he does develop the proof from motion in much more depth in *Summa Contra Gentiles*). Of course, philosophers following Thomas, such as A. Kenny, have written far more about his arguments than Thomas himself ever did. But the point stands that proofs need not be highly complex to be somewhat cogent or believed. So, Pascal's premise 1 does not seem to be clearly true.

However, one could plausibly argue that a high level of sophistication is required for the *proper* evaluation (whether positive or negative) of these proofs. Kenny, for instance, spends over a hundred densely argued pages discussing the Five Ways.[19] He deems this philosophically appropriate and necessary if an adequate judgment is to be made on the value of these arguments.

Consider another case. Nonphysicists attending a popular lecture on recent cosmological theories may understand the rudiments of the theories sufficiently well to discuss the merits of these theories with their peers after the lecture. But this does not qualify them to make authoritative judgments on the ultimate validity of the theories. If this analogy is valid, Pascal's point seems to stand because the subject matter demands an intellectual rigor which is "remote from reasoning" or at least remote from common understanding. (More on what constitutes "remoteness from reasoning" will be discussed below.)

How one assesses the matter of complexity in argument in its relation to rational justification depends on the cogency of the arguments at the various levels of sophistication. An argument one person takes to be complex may be clearly grasped by a very intelligent person and thus not be "remote from [his or her] reason" at all. Although I am not wedded to the following notion, it could be that a relatively simple and straightforward theistic proof is cogent. If so, the one who understands the proof may come to a justified theistic belief without considering further philosophical complexities. This would be the case even if sophisticated critics constructed complex criticisms of the argument far beyond the ken of those believing the simple argument. We can think of any number of sophisticated criticisms of rationally justified beliefs that need not concern one convinced otherwise.

On the basis of a few facts and a basic moral intuition, one may justifiably believe that the United States' entry into the Korean War was warranted, and this position could be rationally held without consulting the revisionist arguments against the military intervention, however sophisticated they may be. One simply cannot chase down every possible refutation of arguments that appear solid.

V. ARGUMENTS AS WINDOW DRESSING FOR FAITH?

But even if simple theistic arguments might succeed, Pascal could claim that these arguments are really just window-dressing for beliefs which are rooted not in philosophical reflection but in an immediate intuition of what he calls "the heart," the organ for the acquisition of nondiscursive knowledge.[20] He might argue that because believers feel obliged to defend their faith and convince the unconverted, they attempt to argue people into belief through proofs. However noble the intentions may be from a religious perspective, the arguments given are not the true basis for the believer's convictions. If the believer's faith were based solely on proofs he or she would not likely be so zealous for conversions because he or she would be concerned for dispassionate philosophical disputation rather than religious conversion.

This reply highlights the fact that one may defend a proposition with arguments that were not the basis for one's original assent to that proposition. One may come to believe in the Christian God through a unique and convincing religious experience and not through metaphysical proofs. One's faith would then be rooted in a situation that cannot be reproduced on command for unbelievers. Nevertheless, once one has come to believe that God exists, it is appropriate to use any valid means available to convince others of God's existence. For there are, generally speaking, various ways of coming to know that the same object exists. The following tale from crypto-zoology should illustrate this principle.

One may come to believe that Sasquatch exists because of a Sasquatch-sighting made when one was in one's right mind and in clear light and at close range. But one might attempt to convince a person not so favorably positioned of the existence of Sasquatch through various other media—reports of sightings, circumstantial evidence such as footprints, etc.—to establish the crypto-zoological claim. The eyewitness of a veridical Sasquatchophany certainly needs no such supports for his or her original belief so long as he or she has good reason to trust the experience as veridical. But that eyewitness may employ non-Sasquatchophanic means in order to convince others of the objective existence of the creature (or to develop a more systematic and epistemically enriched Sasquatchology). This kind of noneyewitness argument may be less convincing than would be the more direct Sasquatchophany, but it might convince skeptics nonetheless.

In the same way, theists converted apart from argument may adduce arguments (that they find convincing after their conversion to theism) to commend their theism to others not yet convinced. There need not be anything epistemically improper about this enterprise if it is carried out with intellectual integrity and avoids propagandizing. (This argument about simple theistic arguments would also apply, *mutatis mutandis,* to more complicated versions.)

VI. COMPLEX PROOFS AND EXISTENTIAL IMPACT

But even if these theistic mini-arguments are not illegitimate in principle, it is certainly true that many metaphysical arguments for God's existence are extremely complicated and intellectually taxing, if not intimidating. Pascal, being familiar with the proofs of Augustine, Aquinas, and Descartes, probably thought that the proofs for God's existence most likely to succeed were the more sophisticated versions. Hence his characterization of them as "remote from human reasoning." Despite our discussion about the possible success of a simple theistic argument, we can grant Pascal this point regarding the complexity of the arguments. Nevertheless, it need not be the case that even every complicated (or speculative) theistic argument must be "remote from human reasoning" in the sense of having "little impact." A complicated and successful theistic argument would, in fact, itself be the result of human reasoning, albeit arduous reasoning, and could have considerable impact.

Before preceding further, a distinction is required to clear up some possible confusion. When Pascal speaks of arguments that are "remote from human reasoning," he may mean arguments that are uncommon with respect to their complexity. Or he may refer to arguments that are remote from the *practical reasoning* used in everyday business transactions (such as balancing a checkbook) or family affairs (such as considering what and who to put in your will). Any ontological argument would likely fit in this category of the uncommon argument because we seldom, if ever, deduce the objective existence of anything, the existence of which is debatable, from the very nature of its concept or definition. An absolutely perfect automobile or island does not exist simply because we can conceptualize or define it. (This comment is not meant to refute any ontological argument but simply to illustrate its uncommon form.) Similarly, Aquinas's attempt to prove the Prime Mover in *Summa Contra Gentiles* (where the argument is longer and more complex than the version in *Summa Theologica*) is a somewhat uncommon form of argument or at least remote from practical reasoning.

Therefore, on the one hand, it can be said that these kinds of complex arguments are "remote from common or practical reasoning." The same is true, of course, for the theory of relativity or quantum physics. On the other hand, the most abstruse and recondite theistic arguments are not remote from human reasoning when they are philosophical projects. If a theistic proof avoids propaganda and preaching and works within the prescribed framework of the law of noncontradiction, the law of identity, the law of excluded middle, *modus ponens, modus tolens,* contraposition, material implication, and all the other stipulations of logic, it would be an exemplary case of human reasoning.

Someone partial to natural theology might contend that the better theistic proofs are models of human reasoning at its best. We might call this intellectual enterprise *speculative reasoning,* not in the sense of "mere speculation" (reckless rumination untethered from epistemic sobriety) but in the sense of rigorous ratiocination on matters philosophical; that is, the contemplation of matters not subject to immediate empirical adjudication. Furthermore, the quality and passion of intellect required to construct a speculative argument could, contra Pascal, conceivably make someone all the more certain of its conclusion. These arguments may be both complex and profound and so deserving of respect and attention.

If an undergraduate philosophy student scrupulously works his or her way through a commendable modern anthology of the philosophy of religion, carefully weighing arguments for and against theism, and comes to the conclusion (rightly or wrongly) that the arguments for theism considerably outweigh the arguments against it such that the student reckons theism to be proved, he or she may view this conclusion as a considerable intellectual achievement that leads him or her to a rather gripping conclusion: *God exists.* The student would claim to have moved from either atheism or agnosticism to theism through convincing arguments.

This philosophical reasoning, contra Pascal's premises 2 and 3 concerning the religious impotence of such reasoning, seems to have some existential consequence. The student might begin to ponder his or her relation to God, what God might want from him or her, whether there is an afterlife, what it might be like, how it impinges on the student's life on earth, etc. He or she might engage in spirited arguments with atheists whose position he or she now rejects. Like C. S. Lewis, who adopted a generic theism before converting to Christianity, the newly convinced theist may even begin to attend religious services out of an ill-defined sense of religious obligation.[21] My point is that these are not unlikely actions for one convinced of theism and that they bear the marks of existential impact, if not a fully mature faith.

Pascal might ask the following: What if the ratiocination requisite for the student's conversion to theism was so esoteric as to render his or her belief tenuous because he or she cannot be sure he or she has reasoned correctly? The student's theism then would obtain only during the moment she understood the demonstration "because an hour later [he or she] would be afraid [he or she] made a mistake."[22] This kind of epistemically episodic and infirm theism is hardly the fiber of robust religious faith. Pascal might put it another way: When considering beliefs concerning the existence and nature of God, on which one's eternal destiny depends, we must be free from the kind of doubts that may assail those who assent to complex arguments, because religious faith involves a deeper certainty than bestowed by any philosophical argumentation.

Three responses to this are in order. First, there is little sense of intellectual achievement in the simple operations of reason such as making change or gauging how much money to put in the parking meter; but more grandiose intellectual enterprises, if successfully executed, can galvanize one's whole being. This often happens in the case of detailed, difficult, and controversial scientific theories—whether in biology, physics, sociology, or elsewhere. A student may labor long and hard to figure out the Pythagorean theorem, only to forget all the steps involved at a later time; but having understood the theorem only once is enough to know that it is true. Not being able to rehearse instantly all its steps upon command does not defeat one's knowledge of the truth of the Pythagorean theorem for one who truly remembers having mastered it. This consideration begins to challenge Pascal's premise 2: *What is remote from reasoning has little existential impact.* An argument may be difficult to execute and understand but still have existential effect because of the subject matter and the discipline required to understand it.

Second, it is not clear that genuine religious faith requires a kind of constant indubitability or incorrigibility to be genuine. It can be argued that so long as one genuinely assents to essential Christian doctrines (however strong that assent may be) and sincerely consents to obey the dicta of Christian conduct, one is comporting oneself as a genuine Christian—even if doubts sometimes come.[23] Believers may identify with the confession made to Jesus: "I do believe; help me overcome my unbelief"—a confession that Jesus is not recorded as rejecting as illegitimate.[24]

Third, metaphysical arguments for God's existence need not be understood as the central bulwark of mature Christian faith. As mentioned earlier, one might be impressed by some recondite theistic argument and begin to investigate the Christian faith. If such a person becomes a Christian, the Christian tradition teaches that he is privy to the internal working of the Holy Spirit that produces a depth of spiritual conviction that while not irrational[25] is not strictly explicable in terms of metaphysical arguments alone. Therefore, a mature Christian faith, even if initially sparked by theistic argumentation, need not be dependent on that epistemic reservoir alone for the fullness of religious confidence. Other sources of cognitive confidence are available.

To critique further Pascal's argument we need to consider the role of habituation with respect to difficult reasoning.

VII. BELIEF AND HABITUATION

Even by Pascal's own reckoning, belief in difficult proofs—mathematical, theological, or philosophical—can be intellectually ingrained through habit because "we are as much automaton as mind." We only need see the truth of the reasoning—that is, its soundness and cogency—once in order to continue to believe the conclusion of the given argument. Pascal further explains this:

> Proofs only convince the mind; habit provides the strongest proofs and those most believed. It inclines the automaton, which leads the mind unconsciously along with it. . . . In short, we must resort to habit once the mind has seen where the truth lies, in order to steep and stain ourselves in that belief which constantly eludes us, for it is too much trouble to have the proofs always present before us. . . . We must therefore make both parts of us [the mind and the automaton] believe: the mind by reasons, *which need to be seen only once in a lifetime,* and the automaton by habit.[26]

Pascal employs two senses of the word *proof.* When he says that "proofs only convince the mind" he means intellectual arguments that compel rational assent. This is an epistemic proof. Understanding the Pythagorean theorem is an example of a mathematical proof convincing to the mind; it is epistemic in nature. When Pascal says that the "strongest proofs" are provided by habit he means proof in the sense of the conditioning required to habituate a belief psychologically. This is, somewhat paradoxically, a nonepistemic sense of "proof." This nonepistemic proof presupposes the epistemic proof and inclines the automaton to believe something more strongly than was the case at the time of original assent.

But what might Pascal have in mind when he speaks of ingraining a mathematical belief through habit? Unfortunately, he never tells us, but several likely candidates present themselves. If Sam finds a mathematical proof to be convincing but difficult to remember and rehearse, he could read it repeatedly in order to become more familiar with its steps. This process could eventually eliminate the strangeness of the proof. Furthermore, one could memorize the proof and refer to it at will to shore up one's understanding through familiarity. This kind of habituation builds up the understanding through repetition that makes the material more familiar and convincing. The certainty of its truth is thereby strengthened. This process would help dissipate Pascal's concern that complex arguments have "little impact" because "an hour later [people] would be afraid they had made a mistake." Any fear over miscalculation (say over the Pythagorean theorem) decreases as certainty is enhanced through repetition.

However, Sam doesn't merely see the truth of the proof "once in a lifetime." He sees it initially, finds it difficult to retain in his understanding, and so becomes more familiar with it through repetition. This construction differs from Pascal's statement in that the cognitive element is repeated through habit until it becomes more psychologically certain. In the fragment above, Pascal speaks of it being "too much trouble to have the proofs always present before us" in connection with only needing to see the proofs' truth once. But the repetition of the proof need not be perennial ("always before us") in order to solidify the certainty.

In these sorts of cases, becoming habituated to a proposition once certainly believed—however obscure the process of reasoning needed to derive the proposition might have been—is the psychological answer to the problem of "remoteness from human reasoning." The remote—or the intellectually involved or complex—can be made more immediate and understandable through repetitive practices. Pascal also mentions this sense of habituation to fortify belief in the context of the believer's thought-life:

> Man is so made that if he is told often enough that he is a fool he believes it. By telling himself so often enough he convinces himself, because when he is alone he carries on an inner dialogue with himself which is important to keep under proper control. . . . We must keep silence as far as we can and only talk to ourselves about God, whom we know to be true, and thus convince ourselves that he is.[27]

Pascal uses "know to be true" in a different sense than "convince ourselves that he is [true]." The former seems to mean an initial intellectual assent whereas the latter has to do with a certainty that is achieved through habituation. This corresponds to the distinction between epistemic knowledge and proof through habituation made a few paragraphs above. Pascal does not specify just what he is speaking of; he could be referring either to God's existence or to God's truthfulness (or trustworthiness). But his central point is that habituation can fortify belief.

However, if one already *knows* God to be true (either in terms of existing, or being trustworthy, or both), what need is there to *convince* ourselves that he is true? Is this not redundant? I know that the Atlanta Braves baseball team lost the seventh game of the 1991 World Series in the bottom of the tenth inning. Do I need further to convince myself of this mournful fact? I may not want to believe it, but it has been amply verified through so many means that I cannot deny it and retain my sanity.

But Pascal is not thinking of these kinds of situations, where persuasion is superfluous. He is considering cases in which religious belief is threatened by doubt about either God's existence or his trustworthiness. In these cases, the stability of one's belief may be rocked by various factors, including an inattention to the very object of faith or inattention to one's previous religious experiences.

Consider Thomas. It might be that Thomas's life becomes cluttered with activities that leave little time for religious reflection, prayer, or worship. As a result, his thought-life wanders from its religious moorings, and Thomas feels unsettled and insecure in his faith. Pascal would counsel him to return to his roots—through talking to himself about God—to convince himself that God is there and is true. Pascal assumes at some level that someone like Thomas already believes in God and his trustworthiness. But through spiritual sloth or worldly busyness this belief has faded in intensity and therefore needs rekindling.

This route to certitude through habituation is similar to Pascal's comments at the end of the wager argument. By acting like a believer, the skeptic may eventually find himself or herself to be a believer. However, in the case of the wager, a prudential decision to believe is advocated in place of any theistic proofs. There is no epistemic certainty through argument about the existence of God that precedes the wager, except to suppose that the odds for God's existence over against his nonexistence are even. Habituation is not used for training the mind to remember a truth once seen but has another function.[28]

A person who is not interested in the subject matter of a complex argument may doubt the conclusion because of insufficient habituation, with the result that the conclusion has "little impact." For instance, I may conclude through the use of the complex sociological method of regression analysis that Asian-Americans tend to watch less television because of their work ethic. But since this fact has little impact on me existentially, I may doubt the veracity of the conclusion if I forget how to do regression analysis. This would not likely be the case if I were doing a well-funded research project related to Asian-Americans or if I had some other incentive to understand the sociological investigation. In this case, the procedure of regression analysis, though initially difficult to master, would have become second nature to me through repeated use.

VIII. CONCLUSION: COMPLEX PROOFS NOT DISALLOWED

Pascal's argument against natural theology confronts the nature of the argumentation involved. He claims that such arguments are too complex to have any religiously significant impact on the unbeliever. These arguments, therefore, cannot deliver any true knowledge of God, because such theological knowledge will have no existential impact.

However, Pascal's argument against the legitimacy of metaphysical arguments loses its force in the case of any successful metaphysical argument (whether simple or complicated) for God's existence that one finds worthy of attention. Such an argument would be a paradigm case of human reasoning in its speculative mode and therefore not "remote from reasoning" at all. The argumentative procedures may be more complex than what is used in the common operations of life, but this in no way diminishes a proof's probative force or its possible existential impact. Assenting to such an argument could even mark the beginning of a more robust Christian faith that draws on other epistemic resources than the metaphysical proofs in isolation.[29]

ENGAGING THE (NEO)PAGAN MIND: PAUL'S ENCOUNTER WITH ATHENIAN CULTURE AS A MODEL FOR CULTURAL APOLOGETICS (ACTS 17:16–34)

J. Daryl Charles

I. INTRODUCTION

Acts 16 contains an account of an unusual directive in the life of Paul. While in the major Aegean port city of Troas in northwest Asia Minor, the apostle is conscious in a dream of a Macedonian appealing for help.[1] Paul's subsequent entry into Europe, as it turns out, is crucial to the spread of Christianity throughout the Roman Empire. Following his arrival at Neapolis, the port of Philippi and terminus of the Egnatian Way, Paul visits Philippi, Thessalonica, and Berea before going on to what was considered the intellectual center of the ancient world, the "university" city of Athens. During Paul's visit to Athens, a rather remarkable opportunity presented itself. What, too, is remarkable is the amount of detail given in Luke's narrative both to the content of Paul's speech at the Areopagus and the social context in which it is delivered.

Adolf Deissmann claimed that Paul's Areopagus address was "the greatest missionary document in the New Testament."[2] Deissmann noted that the apostle's aim was to "exhibit to pagans of a great city in the Mediterranean world what was characteristic of the new religion as concisely as possible."[3] Despite this enthusiastic assessment, it has not been unusual for commentators to view Paul's ministry in Athens as a failure, to the extent that Paul's technique in Athens is deemed ineffective. Writing a century ago, W. M. Ramsay gave credence to the view that Paul became "disillusioned" by his experience in Athens.[4] C. Munsinger has called the Areopagus speech an "unrealistic experiment."[5] A. Daniel-Rops also sees Athens as an "unsuccessful" paradigm. A negative view of Paul's ministry in Athens has even found its way into the notes of the New Jerusalem Bible.[6]

In spite of obvious missiological interest in this narrative, the negative appraisal of Acts 17 raises several questions. Does Paul's preaching at the Areopagus involve compromise with contemporary pagan religious notions? Does it obscure in any way the distinctives of the Christian message? Does it in Luke's mind represent a capitulation to the cultural forces at work in cosmopolitan Athens? Is it possible that Luke is attempting, in veiled fashion, to mirror an "unsuccessful" ministry, or even more strongly, to show that Paul is sidetracked by a "natural theology" that fails to penetrate his audience because of its absence of Christian theological distinctives? Viewing Paul's preaching in Athens as either a success or failure fundamentally guides how one interprets the text of Acts 17. In Luke's mind, does the material in 17:16–34 play the role of the model or the foil?[7] Can Paul's encounter with Athenian culture serve as a model—positively or negatively—for the Christian community of any age?

In the book of Acts there are three speeches of Paul recorded—one to a Jewish audience (13:16–41), one to a Christian audience (20:17–35), and one to a pagan audience (17:16–34). This distribution surely is not by chance.[8] Like most of the preaching throughout Acts, the Areopagus speech is received with both hostility and faith; thus, the reader can assume 17:16–34 to be exemplary of first-century apostolic preaching. The text of Acts 17 itself does not suggest explicitly that Paul's speech at the Areopagus is misguided in a strategic sense. While verses 16–34 are of obvious missionary interest, the reader must come to terms with why Luke is so concerned to present the "human side" of Paul's preaching. Why the preoccupation with detail?

It is in the interest of this concern that we wish to proceed. Acts 17:16–34 raises important questions concerning Christian proclamation and the church's relation to culture—specifically, to "educated pagan" culture.[9] Some of what confronted Paul and the subsequent Christian community in Athens—the little that we know of it—confronts North American Christians as well. What are the lessons that can be drawn from Paul's encounter with "cultured paganism"?

II. PAUL, APOSTLE TO THE CULTURED PAGAN

"I am a Jew, from Tarsus [in the province] of Cilicia, a citizen of a very important city."[10] Thus Paul describes himself in one instance of interrogation. Although Saul was "brought up"[11] in Jerusalem, he returned to his home city of Tarsus after his conversion (Acts 9:30). Doubtless he was proud of his linkage to Tarsus,[12] a university city as well as center of government, banking, and commerce.[13] Paul was hence well acquainted with pagan "high culture"—an acquaintance that, when sanctified, would thrust *him,* not Simon Peter, forward as the apostle to the Gentiles (Rom. 11:13). Roman citizenship and life in a university city, after all, did have its privileges. This background would aid him enormously during his apostolic ministry—particularly in a city like Athens.[14]

Why was Tarsus the city that should produce the apostle to the Gentiles? Uniting oriental and occidental cultural and intellectual life, the institutions of Tarsus were uniquely suited to mold Paul's intellectual development.[15] Cicero was governor of Tarsus in the mid-fifties B.C. It was here that Mark Antony met Cleopatra in 41 B.C. Tarsus was the native city of several famous Stoic philosophers—among them Zeno, Antipater, Athenadorus, and Nestor. In the period of 27 B.C.–A.D. 14, during the reign of Augustus, Tarsus came to be renowned as a center of intellectual life. As a "university" city, Tarsus is said to have surpassed Athens and Alexandria in terms of zeal for learning.[16]

Prosperous and cosmopolitan, Tarsus would have prepared Paul well for engaging Hellenistic culture.

III. ATHENS IN PAUL'S DAY

The cradle of democracy, Athens was the foremost of the city-states in the fifth century B.C.[17] Following nearly thirty years of exhausting strife with totalitarian Sparta, Athens lay politically ruined. In terms of its rich cultural heritage, however, the city remained unsurpassed. Its contributions in sculpture, literature, philosophy, and oratory from the fifth and fourth centuries were unparalleled in the ancient world. In addition to being the native city of Socrates and Plato, it became the adopted home of Aristotle, Epicurus, and Zeno. Demosthenes, an "unsuccessful Churchill"[18] of the mid fourth-century B.C., strove in vain to rouse his fellow Athenians once more to independence and political greatness. Athens was also home to the poet Menander, whose New Comedy as a form of entertainment eclipsed the classical Greek tragedy in the late fourth and early third century B.C.[19] It is worthy of note that the Attic dialect, not its Ionic or Doric counterparts, formed the base of the later *Koinē*.

By Paul's day, the city had lost much of the preeminence that it once possessed. Yet Cicero, writing one hundred years earlier, observed that in spite of its decline in political power, Athens still enjoyed "such renown that the now shattered and weakened name of Greece is supported by the reputation of this city."[20] People generally came to one of three "university" cities of renown—Athens, Alexandria, or Tarsus—to study philosophy, rhetoric, or general education.[21] Apart from its academic reputation,[22] Athens is depicted in the writings of Strabo and Ovid as a tourist center and the site of great festivals, attracting as well various itinerant philosophers and mystics. One such traveling teacher-mystic, Apollonius of Tyana, is described by Philostratus (third century) as having arrived at Athens about the same time as Paul.[23] Interestingly, the account mentions that Apollonius was struck by the altars "to unknown gods." It is to such a city that the apostle Paul would come, adapting himself in astonishing fashion to the dialectical habits of its inhabitants.[24] Simply put, for Luke Athens represents the height of pagan culture. Hence, he infuses the description of Paul's ministry here with notable detail. It should not be lost on the reader that Athens in Paul's day was still the cultural capital of the world.

The intellectual atmosphere of first-century Athens might be characterized as mildly promiscuous, both in a religious and nonreligious sense. A large proportion of the city's population had been initiated into the Eleusian mysteries.[25] Religiously speaking, the city had no discernible knowledge of Old Testament revelation. It basked in the glory of past intellectual strength, yet by Paul's day exhibited a somewhat indiscriminate, almost casual approach to life issues, lacking the seriousness of intellectual pursuit that had typified the classical era. Several of the church fathers allude to Athens as a city of talkers, a people possessed of curiosity.[26] According to one ancient source, Athenians were particularly fond of lawsuits.[27] With hermaphrodites commonplace at house doors and innumerable symbols of phallic worship and sex obsession on public display throughout the city (to some of which were attached religious significance), one can envisage the dislocation in the apostle's spirit as he engages a culture in moderate decline (17:16).[28]

With the passing of the centuries a canonical twelve gods were thought to hold power on Mt. Olympus.[29] Athens was the site of an altar dedicated to this twelve-member pantheon, which included Athena, daughter to Zeus.[30] Religion and politics appear to have been ineluctably intertwined in Athenian culture, as evidenced by surviving literature. One such example is a somewhat turgid speech dating to c. A.D. 155 by Aelius Aristides at the Panathenaic festival. In this speech, the author recounts a legal battle of the gods that is significant for an understanding of Athenian history. In his pursuit of justice, Poseidon sued Ares over the murder of his son, ultimately winning his case in the presence of all the gods.[31] As a record of the event, the purported site of disputation took on Ares' name. Hence, throughout Athen's rich history the Areopagus constituted for some the pinnacle of Athenian respect. It was here that the gods were understood to have convened and disputed. And it was here that justice was to be eternally manifest—even among mortal Athenians. Thus it was that Athenians looked to the Areopagus as a source of knowledge, wisdom, reason, and justice.[32]

Since the mid third-century B.C. the Council of the Areopagus functioned as authoritative in civil-legal[33] and educational matters. The council consisted of about thirty members and was presided over by a κῆρυξ, the president of the assembly who conducted official business. In the Roman era the Areopagus was constituted by several commissions, one of which was educational.[34] This "university" commission, known to us through pseudo-Platonic literature and Plutarch, and on which Cicero is said to have served, was still functioning in the 60s when Paul visited Athens. Acts 17:22–23 may well be Luke's report of the apostle being led before this elite educational commission for an informal inquiry.[35]

IV. LITERARY-RHETORICAL STRATEGY IN ACTS 17:16–34

A. The Narrative Framework of Paul's Areopagus Speech

Acts 14:8–18 and 17:16–34 contain notable similarities. In both Lystra and Athens, the apostle adapts his preaching to his audience by assimilating a more or less Greek view of the universe, with its human quest for God. Luke's narrative in chapter 17 is far more extended, incorporating detail that tantalizingly suggests eyewitness testimony.[36] Supporting his argument by quotations from Epimenides and Aratus of Soli, Paul employs a line of reasoning not unlike that of classical Greek orators. Luke depicts the Athenians' response to Paul in the agora as moderately bemused. Significantly, it is the introduction of the notion of a bodily resurrection that evokes a strong reaction (vv. 18, 32). To the Greek intelligentsia, the idea of somatic resurrection is patently absurd, for it flies in the face of the Platonic-Stoic view of psycho-immortality.

Perhaps Luke has in mind the tradition regarding Socrates, who also was accused in Athens of introducing "new gods" (cf. v. 18). For this we are dependent on the testimony of Xenophon: "Socrates does wrongly, for he does not acknowledge the gods which the state acknowledges; rather, he introduces other new-fashioned gods."[37] Indeed, not only Socrates but also Anaxagoras (500–428 B.C.) and Protagoras (480–410 B.C.) were accused in Athens of introducing foreign gods. In the more recent past, Cicero had criticized the Stoic philosopher Chrysippus for embracing "unknown gods" (*ignotorum deorum*).[38] Hence, it is possible that Luke is attempting to portray Paul in the "Socratic" mold.[39]

After all, Luke had noted that in the agora Paul had "disputed . . . daily with those who happened to be there" (17:17). Showing the apostle to the Gentiles in the marketplace, engaging in dialogue like Socrates and the great philosophers of the past, and then addressing a select audience (perhaps the educational commission of the Council of the Areopagus), Luke has hit an apologetic home run. Paul is seen operating at his apologetic best, engaged in moral discourse with the intellectual and cultural elite of his day. The striking significance of Acts 17:16–34 is the ability of Paul to clothe biblical revelation in a cultured and relevant argument to his pagan contemporaries.

H. Flender has summed up Luke's intention in this way: (1) to communicate the Christian message to his readers in the language of the audience, utilizing pagan categories to express the reality of divine revelation;[40] (2) to build on pagan concepts through illustration, both philosophical and literary; (3) to adjust pagan assumptions in the light of biblical revelation (namely, via creation, transcendence, and self-disclosure); (4) to give evidence of God's self-disclosure (through the Resurrection); and (5) to move toward the goal of repentance on the part of the reader through rhetorical persuasion.[41]

Luke's historiography in Acts 17 has been compared to that of Greek classical writers.[42] A certain kinship to Hellenistic tradition is evidenced both by Luke's express didactic-apologetic intent[43] and by numerous evidences of a secular style of speech.[44] Luke may only be reproducing a distilled essence of Paul's Areopagus address; nevertheless, the Areopagus narrative includes three central apologetic components: natural revelation, conception and character of God, and Christian exclusivity over against pagan inclusivity.[45] A closer look at these three components will aid us in penetrating Paul's rhetorical strategy at the Areopagus. The results commend themselves to the Christian community of any era as it interacts with pagan society.

B. Paul's Rhetorical Strategy

In his speech before the Council of the Areopagus, Paul uses numerous strategic elements to address his social context. Given the fact that Athens was home to several prominent schools of philosophical thought, it is not incidental that Paul's address touches core philosophical assumptions of both Stoics and Epicureans. Forging an apologetic bridge requires that the apostle be conversant with contemporary philosophical constructs, even when sophistry, more than intellectual strength, characterized the Athens of Paul's day. Moreover, Paul demonstrates an acquaintance with and understanding of Athenian culture. Evidence of this can be found not only in his fluency in the idiom of his day but familiarity with literary and historical traditions meaningful to his Athenian audience.

In addition to the apostle's ability to contextualize, strategic elements in the content of his message are worthy of note as well. Against the materialist-rationalist world view of his listeners, Paul demonstrates the folly of the gods of material creation. In his disputation the apostle presumes a monotheistic outlook, adjusting presuppositions in reigning worldview. Paul verifies the claims of divine revelation by introducing the notion of *creatio ex nihilo* and bodily resurrection, the core of the Christian kerygma. Both concepts, inextricably related, are untenable to the Hellenistic mindset, due to contemporary views of the universe, the body, and the soul.[46]

Paul's speech is a masterpiece of eloquence. His mode of addressing his audience with "Men" (ἄνδρες) followed by the designation "Athenians" (17:22)[47] is thoroughly Greek, allowing the audience immediately to feel at home. This is in keeping with Greek custom, yet at the same time it reflects the official character of the address.[48] Paul's message, too, is pregnant with irony. A prominent theme is human "ignorance" (ἄγνωστος, ἀγνοέω, v. 23; ἄγνοια, v. 30), and this not only in a city of great learning but before the Areopagus Court, which was composed of thirty of the most literate men of Paul's day. With the skill of a surgeon, the apostle exploits the language and ideas of his contemporaries. It is indeed fitting that before he is led in front of the Areopagus, Paul is depicted by Luke as engaging in "dialogue"[49] with Athenians in the agora.

Acts 17:16–34 conforms to a pattern of Hellenistic discourse, with its epistemological and teleological emphases. Paul's preaching thus cannot be confined narrowly to a normative Old Testament pattern, as some commentators have sought to do. Rather, it wraps universal truth in the language and idiom of the day, culminating in a uniquely Christian expression of biblical revelation and inviting the listeners to a higher metaphysical ground.

In sum, Acts 17:16–34 mirrors apostolic Christian contact with pagan culture. It begins with the epistemological assumptions of its hearers, it builds on a common understanding of the cosmos, yet it climaxes in the fullest self-disclosure of the Creator—the resurrection of the God-man.

The modern reader is apt to sense a dichotomy that the ancients would not have understood: is Paul's speech mainly philosophical or theological? Some commentators, in their attempts to explain the derivation of Pauline categories, look chiefly to Jewish and Old Testament sources for the apostle's Areopagus speech. Others argue that Jewish/Old Testament notions are absent altogether. An Athenian worldview, it should be remembered, was probably an amalgam of Olympian religion, magic, and some philosophical commonalities, all of which was overlaid with heavy doses of fatalism. Given the exigencies of the social situation, part of which is dictated by Athenian intellectual culture and the limitations of audience comprehension, Paul can be viewed as dealing with "ultimate issues" that are simultaneously philosophical and theological. Touch points with Stoic and Epicurean worldviews (with prominence given to the former) run throughout Paul's message, while the biblical doctrines of creation, God, man, and the resurrection are key aspects of his proclamation. The movement in his address from creation to resurrection, calculated with great precision, engages the philosophical assumptions of the hearer at the most fundamental level.[50]

1. The Appeal to Natural Revelation[51]

Because Acts 17:16–34 follows a different rhetorical pattern than Romans 1, the theological character of Paul's Areopagus speech has been doubted both by traditional critical scholarship as well as by religious conservatives. In spite of the differences between Acts 17 and Romans 1, a common apologetic bridge to the pagan mind is employed: nature itself.[52] It is impossible to miss the inseparable connection between creation, the moral order, and human accountability. This movement, articulated in the idiom of his day, is present in Paul's Areopagus speech as well. Pagans "know" because of creation and conscience; their "ignorance," ultimately, is "without excuse."[53]

"Natural theology" in Romans 1 and Acts 17 has the function of pointing to human accountability. To the extent that the Athenians—and the men of the Areopagus—have no Christological understanding, Paul's discourse on creation and the cosmos serves as a necessary "pedagogical-missionary preamble."[54] In both Romans 1 and Acts 17 the phenomena of creation are accessible to all.[55] For Paul, this knowledge of the Creator-God is innate. Even pagans without knowledge of Christ have a fundamental awareness of moral accountability. Pagans "by nature" do the moral law of God, even though they do not have the law (Rom. 2:14). Thus, the apostle can speak of universal norms.[56] Ultimately, whether he is writing to Christians living in the imperial seat of Rome or addressing academics sitting on the council of the Areopagus in Athens, Paul's purpose is to stress that *all people* are morally accountable. All, though "ignorant," are without excuse.

2. Conception and Character of God

What are the spheres of natural revelation delineated by Paul in his Areopagus speech? Three realms can be detected: creation and maintenance of the cosmos, history and the nations' boundaries, and human dependence on God.[57] All three touch commonly recognized Stoic assumptions. (To be sure, a vast chasm separates the Old Testament and the Stoic view of God, about which Paul is not naive.)

For the Stoic, the divine essence is *logos,* reason. "Right reason" (*logos orthos*), as taught by Zeno, "is the same as Zeus."[58] Accordingly, in the structure of the physical universe lie the seeds of knowledge, the *logos spermatikos* of Stoic thought,[59] which gave rise to the universe. Reason, hence, was viewed as the highest expression of nature.[60] Paul bridges the chasm between Stoic and Christian thought by appropriating common philosophical ground, asserting that the use of reason can lead to the knowledge of God. Observing the universe (17:24–25) rouses the individual to seek after God; in truth, this Creator-God is not far removed from humankind (17:27).

Allusion to God's immanence and human kinship with God, both of which immediately follow, places Paul squarely within the Stoic understanding of the divine.[61] Paul does not remain, however, at the level of human reason, even though he will go as far as Greek assumptions will allow him. Creation *ex nihilo* and divine self-disclosure require more from the philosopher.[62] The apostolic message achieves continuity (kinship with God) as well as radical discontinuity (transcendence) with the Hellenistic worldview.[63] While the materialistic pantheism of Stoic belief corrupts Stoic "theology," Paul first utilizes the "common ground" shared by all. Athenian "ignorance" is initially related in a positive sense ("You are very religious . . . you worship . . ."), then negatively (with the admonition to repent).[64]

At this point it is useful to consider Paul's acquaintance both with Athenian historical tradition and literary sources meaningful to his audience. That there were many "unknown gods"[65] in Athens is a well established fact. With an atmosphere of religious inclusivity reaching to a "lowest common denominator," no theological distinctives are discernible in Athenian culture. Paul's strategy hence is to take this "given" and build upon it for the purposes of expressing Christian exclusivity. Paul may well be infusing the altar "to the unknown god" with a "monotheistic" adaptation in order to exploit it for his own purposes.[66] To be sure, Athenians would not have understood Paul's monotheism as Jews would have.

Paul's qualification of God's nature also involves the enlistment of conventional literary sources. Theological "common ground" is sustained by two citations from well-known "poets." The statement "in him we live, move, and have our being" expresses the Stoic belief in closeness to/kinship with God. No pagan philosopher could reject this assertion, since any Stoic worth his salt readily conceded that God "fills" the universe, that a union exists. (This quotation is generally attributed to a sixth-century B.C. poet, Epimenides of Crete.)

The second citation, "We are his offspring," stems from the third-century B.C. Stoic philosopher Aratus, who, significantly, hailed from Paul's native Cilicia. Aratus penned these words in a poem in honor of Zeus. Titled *Phaenomena,* the poem is an interpretation of constellations and weather signs. It reads that "in all things each of us needs Zeus, for we are also his offspring." Without question, "his offspring" is sure to resonate with any Stoic present in the audience.[67]

3. Pagan Inclusivity and Christian Exclusivity

We have already observed the religiously "inclusive" environment pervading Athenian culture. The universalist and pantheist stamp of the Areopagus speech is a clear reflection of Luke's intention. Although religious "ignorance" in Athens of the one true God is universal and absolute, the times of *agnoia* are nevertheless pronounced by the apostle to be past: "Now God commands all men everywhere to repent" (v. 30). As evidence that epistemological ignorance is not bliss, the "one true God" has ordained "a day" on which "the man" Jesus "will judge the world in righteousness" (v. 31). Whereas Adam was the starting point of all humanity, Jesus, the counterpart to Adam, is the culmination of all things, by virtue of having mediated all history. Paul has thus dismantled the Stoic view of universal continuum. The Judeo-Christian understanding of history, which begins and ends with divine fiat, marks a "radical discontinuity" with the world view of Paul's audience. At this point, one can assume that polite tolerance by the council members turned into indignation. Paul's declaration, an intellectual stumbling-block for his audience, is that "one man" will judge the cosmos, that it will not be perpetual in the Stoic sense. Assurance of the proposition that God *has disclosed* himself is the linchpin of Christian revelation; hence, Paul's emphasis on the resurrection.

Three times in the Lukan narrative the resurrection is mentioned—verses 18, 31, and 32. While 17:16–34 contains no explicit Christology, the seal of divine truth—and thus, a key to an effective apologetic in pagan culture—is the bodily resurrection of Jesus Christ. It is by no means incidental that at this point in Paul's speech the mood of his audience shifts. Scorn and derision surface both in the agora, where Paul had earlier been "dialoguing," and at the

Areopagus. While Paul utilizes the utmost in skill and erudition to ensure that the packaging of his message does not offend his audience, the content of the Christian apostolic kerygma inevitably is scandalous.

Summing up Paul's rhetorical strategy in Athens, we may note that the apostle was knowledgeable, dialectical, well-read, relevant, and rhetorically skillful. What particularly strikes the reader is his ability to accommodate himself to the knowledge base of most Athenians. Viewing Paul's encounter with Athenian culture as such, we may conclude that his ministry was not a "failure." Nor is it necessary to assume that his not-too-distant reflections about the power of the cross, recorded in 1 Corinthians 1–2, were penned with a wrong apologetic model (i.e., Athens) in mind.

To the contrary, a more accurate assessment of Paul's ministry in Athens may be summed up by his own testimony to the Corinthians: "I have made myself a servant to all, that I might win more. To the Jews I became a Jew . . . ; to those without the law [pagans], [I became] like those without the law . . . I have become all things to all men, that I might by all means save some" (1 Cor. 9:19–22).

V. THE APOLOGETIC TASK OF THE
LATE TWENTIETH-CENTURY CHURCH

It is worth remembering that Paul, not Peter, was called to be the "apostle to the Gentiles." It was Paul who could dispute with philosophers in Athens, argue from the Scriptures with the Jews in the synagogue, persuade imperial magistrates—indeed even procure an audience with the Caesar himself. Everything that God took away from Saul of Tarsus following his conversion— his pride, his zeal, his cultural pedigree, his learning, his knowledge, his rhetorical ability—was restored to the apostle after he lay broken in the presence of Almighty God. Having been sanctified, Paul's past was now to serve the greater purposes of God as the Holy Spirit would see fit.

In many ways, Western culture in general—and North American culture in particular—resembles that of Athens in Paul's day. Like the Athenians, to whom belonged an illustrious cultural past, ours is what Alexander Solzhenitsyn has called a "culture of novelty." We are obsessed with that which is novel; truth and its consequences are of little value.

For this reason, Paul's ministry model in Athens beckons to us. It invites us to learn on two plains: (1) how to relate biblical truth in culturally relevant ways (i.e., contextualization), and (2) how to formulate a cultural apologetic that retains its theological integrity in the midst of a culture of compromise.

Consider the amount of attention given to detail in Acts 17:16–34. By Luke's account, Paul has "earned the right" to an audience in Athens; he demonstrates an apprehension of Athenian culture and thus is able to accommodate theological truth to the prevailing cultural *Zeitgeist*. This should be paradigmatic for the church of any era. The Christian community must understand the culture in which it has been placed by the sovereign Lord. By demonstrating an understanding of culture, it is then able to engage culture with a measure of credibility. Finally, having humbly sought to be a student of and active participant in culture, the church is able to confront the false values that are lodged within culture. Perception, engagement, and confrontation necessarily follow—in this order.[68]

Paul's model also has profound implications for the church's message in a pagan cultural environment. Three theological "non-negotiables" on display in the Areopagus address guide the apostle in his ability to address reigning philosophical assumptions. First, the apostle stresses the sovereign lordship of the one true God. This lordship is manifest in creation *ex nihilo*[69] and in maintaining the history of nations. Second, proof of divine self-disclosure can be found in the resurrection of the God-man, Jesus Christ. A stumbling-block to any generation, the Resurrection "forces the issue," as it were, in validating Christianity's truth-claims.[70] As cultural apologists, Christians need to be equipped with an understanding of philosophical and theological "first things." Competing in culture are diametrically opposed worldviews,[71] and the ultimacy of Christian truth-claims stands or falls with the Resurrection. Third, the movement of a faithful apologetic is always in the direction of moral accountability. By underscoring the reality of future judgment, the apostle dismantles religious inclusivity: all people everywhere must repent and confront the knowledge of the Creator that has been imparted to them.

VI. EPILOGUE

The story of Paul's ministry in Athens does not end here, however. A concluding observation remains. It is fair to say that Luke's rather abrupt ending of the narrative (vv. 32–34) does not strike the reader in any way as impressive. Almost as an afterthought, as if to say, "Oh, by the way . . . ," Luke appends one sentence that mentions two individuals by name who happened to "believe." One is a woman named Damaris; the other is a member of the Council of Areopagus by the name of Dionysius.

Neither Damaris nor Dionysius appear again in the New Testament, and Luke leaves us with no clue as to the significance of either. And yet, a bit of extra-biblical reading changes the complexion of the entire Acts 17 narrative. Thirty years ago E. M. Blaiklock wrote of the mix of ancient and modern that strikes the person visiting Athens today. Describing the city over nineteen hundred years after Paul's visit, Blaiklock was intrigued to find that the street that today runs around the south side of the Acropolis ruins bears the name of Dionysius the Areopagite. What sort of person was this Dionysius, anyway?

The only surviving source in this regard is Eusebius. We are informed by Eusebius that Dionysius the Areopagite, a member of the elite Areopagus Council, converted to Christ through Paul's preaching and then went on to become a bishop in the church. Eusebius writes that Dionysius ended up being martyred for his faith. One wonders that still one thousand years later in parts of the Near East a body of pseudepigraphic literature (Pseudo-Dionysius) was still being attributed to the Areopagite of Paul's day. One can only guess that this was an extraordinary individual. Perhaps a moral of the story is that one never knows what faithfulness to God will yield. To the natural eye, Paul's ministry in Athens may have seemed a "failure." Another perspective, however, reminds us that the church did grow in Athens and Greece in the fullness of time.

CHAPTER ELEVEN

APOLOGETICS, WORLDVIEWS, AND THE PROBLEM OF NEUTRAL CRITERIA

Harold A. Netland

Therefore go and make disciples of all nations, baptizing them in the name of the Father and of the Son and of the Holy Spirit, and teaching them to obey everything I have commanded you (Matt. 28:19–20a NIV).

Generally known as the Great Commission, the command of our Lord quoted above has traditionally been regarded as constituting one of the primary reasons for the missionary enterprise. Implicit in the command is the universality of the person and message of Jesus Christ: disciples of Jesus Christ are to be made from "all nations" (πάντα τὰ ἔθνη), regardless of cultural or religious affiliation. The person and teaching of Jesus are assumed to be universally binding and normative, and it is the task of Christ's followers to endeavor to bring others from all cultural and religious contexts into a relationship of proper allegiance to Him. The modern missionary movement is in large measure a testimony to the seriousness with which Christ's disciples have set about to obey the Great Commission.

But what may appear to the believer to be perspicuous and entirely legitimate often seems to the nonbeliever to be hopelessly muddled and unfounded. The notion that one particular religious figure and one religious tradition can be normative for all peoples in all cultures at all times—an assumption central to the Great Commission—is today increasingly being dismissed as obscurantist and out of touch with the realities of our pluralistic world. A pervasive epistemological skepticism, combined with a highly relativistic ethos that virtually refuses to reject any perspective as false and that champions an undisciplined tolerance as the quintessence of virtue, compels many today to look with incredulity upon any religious claims for exclusive or definitive truth.

I. APOLOGETICS AND ALTERNATIVE WORLDVIEWS

The Christian faith includes some profound and far-reaching truth claims about the nature of the universe, the existence and nature of God, the human predicament, and the possibility of salvation. Now part of the price of making such claims to truth is exposure of such assertions to rigorous scrutiny and the demand for corroborative justification. For we normally do not blindly accept just any claim to truth, nor should we expect others to do so. Although notoriously difficult to formulate precisely, there is a direct correlation between the proper acceptance of a truth claim p and the warrant or justification for acceptance of p. The more significant and controversial a claim, the greater will be our expectation of corroborative justification for the claim. The central claims of biblical Christianity are controversial indeed. Thus those who take it upon themselves to proclaim the truth of the Gospel to a largely unsympathetic audience owe it to their audience to be prepared to respond in an appropriate and informed manner to criticisms raised against the Christian message. And this has generally been regarded as the task of the Christian apologist.

Christian apologetics has been defined by Mark Hanna as "a systematic response of the reflective and culturally informed Christian to attacks that inevitably come upon the truth claims of the Christian faith."[1] Hanna also draws a very helpful distinction between *pure* and *applied* apologetics.[2] Pure apologetics is concerned with the objective justification of the Christian faith irrespective of human response. Its purpose is to answer definitively certain fundamental questions about the acceptability of Christian truth claims. Among these questions are the following: How do we acquire religious knowledge? Can we know whether God exists, and if so, how? Is the Christian understanding of God, sin, and salvation significantly different from that of other religions? If so, which, if any, is correct? Are the Scriptures a reliable revelation from God? Did Jesus rise from the dead, and if so, what is the significance of this?

Clearly each of these questions has an answer, regardless of whether anyone knows the answer or can demonstrate that he knows the answer. Pure apologetics tries to ascertain and clarify these answers. Thus it is primarily concerned with establishing answers to these questions, not with trying to persuade any given target audience of the truth of the answers. The distinction here is simply that between finding the answers to certain questions and persuading others that you have indeed done so. Presupposed by this distinction is the objectivity of truth and that the answers to basic questions in apologetics are logically independent of any human response to them. Given the complexity of basic questions raised on this level, we should expect that pure apologetics as a discipline is highly specialized and involves rigorous analysis. Although a variety of disciplines (such as history, archeology, anthropology, the sciences, etc.) are involved, central to pure apologetics is epistemology.

Applied apologetics, on the other hand, is very much concerned with human response to the proclamation and defense of the gospel message. For applied apologetics is the utilization of justification procedures and relevant data in the actual presentation and defense of the Gospel to a particular target audience. Its purpose is to elicit a favorable response from the audience—it actively seeks to persuade. The methods and levels of sophistication of applied apologetics will vary greatly depending upon the nature of one's audience. What is appropriate with a university professor will not necessarily be effective with an automobile mechanic. What works in Kyoto may not be acceptable in Mexico City. Considerable variety and creativity in approach are essential. But the answers to questions raised on the level of applied apologetics are logically dependent upon answers to corresponding questions in pure apologetics. Thus responsible and effective applied apologetics presupposes some familiarity with pure apologetics.

Now Christian apologetics in the modern era has generally been concerned with issues stemming from the Western philosophical heritage, particularly with problems arising from the post-Enlightenment humanistic and secularistic mindset. Thus the subject matter of most recent texts on Christian apologetics is quite predictable and includes such standard topics as the existence of God, the problem of evil, miracles, the reliability of the biblical documents, etc.

But I would suggest that the legacy of post-Enlightenment secular humanism presents just one—and by no means even the greatest—among many challenges to Christian faith today. Perhaps the most daunting task for the Christian apologist in the coming decades emerges from the fact of competing religious and secular worldviews and the accompanying problem of determining acceptable criteria for the assessment of alternative worldviews.

Whether one today lives in London, Chicago, Nairobi, Caracas, Hong Kong, or Tokyo, one is apt to confront a bewildering variety of worldviews. Many are religious in nature and thus pose the cluster of troublesome questions arising from religious pluralism. Other worldviews are explicitly secular and are atheistic or agnostic. Buddhist, Hindu, Muslim, Christian, animist, Mormon, philosophical materialist, Marxist, hedonist, New Age cultist—each claims to have a distinctive worldview that accurately reflects the nature of reality. Which, if any, is true?

The problem of alternative worldviews is especially acute in the great urban centers of Asia, where one encounters not only the resurgent indigenous traditions of Hinduism, Buddhism, Taoism, and Shinto but along with these also the pervasive impact of modernism and secularism. The question in Asia then is not merely that of a simple choice between theism and atheism or between Christian faith and secular humanism. The central issue for the Christian apologist in Asia—and increasingly in the West as well—is: Given the many alternative worldviews available today, both religious and secular, why should one become a Christian? The Christian is thus put in the position of justifying the Christian alternative in the face of many other plausible and attractive options. Could this be part of what Peter had in mind when he enjoined believers to be ready to give a defense or reason (ἀπολογία) for the hope that is in us (1 Peter 3:15)?

II. THE PROBLEM OF CRITERIA

Why should one be a Christian instead of a Buddhist, Muslim, or secular humanist? It would seem that there are several senses in which this question could be answered. For example, there is an important sense in which the Christian can answer it from within the Christian worldview. Orthodox Christians hold that God has revealed Himself in a definitive manner in the Incarnation and the written Scriptures. The Bible is taken to be the very Word of God, true and fully authoritative. If indeed this is the case, then clearly anything that is incompatible with the teachings of Scripture must be rejected as false. And thus the Christian—as a Christian—is fully entitled to reject any worldview or teaching that is incompatible with the claims of Scripture.

But this response, although legitimate as far as it goes, hardly settles the matter. For although from *within* the Christian worldview one can evaluate competing alternatives on the basis of principles and values internal to the Christian perspective, there is a logically prior question which demands attention: How do we determine which religious worldview is in fact true? On what basis do we accept the Christian worldview as in fact the true one?

This is not merely an academic question, for each of the major religions claims to be true and to provide the standard by which to evaluate other alternative worldviews. The Christian appeals to God's definitive self-revelation in the Bible as the supreme authority for settling religious questions; the Muslim claims that Allah dictated his revelation to Muhammad through the angel Gabriel; the Zen Buddhist maintains that he has direct access to the ultimate nature of reality through the experience of *satori;* the Advaita Vedanta Hindu calls upon the authority of the Upanishads and the experience of *samadhi* as validating his claims to truth; and so on. Obviously, simply appealing to divine (or other) authority in and of itself settles nothing, for each tradition has its own authoritative structure. The inescapable question is, Which "authority" is in fact ultimately authoritative? Which claim (if any) is true?

It would seem that in order to answer these questions some acceptable criteria that can legitimately be applied in the evaluation of competing worldviews are necessary. Now it has traditionally been held that there is such a thing as objective truth, that fundamental epistemological questions have answers, and that we can ascertain answers to at least some of these basic questions. Moreover, it has generally been accepted that there are procedures and principles that can legitimately be applied to the evaluation of competing worldviews and that one can appeal to certain criteria in determining the truth or falsity of a given worldview. That is, there are at least some criteria that are neutral in the sense that they are not simply the product of, and thus restricted to, particular contexts or worldviews. They are context-independent and normative in the sense that they can be utilized in critically evaluating competing worldviews. It seems to me that this approach, although not without its problems, is in the main correct and that Christian apologetics in the coming decades should give careful attention to the formulation and application of criteria that can legitimately be applied in the evaluation of competing worldviews.

But the suggestion that there are such context-independent criteria is today being vigorously challenged from at least two distinct quarters. On the one hand, due in no small measure to the influence of the social sciences, various forms of relativism today reject the notion that there are any principles or criteria that are not context-dependent.[3] All criteria for evaluation are said to be the product of particular contexts, whether linguistic, psychological, sociocultural, historical, etc. Thus, although such criteria can be employed for evaluation *from within* a given context, they cannot legitimately be used for making critical evaluations of competing worldviews *from the outside.* Although relativism in its various forms is pervasive today in the academic world and obviously presents a serious challenge to Christian faith and mission, we will not be concerned explicitly with it here.

Curiously, however, there is another sector that, while highly critical of relativism, also rejects the suggestion that there are neutral or context-independent criteria that can be applied in evaluating competing worldviews. I refer here to a small but influential theological tradition generally but by no means exclusively identified with certain segments of Reformed theology and with the work of Cornelius Van Til and his disciples in particular. Often labeled "presuppositionism" or "theological fideism," this tradition stoutly resists the suggestion that there are any neutral principles or criteria that can be appealed to in order to settle disputes between the conflicting worldviews of biblical theists and atheists. The motivation behind presuppositionism—the desire to preserve the absolute sovereignty of God and to bring everything under the lordship of Jesus Christ—is certainly laudable, but I would suggest that in this case zeal has outstripped wisdom, and a worthy objective has resulted in a theologically misleading and epistemologically unacceptable position. For it seems that presuppositionism, as generally formulated, suffers from largely the same epistemological difficulties which vitiate relativism.

III. JOHN FRAME'S PRESUPPOSITIONISM

Fideism, or presuppositionism,[4] occasionally manifests itself in rather unlikely places. Although certainly no disciple of Van Til, the respected missiologist Lesslie Newbigin makes unnecessary concessions to fideism in his otherwise fine book, *The Open Secret:*

> The framework which I devise or discern is my ultimate commitment or else it cannot function in the way intended. As such a commitment, it must defend its claim to truth over against other claims to truth. . . . At the risk of wearisome reiteration I must repeat the simple truth that no standpoint is available to any man except the point where he stands; that there is no platform from which one can claim to have an "objective" view which supersedes all the "subjective" faith-commitments of the world's faiths; that every man must take his stand in the arena, on the same level with every other, and there engage in the real encounter of ultimate commitment with those who, like him, have staked their lives on their vision of the truth. . . . Jesus is for the believer the source from whom his understanding of the totality of experience is drawn and therefore the criterion by which other ways of understanding are judged.[5]

Newbigin's statements occur in the context of discussion of broader missiological issues and perhaps should not be pressed for epistemological significance, but they illustrate graphically the epistemological bankruptcy of fideism: if indeed each of our worldviews reduces to one or more "faith-commitments" or presuppositions, and if there is no "objective" perspective, no neutral criterion, from which to evaluate other competing worldviews, then surely all talk of "truth" in religion calls for radical reinterpretation. Furthermore, given Newbigin's premises it is difficult to see how he can, in the same paragraph in which he rejects the possibility of neutral criteria and objective perspectives, advocate defense of the Christian truth-claim over against other claims to truth and assert that Jesus is the "criterion by which other ways of understanding are judged." After all, why Jesus and not the Buddha?

Newbigin may not have intended to put forward presuppositionism as an epistemological thesis, but other thinkers have done just that. The most vigorous recent statement of epistemological presuppositionism comes from Van Til's disciple John Frame in his work *The Doctrine of the Knowledge of God*

(Phillipsburg, N.J.: Presbyterian and Reformed, 1987). Frame's discussion is rich and stimulating, and a comprehensive response to it would take us well beyond the limits of this chapter. Accordingly, we must restrict our attention to those aspects of his thesis that are directly relevant to the question of neutral criteria for assessing competing worldviews.

A useful point of entry into Frame's thesis is his understanding of presupposition.

> A presupposition is a belief that takes precedence over another and therefore serves as a criterion for another. An ultimate presupposition is a belief over which no other takes precedence. For a Christian, the content of Scripture must serve as his ultimate presupposition. Our beliefs about Scripture may be corrected by other beliefs about Scripture, but relative to the body of extra-scriptural information that we possess, those beliefs are presuppositional in character. This doctrine is merely the outworking of the lordship of God in the area of human thought.[6]

A presupposition is "a basic commitment of the heart," an "ultimate criterion." Frame holds that everyone, believer and unbeliever alike, has presuppositions. "Everyone has them because everyone has some commitment that at a particular time (granted, it may change) is 'basic' to him."[7]

Frame emphatically rejects the suggestion that there are any neutral criteria or neutral principles on the basis of which competing worldviews (Christian and non-Christian) can be evaluated. There seem to be at least two distinct reasons for this, one philosophical and the other theological. First, he holds that all knowledge is ineradicably interpretive in nature and that we have no access to "pure" or "objective" data that could serve as neutral criteria. "Facts" and their interpretation are inseparable.

> It will serve us adequately if we think of "facts" as the world seen from God's point of view (or, perhaps, when truly seen from a human point of view) and "interpretations" as our understanding of those facts, whether true or false. Often in philosophy, however, the "fact" is thought to be a kind of reality-in-itself, a reality totally devoid of any interpretation—divine or human—by which all attempts at interpretation are to be tested. In reply, (1) we must insist that there are no facts utterly devoid of interpretation; there are no "brute facts," to use Van Til's terminology. . . . (2) We must also insist that human interpretation is involved in any knowledge of facts. We can have no knowledge of facts devoid of human interpretation, for knowing itself is interpretation. We have no access to reality apart from our interpretive faculties.[8]

A second reason for rejecting the idea that there can be neutral criteria is Frame's contention that the search for neutral criteria is really merely a refusal by rebellious creatures to recognize and submit to the lordship of God in the realm of knowledge.

> The idea of "brute fact" is an invention intended to furnish us with a criterion of

> truth other than God's revelation. . . . We have no access to reality apart from our interpretive faculties. To seek such access is to seek release from creaturehood. . . . The desire for a "fact" totally devoid of human interpretation that can serve as an authoritative criterion for all interpretation is a non-Christian desire, a desire to substitute some other authority for the Word of God.[9]

Any attempt to find a foundation, bedrock, or criterion for knowledge apart from the Word of God must be rejected as an idolatrous attempt to substitute the human mind for the authority of the Word of God.

Frame maintains that since everyone has presuppositions the question is not whether or not we will be governed by our presuppositions but rather which presuppositions we will accept. Frame holds that the only legitimate presupposition is God's self-revelation in Scripture. Anything less than this results in epistemic idolatry. For Christians the Word of God must be the basic presupposition. "Thus this doctrine of presuppositions purely and simply asserts the lordship of Christ over human thought. Anything less than this is unacceptable to Him."[10]

Given our religiously pluralistic world an obvious question arises here: Why should one accept the Christian presupposition instead of the Hindu or Buddhist presuppositions? Since Frame has already ruled out the possibility of there being any neutral principles or criteria by which to judge between competing worldviews, we would hardly expect him to argue for the justification of the Christian presupposition on the basis of something other than Scripture itself. And, as expected, Frame insists that Scripture provides its own justification.

> If Scripture is the ultimate justification for all human knowledge, how should we justify our belief in Scripture itself? By Scripture, of course! There is no more ultimate authority, no more reliable source of information, and nothing that is more certain by which Scripture might be tested.[11]

Scripture must be self-justifying because, as the "highest law of thought" for all human beings, it justifies all knowledge. Nothing is epistemologically more basic than Scripture. Ultimately Scripture is the source and "foundation" for all knowledge.[12]

Are we then reduced to exercising a blind faith in which one simply chooses to accept the authority of Scripture, and that is that? Is there no room here for corroborative evidence? Curiously, although he contends that ultimately Scripture is self-justifying, Frame allows that there is a sense in which it is legitimate to appeal to "evidence" from history, archeology, cosmology, etc., to support the Christian presupposition. He emphatically denies that the Christian presupposition is merely the product of arbitrary choice. To the contrary, he claims that "the Christian presupposition has the strongest possible rational ground: it is based upon God's revelation."[13] Frame is even willing to say that the Christian presupposition can be "proved" by a kind of circular argument.

> Does Scripture's self-attestation imply that we may not use extrabiblical evidence in arguing for Biblical authority? We may use such evidence, and indeed we ought to. . . . But even as we select, interpret, and evaluate evidence, we must

presuppose a biblical epistemology. Therefore, in a sense, our argument for Scripture will always be circular. Even in our use of evidence, Scripture will be, in effect, justifying itself.[14]

Frame is fully aware that the appeal to evidence by presuppositionists is circular. That is, in appealing to arguments from history or archeology to confirm the truth claims of Christianity one is not employing a neutral criterion, for the arguments from historical or archeological evidence are themselves ultimately dependent upon the Christian presupposition. But, he urges, such circularity is hardly cause for alarm since everyone—theist and atheist alike—is in precisely the same predicament. No one can escape circularity in argument.

> [N]o system can avoid circularity because all systems (as we have seen)—non-Christian as well as Christian—are based upon presuppositions that control their epistemologies, argumentations, and use of evidence. Thus a rationalist can prove the primacy of reason only by using a rational argument. An empiricist can prove the primacy of sense-experience only by some kind of appeal to sense-experience. A Muslim can prove the primacy of the Koran only by appealing to the Koran. But if all systems are circular in that way, then such circularity can hardly be urged against Christianity. The critic will inevitably be just as "guilty" of circularity as the Christian is.[15]

Frame is to be commended for explicitly recognizing the circularity of his position, although his apparent lack of awareness of the implications of such circularity is hardly reassuring.

Frame attempts to distance himself from the charge of fideism by qualifying the circularity in question in two respects. First, he states, "Circularity in a system is properly justified *only* at one point: in an argument for the *ultimate* criterion of the system."[16] Thus circular arguments for propositions within a given system are not legitimate, whereas they can be legitimate when the proposition in question serves as the ultimate presupposition upon which the system is based.

This leads naturally to a second qualification of circular argumentation, the restriction of circular argumentation to "broadly circular arguments." Frame distinguishes between "narrow" and "broad" circles.[17] A "narrow" circular argument is one like the following: "Scripture is the Word of God because it says it is the Word of God." Such circularity is rejected by Frame as unwarranted. But, he claims, it is possible to "broaden" the circle by appealing to the volume and variety of data upon which the conclusion is based: "Scripture is the Word of God because archeology, history, and philosophy verify its teachings" is said to be still broadly circular, and yet, according to Frame, such circularity is acceptable.

> If used rightly, that argument will still be circular, because the archeology, history, and philosophy in view will be *Christian* sciences that presuppose the biblical world view. But that argument will be more persuasive than a *bare* circle. Thus to say that our argument for Christianity is circular need not imply a *narrow* circle. That fact removes some of the sting from our admission of circularity.[18]

Ancient history and archeology are important disciplines that help us to understand the meaning of the Bible and to verify its reliability. In that second function of those disciplines, historical data becomes part of a "broad circle" that confirms the presuppositions of the Christian faith. Those Christian presuppositions, in turn, serve as the historian's ultimate criterion of truth.[19]

It is interesting that Frame puts his statement in terms of the *persuasiveness* of a broadly circular argument. But this evades the basic issue. A broadly circular argument might indeed be more persuasive than a narrowly circular argument, as Frame suggests, but the crucial question here is whether it *should* be more persuasive. After all, complex circular arguments can be highly persuasive and still be unsound.

IV. EVALUATION

Anyone envisioning the kind of role for Christian apologetics outlined at the beginning of this paper must be prepared to respond to the thesis of presuppositionism. Frame's presuppositionism clearly rules out the possibility of appeal to any neutral criteria. All principles or criteria used for evaluation are derived from one or more basic presuppositions, and these presuppositions, it is said, cannot be neutral. They are either basic Christian presuppositions or basic anti-Christian presuppositions. Neutrality is a chimera.

A thorough critique of Frame's presuppositionism would require careful treatment of a number of theological and philosophical issues that cannot be pursued here. Our concern is strictly with the question of neutral criteria by which to make judgments concerning the truth or falsity of competing worldviews. Although there is undeniable appeal in presuppositionism (after all, it *seems* to be simply drawing out the epistemological implications of the doctrine of God's sovereignty over all of life), lurking beneath the surface are some disturbing epistemological implications. The epistemological inadequacy of Frame's presuppositionism can be seen from the following brief points.

1. Frame suggests that there should not be anything particularly alarming about Christian presuppositionism since every worldview is in the same epistemological boat. Every perspective on reality is based upon certain ultimate presuppositions (commitments) that are simply accepted. And if this is permissible in other cases then surely the Christian presuppositionist is not in an epistemically inferior position.

Now there is an initial plausibility to Frame's position. He correctly points out that not every belief can be expected to be justified in terms of more basic beliefs, or an infinite regress would ensue. Some beliefs must be such that they "stand on their own" and do not need to be justified on the basis of more basic beliefs. Otherwise epistemic justification is impossible. A recurring theme in the history of philosophy has been the search for these "basic beliefs" and the formulation of acceptable procedures for their identification. To be sure, there has been no lack of dispute concerning just what beliefs are to be included in the set of "properly basic" beliefs, but such disagreement should not be exaggerated as there is widespread agreement that certain beliefs (e.g., belief in the existence of an external world and other minds, or belief that the universe did not appear two seconds ago, etc.) are entirely warranted even though it is not at all clear that they are to be justified on the basis of other more basic beliefs.

But considerable care must be exercised at this point. It is one thing to recognize that knowledge is based upon certain epistemically basic beliefs that do not derive their justification from other beliefs and then to try to identify such beliefs and establish their relation to other beliefs. However, it is an entirely different matter to suggest that every perspective is based upon certain ultimate presuppositions (commitments) that can be accepted or rejected at will and that we must simply choose our ultimate commitments and proceed accordingly.

Part of the inadequacy of Frame's discussion lies in his failure to distinguish clearly presuppositions from epistemically basic beliefs. A presupposition is generally held to be an assumption or postulate, that is, a belief that is assumed to be true or is taken for granted as true apart from any corroborating evidence. Essential to the meaning of presupposition is the volitional element; *there is an important sense in which one chooses to accept a presupposition.* If *p* is a presupposition of *S,* then in some sense *S willfully presupposes p.* This volitional element is clearly reflected in Frame's characterization of a presupposition as "a basic commitment of the heart." Everyone, he says, has ultimate presuppositions because "everyone has some commitment that at a particular time . . . is 'basic' to him."[20] Thus presuppositionists frequently speak of "faith" or "commitment" as being prior to "knowledge." Ultimate presuppositions are said to be basically of two kinds: those that include God and His revelation as the fundamental presupposition from which everything else is said to flow and those that substitute some other starting point apart from God as the basic presupposition. One either begins with God or with something apart from God. In either case it is a matter of personal commitment or choice.

No informed Christian would deny that ultimately all human beings fall into one of two mutually exclusive classes: those who recognize and respond appropriately to God as sovereign Lord and those who reject God and substitute something else apart from God as a focus of ultimate concern. But it does not follow from this that all epistemological perspectives can be reduced to two kinds of basic presuppositions: those that begin by postulating God and His revelation and those that begin by presupposing something other than God as epistemically basic.

Now it is crucial to see that the notion of presupposition is itself highly inadequate for depicting that class of beliefs that are epistemically basic. Epistemically basic beliefs cannot be presuppositions for they are (logically) necessary for there to be any presupposition in the first place! In other words, epistemically basic beliefs are necessary conditions for there even being presuppositions. For example, one cannot presuppose anything—whether it be God or some other object of ultimate commitment—without appealing to (among other things) the principle of noncontradiction. And the principle of noncontradiction cannot itself be a presupposition for it is a logically necessary condition for any presupposition whatsoever. In their discussions of presuppositionism, presuppositionists, including Frame, make widespread appeal to principles and categories that are not presuppositions and that are logically independent of their presuppositional systems—e.g., the general principles of adequacy, simplicity, coherence, consistency, the logical principles of non-contradiction and identity, etc. This in itself indicates that a thoroughgoing presuppositionism cannot be an adequate epistemological perspective.[21]

2. As noted above, Frame explicitly accepts the circularity of appeals to evidence from within Christian presuppositionism, but he claims that there is a crucial difference between "narrow" circularity and "broad" circularity in arguments and that whereas narrowly circular arguments are not legitimate, broadly circular arguments can be. But it is difficult to see how Frame can expect this assertion to be taken seriously. The issue is not the size or complexity of the circle, for a circular argument—regardless of size or complexity—is still a circular argument. If indeed there are no neutral principles or criteria for assessment and if all criteria are internal to a given worldview in the sense that they are derived from certain basic presuppositions that define that worldview, then it matters little whether one employs a short, clear, explicitly circular argument or a longer, complex, and only implicitly circular argument. Epistemologically one is in precisely the same position in either case: the argument appeals to factors, principles, or criteria that are strictly internal to the worldview in question and thus cannot be used legitimately to make judgments about competing worldviews. Epistemologically it makes no difference whether the worldview in question is Christian theism or Advaita Vedanta Hinduism.

3. Frame presumes that his presuppositionism renders Christian theism immune from attack by secularists. After all, everybody ultimately is dependent upon certain basic presuppositions that cannot be proven to be true, so why should the Christian theist be regarded as in any way inferior epistemically to the secular humanist? But what Frame apparently fails to notice is that if presuppositionism protects Christian theism from its secular critics it does so at the price of forfeiture of the right to make any claim to universal truth. For if there are *no* criteria that are neutral in the sense that they are not context-dependent—if ultimately all criteria for assessment are simply the products of basic presuppositions within a given worldview—then it hardly makes sense for a Christian theist to claim to have the truth that is universally binding upon all persons, irrespective of worldview, and to be able to dismiss other competing worldviews as false. For given the presuppositionists' premises even the Christian's claim to truth is ultimately dependent upon the Christian presupposition. Thus if one accepts presuppositionism one forfeits the right to criticize other competing worldviews!

4. Frame takes a remarkably cavalier approach to the history of philosophy, categorizing philosophers as "rationalists," "empiricists," or "irrationalists" and then casually dismissing them for allegedly refusing to submit to the sovereignty of God's Word in the area of knowledge.[22] Fundamental epistemological problems are reinterpreted and dismissed as being largely spiritual in nature. It is difficult to escape the impression that Frame has simply failed to grasp the nature and significance of basic epistemological issues that have defined the course of Western philosophy.

Now it would be foolish to pretend that philosophers have never been guilty of suppressing God's truth and deliberately rejecting God's revelation. Obviously many have. But neither should we overlook the fact that throughout the history of philosophy, and even today, some of the most brilliant and influential philosophers have been very orthodox and highly committed Christians, although their views on epistemology are not likely to be compatible with Frame's presuppositionism.

But more than simply misrepresenting the historical tradition, Frame seems not to have grasped the significance of basic epistemological issues that have been at the center of debate for centuries, and it is this failure that keeps presuppositionism from providing a genuinely viable epistemological perspective. For example, Frame states that for the Christian the most basic presupposition must be "the content of Scripture."[23] Belief in God and His Word is the ultimate presupposition. But how does one know the content of Scripture? Presumably by reading the Bible. But reading anything, including the Bible, is a highly complex activity that includes proper application of basic epistemological, semantic, and logical categories and principles. Minimally, application of fundamental logical principles such as those of noncontradiction and identity, and semantic and syntactic principles that enable one to derive meaning from the marks of ink on the page, and hermeneutical principles that help one to interpret properly the data of Scripture will be necessary. Christian philosopher Paul Helm correctly points out that the following five principles, at least, are necessary for understanding any passage of Scripture: (1) everything is identical with itself and distinct from anything else; (2) if A is identical with B then whatever is true of A is true of B; (3) no proposition can be both true and false; (4) if a proposition p is true, and q follows logically from p, then q is true; and (5) if p and q contradict each other then they cannot both be true.[24]

Contrary to presuppositionism, then, all of these principles must be logically and epistemologically prior to "the content of Scripture" in the sense that they must be utilized in order even to understand the content of Scripture. Furthermore, on an even more basic level, in reading the Bible and thus being confronted with the content of Scripture one holds in one's hands an empirical object—a book with a cover, pages, and ink marks on the pages, etc. But how can one be sure that he is indeed holding a Bible? How does one know that the Bible is an extramental object and not simply the product of one's own consciousness or indeed of some Cosmic Consciousness? Now to be sure, few people ask these questions genuinely wondering whether the book in their hands has extramental reality or not, but that is largely irrelevant. The history of philosophy amply demonstrates the difficulty of settling fundamental questions about the epistemology of perception. The point here is that these are significant questions with which any adequate epistemological theory must grapple and that, since they are logically prior to any apprehension of the "content of Scripture," they cannot be answered satisfactorily in terms of presuppositionism. "The content of Scripture" cannot be held to be epistemologically basic for we only come to know the content of Scripture through reading the Bible, and the very act of reading the Bible presupposes, among other things, that one's senses are (generally) reliable, that one perceives an external object (a book), that one is warranted in taking the object to be a book that is to be read, and that one can apply proper logical, semantic, and hermeneutical principles in reading and understanding the book.

5. But surely, one might suppose, presuppositionists recognize that basic logical principles are context-independent and thus provide some basis for making judgments about alternative worldviews. Can we not appeal to the principle of noncontradiction, for example, as at least one neutral criterion? Surely it provides a negative criterion for truth in the sense that anything that is implicitly or explicitly contradictory cannot be true? In a lengthy section Frame considers the question of logic, but his discussion reveals both serious misunderstandings of the nature of logic and the peculiar difficulties presuppositionism faces. Two issues in particular demand brief attention.

First, Frame maintains that, although logic has an important role to play in critical thinking, it is subordinate to Scripture.

> Logic is a law of thought, if you will, but as such is subordinate to Scripture, which is our ultimate law of thought. It is Scripture that warrants our use of logic, not the other way around. As such, logic is in a position similar to linguistics and history—a discipline that gives us information that is useful in the application of Scripture, information that ought, indeed, to govern our thinking about Scripture but information that itself is subject to biblical criteria.[25]

But how can Scripture "warrant our use of logic" or how can logic be "subject to biblical criteria" when, as noted above, fundamental logical principles are necessary for understanding the meaning of Scripture in the first place?

Second, we are informed that there is a difference between "human logic" and "God's logic" and that "Human logic is fallible, even though God's logic is infallible."[26] Frame contends that

> There have been many systems of logic throughout history. . . . Nevertheless it should be clear to all that logic as a human science is no different from physics, chemistry, sociology, or psychology; it changes over the years. What is accepted in one century may not be accepted in another, and vice versa. These are fallible systems, human systems. They may not be equated with the mind of God. God's logic is divine; human logic is not.[27]

But what is meant by "logic" here? The way people do in fact reason (descriptive) or the rules of valid inference, the way they should reason (normative)? If the former, to say that human logic is fallible is to state the obvious, but we must emphasize that this is not what philosophers normally mean by logic. If the latter, we are left with the perplexing conclusion that the rules of valid inference—the ways in which we *ought* to reason—are fallible. But what then does "ought" mean in this context? How can we be obligated to do that which is improper? What does Frame mean here? That argument forms such as *modus ponens* or *modus tollens* can be valid and binding for humans but not for God? That the principle of noncontradiction is binding for humans but not for God? Can God then contradict Himself? To draw a sharp dichotomy between "human logic" and "God's logic" in this manner is to remove the epistemological basis for holding that there can be genuine knowledge *of God*. Furthermore, to equate logic with psychology or sociology, as Frame does, is to demonstrate failure to have grasped the prescriptive and normative dimension to logic.[28] Although the term *logic* has many uses and meanings, strictly speaking it refers to the nonempirical and nonpsychological domain consisting of certain principles, rules of inference, and relations that apply to propositions and arguments and thus by extension to thinking and reasoning.[29] Logic in this sense is objective in that its reality is independent of the mental processes or psychological states of any human being. The basic principles of logic are normative; if reasoning and thinking are to be done correctly they must conform to these principles. Furthermore, their normativity is not dependent upon or restricted to particular linguistic or cultural contexts. They are translinguistic and transcultural. Basic logical principles and relations have extramental ontological reality; they are part of the "stuff" constituting reality. As such, they do provide some neutral criteria for the evaluation of competing worldviews or truth claims.[30] I have elsewhere suggested ten principles that can function as neutral criteria for the evaluation of competing worldviews.[31]

V. CONCLUSION

I have argued that perhaps the major challenge for Christian apologetics in the coming decades lies in the cluster of problems arising from our increasing awareness of alternative worldviews and that central to this challenge is the problem of formulating acceptable criteria for evaluating competing worldviews. I have further argued that an influential objection to such an enterprise, exemplified in the presuppositionism of John Frame, is seriously flawed and thus does not rule out the legitimacy of attempts to establish neutral criteria.

In concluding our discussion it might be helpful to note a distinction that is sometimes drawn between *offensive* (or positive) apologetics and *defensive* (or negative) apologetics.[32] Defensive apologetics is primarily concerned with responding to direct challenges to the truth or rationality of the Christian faith. The objective here is to demonstrate that the Christian is justified, or is within his epistemic rights, in accepting the truth-claims of Christianity. Arguments against the Christian faith are shown to be unwarranted.

Offensive apologetics, on the other hand, is concerned to show that non-Christians too *ought* to accept the truth-claims of Christianity. The apologist is very much on the offensive, trying to demonstrate that non-Christians too are epistemically obligated to accept the claims of Christianity, that it is unreasonable or irrational for them not to do so. Obviously offensive, or positive, apologetics is a much more difficult endeavor than negative apologetics. And yet I suggest that this is precisely where apologetics today can make its greatest contribution. In a world in which there are many different religious and secular worldviews competing for the allegiance of humankind it is imperative that the Christian be able to show why one ought to accept the central truth-claims of Christianity instead of those of, say, Islam, Buddhism, Advaita Vedanta Hinduism, or secular humanism. And central to such a demonstration must be rigorous argument for the truth of the defining tenets of Christian faith.

Although many Christians will readily acknowledge the importance of defensive apologetics, some object to offensive apologetics, regarding it as somehow theologically inappropriate. Although I cannot argue the point here, I am convinced that a careful study of the biblical data makes it clear that it is legitimate for Christians to engage in both defensive and offensive apologetics (cf. Mark 2:1–12; Luke 24:25–27; John 4:53; 5:36–40; 10:25, 38; 11:45; 20:30–31; Acts 9:22; 13:16–41; 17:2–3, 22–31; 1 Cor. 15:3–19). Cambridge theologian Brian Hebblethwaite astutely observes,

> there is something extremely odd in the common preference in Protestant and Catholic writing today—one thinks of Plantinga and Küng in this respect—for negative over positive apologetic. The idea that arguments against naturalism may clear the way to faith while arguments for the existence of God are somehow religiously improper is incoherent. Certainly faith is more than intellectual assent. But faith is undoubtedly assisted in its dispute with unbelief by positive natural theology. Moreover, if positive and negative arguments are two sides of the same coin, then both sides should be welcomed. There is no reason for religious minds to be coy about this.[33]

To be sure, apologetics in and of itself will not result in the salvation of anyone. Apologetics, just like the simple proclamation of the Gospel, evangelism, is ineffective without the power and work of the Holy Spirit. For ultimately it is only the Holy Spirit who can bring about conviction of sin (John 16: 8–11) and liberate the spiritually blind person from the grasp of the adversary to new life in Christ (John 3:5; 1 Cor. 2:14–16; 2 Cor. 4:3–4; Titus 3:5). But, of course, this fact does not make apologetics unnecessary any more than it renders evangelism unnecessary. Both evangelism and apologetics must be carried out with much prayer and conscious dependence upon the power of God. Christian apologetics is not the same thing as evangelism, nor should it ever take the place of evangelism. In our witness to an unbelieving world primacy must always be given the simple, direct, Spirit-anointed proclamation of the Gospel (Rom. 1:16; Heb. 4:12). But this does not mean that apologetics is optional or unnecessary. Properly construed, apologetics is ancillary to evangelism and is unavoidable in effective proclamation of the Gospel.

PROCLAIMING THE GOSPEL

CHAPTER TWELVE

PREACH THE WORD — GRIPPINGLY

Victor L. Walter

Preachers listen restlessly to the proclamation of the Gospel in tones other than their own. A preacher listens most critically to any homiletical practitioner other than himself. So a charge against contemporary evangelical preaching by someone who both preaches and teaches preaching begins with two strikes against it. Let me get the charge off my chest anyway: there is an enormous and inexcusable amount of dull and mind-numbing preaching going on in evangelical pulpits today. Evangelical laymen point this up in the often-heard lament, "Our pastor just does not feed us"; and equally evangelical preachers defensively rejoin, "At least I am biblical" or, somewhat more negatively, "This television generation just is not interested in the Word of God!" But there you have it—my growing gripe and conviction: a lot of honestly biblical sermons are honestly boring.

I. RAMIFICATIONS OF THE PROBLEM

When the pulpiteer falls into a dull routine behind his local version of the sacred desk, the faithful pew occupant is in for a rough time, because in evangelical circles "faithful" means "present every time the sanctuary door opens." That means that the hapless pew occupant trapped under a dull pulpiteer has the opportunity to be bored in the name of Jesus 104 times per year. Should the same layman prove especially faithful and meet the same preacher at midweek service also, one can increase that count of dull interludes per annum to 156. In our more free evangelical call systems of placement one can hardly blame such laymen if they begin to think in terms of calling a different pastor, hope springing eternal in their faithful breasts that this time God will send them a modern Elijah and Isaiah rolled in the same M.Div. diploma.

Given the fact that the Bible is seen by everybody—whatever their doctrine of inspiration—as the most interesting book ever authored, it stands as a strange contradiction that any dedicated to its proclamation should be charged with enervating dullness. Add the evangelical's clear assertion that every word of Holy Writ was inerrantly prompted by the eternal God and the practice of enervating dullness in its proclamation becomes a sin as monstrous in one bracket as pastoral adultery is in another category. Let any other orator of history prove boring, but never the preacher of the Word:

> He lights his torch at all their fires, and then has a torch lit not by their flaring lamps, but at the sun, which sun is Christ. The preacher has all they had, and

155

more—and more, aye, gloriously more! No interest vital to the world which he does not touch. He stands at the center of a circle whose entire rim is fire. Glory envelops him. He is a prisoner of majesty. A dumb man would stumble into luminous speech on such themes as the gospel grapples with. We dare not be ineloquent when we have themes which do as Aaron's rod did, burst forth into perfumed bloom. We must not be insipid. There is not a dull page in all this age-long story of the redeeming of the race. The minor prophets leap into eloquence which silences Demosthenes; and the major prophets take the thunders for a trumpet on which to blow their universal summons; and the apostles stand in the highway where the peoples throng and exact a tribute of a hearing from the unconcerned; and the evangelists forget bookkeeping and fishing, in eloquence which time has not had the effrontery to dim.[1]

Even more damaging to the church than the bored layman, however, is the bored proclaimer—the pulpit craftsman who finds his preparation routine, his sermons all ringing the same in his own ears, and his parish assignment about as long lasting as a pair of good shoes. With his preaching pattern in familiar wrinkles and creases and the sole of his content worn thin through much treading of the same terrain, his ears are soon cocked for a "new call," hope springing eternal in his breast for a more appreciative people or new preaching vitality through "a new challenge."

Constant shuffling of preachers among churches fueled by auditor hope for an interesting proclaimer and proclaimer hope for a challenging auditor leaves auditor and proclaimer alike dispirited. The answer to the charge of dullness in evangelical pulpits lies in the recovery of urgency, depth, power, and appeal in sermon preparation and delivery. Once again we must come to the point where

[t]he making of the sermon is actually a moment of revelation, a trip into the holy mountains, for . . . (preachers), and the delivery of the sermon is such a moment for their congregations. Their preaching galvanizes men—upends them, probes them, haunts them, follows them into their most remote hiding places and smokes them out, drives them out coughing and sputtering and crying into the open light of new grace and new freedom and new love. The withered are made whole, the lame leap for joy, the dumb find articulation, the confused discover direction, the harried find resources for slowing down—in short, there is an apocalypticism about such preaching, an immediate grasp of what is yet distant and still to come, a taste of what is promised.[2]

Recovery of this kind of proclamation is inevitably the responsibility of the evangelical proclaimer. Recovery of this kind of sermonizing will inevitably interrupt our contemporary shuffle of pastors with the bonding of a proclaimer to a local people in the delight of the shared preaching experience. Establishment or recovery of this kind of preaching is a worthy goal for any pastor who finds himself in a postseminary, midcareer crisis that features boring preaching, whether in preparation or delivery, as a major ingredient.

To add to the brashness of a charge of dullness in evangelical preaching the audacity of a claim to cure can only be folly, hubris, or both. But if drown we must in such a sea of homiletical folly, let us, before expiring, at least attempt a life raft constructed of planks of observation and suggestion.

II. HISTORICAL REFLECTIONS

The history of preaching can rapidly be epitomized through its so-called great centuries. In the almost twenty spans of one hundred that separate the modern Christian from the cross, the first, fourth, twelfth, sixteenth, and nineteenth centuries are generally considered the highlights of proclamation. During that first century the seed of the Gospel was broadcast to the ancients by the apostles. Peter and Paul represent the force of that pristine preaching. The next century of outstanding preaching, the fourth, postdates the triumph of the Christ over the Caesar, and midst the collapse of all things classical, Augustine of Hippo and Chrysostom of Antioch and Constantinople represent, respectively, the passing Latin and Greek patristic orders. As the scholastics froze the church in useless and endless debate and the mass totally supplanted the sermon in the worship of the congregants, preaching burst again upon the world in the brilliant twelfth-century work of St. Francis and St. Dominic. Growing fires of reformation made the sixteenth century great in preaching power, and Luther and Calvin were followed by a phalanx of only slightly less luminous pulpiteers of reformation. Where the fruit of this reformation grew most profusely, the English-speaking segments of Christendom made the 1900s the fifth century of great preaching, and Charles Haddon Spurgeon and Alexander Maclaren, though both British and both Baptists, can perhaps best represent that epoch.

Such a quick survey of the history of preaching yields an instructive observation when confronted with the question, "Where did preaching occur?" The difference two thousand years brought is immediately apparent. As the infant church took its first steps into pagan culture, preaching largely occurred outdoors and in often furious interchange with auditors caught up in street, forum, or on the riverbank. Now as the aged church totters toward the end of the age, preaching among English-speaking folks at least is almost inevitably indoors and in the context of the worship service. When you cage the sermon behind mortar and stained glass, sustaining and surrounding it with the whine of organ—electronic or pipe, when you tame the sermon to twenty minutes tailored to the latest fashion in liturgy, when you display the sermon only to those who voluntarily come into the cage to behold it, the domestication of preaching has been completed.

None can deny the benefits of domestication: sermons are well mannered (no Petrine prying), shortened (no Pauline length), to the point (no Chrysostom circumlocution), apolitical (no Luther needling the state), and scholarly (no bosom-heaving Spurgeonic flights of oratory). Indeed the sermon has been domesticated; but dare we deny that we have lost some things in the transition? What has happened to the trigger tension, even excitement, of the proclaimer when he never knows the challenge of a shouted rebuttal, to say nothing of a well-aimed stone or wielded club? Where has the electricity of the mixed audience gone that had the sermon carried to it in two sandals via loud voice when that audience is replaced by all those sufficiently in agreement to come to the sermon in a thousand shoes?

Let it be suggested in passing that one thing that might assist in reinvigorating preaching would be the resolution on the part of every twentieth-century pulpiteer to preach at least twelve times a year to a secular audience, a congregation latently or openly hostile to the Gospel. Reverse the drive-in church rage of hyperaffluent suburbia and drive yourself to the nearest park or campers site and set up a preaching situation. When the weather is too bad for that, be enough of a man *in* your world (not *of,* you will note) to be invited to give a P.T.A. devotional, the high school baccalaureate, the county medical association ethical discussion, the town council Christmas emphasis, or the jail sermon. Every preaching year, carry some of your proclamations back out of the sanctuary cage and into moments untamed by worship.

III. TWENTIETH-CENTURY DEVELOPMENTS

Several concomitant developments make the domestication of preaching especially debilitating to modern seminary graduates. One is the loss of status accorded the pastor by his community. When the pastor was an authority figure respected by village friend and foe alike the sermon could afford a certain amount of domestication. A second is the rivalry offered the learning of the rector by every field of endeavor. As long as the rector was the most educated man in his hamlet his preaching could face domestication without total loss of clout. Naturally the vigorous competition afforded the preacher by the entertainment media readily available in every home and town square is a third factor that has imperiled the totally domesticated sermon.

A little more sober consideration needs to be given, however, to the fourth and fifth factors concomitant upon this domestication, factors that are threatening the vitality of preaching. When Phillips Brooks, that warm-hearted Episcopal bishop from Massachusetts, stood before those Yale classes of 1877 to lecture on preaching, none perhaps realized that his distilled thought would come to be seen as some of the best in that distinguished series. His classic definition of preaching, great for its very simplicity, took the American homiletical world by storm.

> What, then, is preaching, of which we are to speak? It is not hard to find a definition. Preaching is the communication of truth by man to men. It has in it two essential elements, truth and personality. Neither of those can it spare and still be preaching. The truest truth, the most authoritative statement of God's will, communicated in any other way than through the personality of brother man to men is not preached truth.[3]

Everywhere English-speaking homileticians of all stripes were happy to chorus, "Preaching is the communication of truth by man to men."

Since those heady days of ecclesiastical and political optimism in American public life the higher criticism battles reaching our shores expressed themselves in the practical realms of churchmanship in the liberal-fundamentalist clash. In the light of these twentieth-century tensions the word *truth* in connection with preaching became suddenly suspect. Fundamentalists were not interested in preaching *truth* for that word could be and often was abused by many varieties of relativism. Fundamentalists were interested in preaching Bible and saw Bible, interpreted in orthodox fashion, as the only valid expression of truth worthy of the pulpit.

Today evangelicals and fundamentalists both would rather speak of biblical preaching than preaching; and they favor, in practice, the expository sermon as the only (or best) expression of biblical preaching. If the sermon is biblical and expository it is assumed that truth is presented by virtue of the message's "biblicalness."

One need not quarrel with the conclusion drawn by evangelicals and fundamentalists alike as to the value of biblical preaching to observe that this attitude, this approach, adds a certain narrowing to the already domesticated sermon. If a man preaches only in an expository pattern considering the major and subsidiary ideas of a biblical paragraph largely in the order of the text, that man is set to traverse the domain of Scripture year in and year out in ways largely familiar to the faithful and thoughtful layman. If that "preacher man" finds himself so busy that his devotional life is arid and his sermon preparation a hurried and cursory exercise, this narrowing of the understanding of preaching is tilted doubly toward the enhancement of boredom.

Fortunately thoughtful voices in evangelical homiletical materials are reminding us again of our rich heritage as preachers, for the history of preaching and the study of sermons suggest forcefully that there are two modes of preaching and both can be powerfully biblical. One mode is to present the content of the Bible itself (the "ranger-on-the-text" oral exegetical pattern, however stylistically adapted); the second mode is to present truth that is in harmony with the Bible (the more topical and broad-ranging approach that has always been productive of the greatest doctrinal preaching, for example).

> This *total* reduction of the modern preacher to a Christian scribe, expounding ancient documents in traditional ways, comes near to "quenching the Spirit" and denying the promise that He should guide ongoing disciples into all truth. . . . We are led to a wider meaning of expository method than that of microscopic analysis of the words of a given text. The essence of that wider interpretation of "exposition" is, *that all we preach shall be expository of Bible truth, whatever its method or approach, and shall bring that Bible truth out of the past into the present* in the power of the Spirit Who first gave it.[4]

All of this suggests that if evangelical preaching is going once again to seize lethargic congregations by their ears and thereby fire their imaginations and hearts toward active service for God the evangelical preacher must not only take apart every text exegetically but also must learn to put the pieces together again in bombshells of truth. One does not dish up a grenade in components to an enemy or in support of compatriots. Devour the text, preacher; but do not be content just to regurgitate it. Rather incarnate it in example and message of luminous truth using the full range of preaching types, expository, textual and topical.

The sixth factor concomitant with the domestication of preaching that must be considered at some length is the relationship of the sermon to modern studies in communication. Probably no one has done this more succinctly than Clyde Reid in his provocative little volume, *The Empty Pulpit*. Studies in communication abound chin deep in any library these days. To put it summarily there are seven stages to full-fledged communication. They are

1. transmission, the preacher articulating his message;
2. contact, the auditor actually hearing the message;
3. feedback, the return process by which the auditor reflects what he heard to the preacher for verification;
4. comprehension, the auditor genuinely understands what the preacher articulated and the preacher knows he does;
5. acceptance, the auditor's personal decision to receive or concur with the message (if the auditor chooses to reject the message the communication process stops here);
6. internalization, the time and quiet needed by the auditor to turn initial, superficial acceptance into profound personal determination; and
7. action, the common, shared understanding and action or response of the auditor to the message in concert with the preacher.[5]

Communication specialists now know that no significant change of thought or action occurs without feedback and internalization. Dialogue changes lives; monologue reinforces the status quo. When the sermon was domesticated out of the street and into the worship service it became a monologue. And while a good shepherd can view his calling, counseling, and small-group ministries as opportunities for significant feedback, the fact remains that some of the frustrating futility in preaching may very well be the result of the loss of meaningful dialogue.[6] Hence most sermons tend to be an exercise in stroking those who already agree with the message, as far as communication theory goes. This cannot help but be exacerbated by the modern spirit which announces, "I am going to be a preaching pastor." This strange contradiction in terms means that the nitty of visitation and the gritty of counseling are going to be left to underling or accident. Such a man, enthroned in the solitary splendor of his exegetical study, cuts off all significant feedback or dialogue with his people and cannot expect seriously to affect thought or action by thrice weekly delivered expositions, however polished.

Short of inviting street gangs to come with rocks to stone us or encouraging differing brethren to pepper our sermons with shouted abuse, how can we modern preachers recapture some feedback, some dialogue, without abandoning worship? Here are five suggestions:

1. Use some pre- or postsermon discussions. Appoint selected speakers for five minutes of rebuttal before you conclude.
2. Try interruptive preaching, accepting reactions and questions as they come. Of course it follows that the content would need to be worthy of a reaction.
3. Follow up a sermon with an I-tried-it-report-back a week later.
4. Instead of a closing hymn, break into small discussion groups or let people move around the sanctuary sharing a response while the pianist plays. The old-fashioned altar call or seeker's room is pointed dialogue.

5. Set up one month a year to address controversial issues biblically and invite a different, carefully selected group into the parsonage for coffee and a free-wheeling discussion each Sunday evening of that month. You will discover that feedback need not dislocate worship and worship context does not need to stifle feedback. Every sermon need not be a monologue.

IV. THE REVIVIFIED SERMON

When the evangelical sets out to speak of the recovery of gripping, transforming preaching he assumes rightly that the preacher is a born-again man, growing in the likeness of Christ, under the call of God to the proclamation of the Gospel, filled with the Spirit, evidencing the Spirit's gifts, fruit, wisdom, and immersed daily and reverently in the study of the Scriptures. These are at once the spiritual foundations, armor, and disciplines of the preaching process without which any discussion of preaching is a presumptuous futility. It cannot be asserted too strongly that these are the other-worldly givens of our trade. No man can grasp for them; no homiletician dare think he can deliver them through training.

Any great sermonic moment is made up of six components. There is the power of the Spirit of God present to convict, bless, intercede, and lead preacher and hearer alike. This is the primary factor in sermonic greatness and it rests upon the givens just discussed. As D. Martyn Lloyd-Jones so rightly reminds us, it is displayed in the anointing of the Holy Spirit upon people, preacher, and sermon in its delivery. You can plan only 50 percent of the sermon situation; the other 50 percent is up to God.[7] An old-fashioned term for this mandatory ingredient is *unction*. Secondly, there is the excitement of discovery, which rests in the pastor's study and in the pastor's discipline of careful, prayerful, faithful daily devotional scriptural study. When he has been gripped, changed, compelled by his own work in the Word, even though the preacher may be dealing with a truth as old as Adam, he communicates freshness and enthusiasm in powerful and intangible ways to his hearers. In homiletics this quality is technically termed *originality*.[8] The third component in a great sermonic moment is the compelling application of the truth proclaimed and the appeal made to the audience to respond. One can apply the term *relevance* to this component. *Structure* is the word for our next component, and that involves clarity and matters of logical organization. Fifth in our list would be the matter of *style*— gripping language full of imagination, narrative, and color. No mastery of this has ever surpassed the Master's parables. The sixth and final component in the great sermonic moment is the full and free use of attention-holding factors. The very abused term *charisma* can be assigned this factor. A great sermon thus has *unction, originality, relevance, structure, style* and is delivered with *charisma*. Not only must the homiletician realize that he dare not think he can deliver the other-worldly givens of his calling; he must candidly and humbly admit that of the six components of the great sermonic moment he can only moderately affect the last and least significant four—*relevance, structure, style,* and *charisma*. Let this chapter conclude by way of a quiver full of arrows of suggestion to be drawn across the bow of homiletical practice in the studies of those pastors concerned with avoiding dullness in proclamation.

V. SUGGESTIONS FOR RELEVANCE, STRUCTURE, STYLE, AND CHARISMA

Genuine relevance is born in application with bite. Application involves focusing the truth being dealt with on the hearer, expressing explicitly what the hearer is to do in response, or how he or she is to do it, and motivating the hearer to do precisely that.[9] As every preacher knows, the third of these applicational factors is the most difficult. Motivating a hearer involves a clear plea so that he or she knows exactly how to "obey" the truth; it involves the speaker's own heightened feelings so the hearer senses the speaker's urgent concern; it involves the use of pungent, moving material so the auditor's emotions are stirred to fire his or her will to act; and motivation finally involves the technical element of appeal, which refers to the speaker's tug on the legitimate desires of the hearer so that he or she will will to act. A suggestion for revivifying preaching: "biblicize" the psychological desires of a hearer and check to see that every main point of your sermon incorporates one to three of these elements of appeal. Take any psychologist's list of basic human drives you wish and translate them into legitimate biblical desires or drives and you will obtain a list something like this:

Psychologists say every man has a drive for . . .	The Bible says every man legitimately desires . . .
entertainment, distraction	freedom from guilt fellowship understanding of God's program knowledge of godly character insight into prophecy
preservation of life	eternal life hope in the midst of a despairing world perseverance to avoid death and hell
status	Lord's "well done" healthy operation of the church self-control self-acceptance and respect confidence and approval of brothers
food and water	Lord's provision fulfilled promises of God knowledge of the Word's content
shelter	caring family of the church security joy and peace in crises

love	fulfilling marriage
	sound home
	love of God
	holy sex
	winning of others to Christ
	worship and adoration of God
power	leadership in the church
	rulership in the kingdom to come
	triumph over social evils

By the prayerful use of a battery of appeals in every message the preacher can, with the help of the Holy Spirit, move the man off the cultural street toward the heavenly path, and even though he may have entered the church giving no credence to biblical authority, that man off the cultural street is brought to the place of obedience to God and the great discovery of every secularist: "This is what the Bible has taught all along."[10]

A further suggestion for revivifying preaching: identify your present, most-used outline organization (*structure*) and deliberately set yourself over the next few months to learn and use two or three new contrasting ways of structuring a sermon. Outline organization can be chosen then in terms of what will best project the particular Bible content or Bible truth to the particular audience, and with an eye to variety in structure, the preacher does not bore himself with his methodology. If your organization is ragged and you feel the need for a clear, clean beginning in structure building, the best step-by-step instructions in all of homiletics are those by Lloyd Perry in *Biblical Preaching for Today's World* (Chicago: Moody, 1973), 42–62. Begin here. On the other hand, if you have a solid basic structure, turn to the ninth and tenth chapters of H. Grady Davis, *Design for Preaching* (Philadelphia: Fortress, 1958) and learn his five forms of a subject—subject discussed, thesis supported, message illumined, question propounded, and a story told. Demonstrate for yourself Davis's theme *that form of subject determines structure* by writing main points according to his rule for each of the types of messages he envisions springing from biblical materials. If you want to challenge yourself with a keenly persuasive structure, the most cogent organization in public address is that clearly developed by Alan Monroe (which he calls the motivated sequence) in *Principles and Types of Speech* (New York: Scott, Foresman and Company, 1962), chapters 16 and 17. Preach to persuade under five points (Monroe's adaptation of man's thought process): attention, need, satisfaction, visualization, and action. Begin now to cultivate challenging structural variety.[11]

If one is to improve *style*—the matter of language that is full of color, narrative, and imagination—one must begin in a kind of devotional meditation that walks in the sandals of the biblical characters and sits in the catacomb seat of an epistle recipient and then comes from that meditation able to make the hearer have that "you were there" experience.[12] This demands an integrity in the treatment of the biblical materials that goes beyond mere fairness to the content. It makes mandatory the preacher's handling of that content while doing full justice to the biblical mood. Thus if the biblical content is exuberant in spirit, the preacher does not give it a judgmental mien; if the passage breathes a somber and reflective air, the preacher should not give it a lighthearted and humorous thrust.[13] These two demands of style meet; for if the preacher in meditation has lived the scriptural passage, he is well enough acquainted with its mood to be fair to it. Beyond the qualities of imagination and fairness to the mood, style also involves clarity, clear thinking.

> Miracles apart, a muddled sermon cannot well be sound in theology, interesting to listen to, effective in persuasion, memorable as an experience, or make any useful contribution to worship. Unclear speaking dissipates attention, destroys persuasiveness, defeats the intention of the speaker from the outset. To any man in earnest about communicating truth, the necessity of clarity is clear enough.[14]

Suggestion for revivifying preaching: at least once a month write out a sermon verbatim (or have a secretary transcribe it from a tape after it has been delivered). Compare its mood to the mood of its lead Scriptures and adjust accordingly. See that at least one imaginative description or application occurs in each main point. Next turn your attention to each word in the sermon. Replace every ambiguous word with an unequivocal one; turn every abstract term into a concrete one; check for emotive, prejudicial expressions and remove them; and finally replace every negative turn of sentence with a positive unless the negative is absolutely essential for your meaning. This discipline corrects obscurity inherent in message language.[15] On the third time through your verbatim message confine your attention to the sentences and their logical pattern. Replace selective observations with statements that are fair to all sides; remove exaggerations ruthlessly and discipline yourself to follow the purged text; correct false or unfair analogies; think about your assumptions and modify those which are unwarranted; and remove all sloganeering or lazy cliches. Such a sentence check will remove fuzzy thinking.[16]

From the human level *charisma* is the ability to rivet attention on the message, messenger, and the whole communication process. Three things are involved in this: controlled, expressive gestures with variety in level; abundant use and variety of supporting or illustrational materials; and the conscious attention paid to writing attention-holding change factors into the sermon itself. Suggestion for revivifying preaching: Round up three or four trusted and sympathetic friends who listen to you preach regularly and dare to submit a sermon to their critical analysis once every month or two. Set one of them to monitoring your gestures. Have them note down mannerisms and constantly repeated or awkward gestures. In practice preaching sessions, work to remove or bring these under control. Remember that meaningless sameness, repetitious gesturing is more distracting to attention than no gesturing at all. Ask this person to keep track of the number of times you gesture into the upper and lower levels. Belt line to shoulder is the middle level where most gestures must occur: variety depends on movement runs that go above the shoulder or below the belt line. If this individual is a perceptive observer set him to checking the number of emphatic gestures (those that express your feelings) as over against the number of descriptive gestures (those describing scenes or objects). There should be a balance in these.

Set a second person to recording instances of supporting material. On a sheet of paper range the types of supporting material down the left hand side: figures of speech, comparisons and contrasts, parables, historical allusions, biographical incidents (from others' lives), personal testimony, anecdotes or stories, poetry or hymn lines, quotations, and building hypothetical situations.[17] Across the top of the paper march the Roman numerals for the points of your sermon. This individual just needs to place a check mark on the paper opposite the type of supporting material used under the column for the point of your sermon in which it occurred to establish a visual representation of your supporting material effectiveness. The check marks should be evenly distributed over the entire sheet, for adequate variety demands many types of supporting material in all points of the sermon.

Set your most perceptive volunteer friend to check the attention-holding factors in your sermon, for these are the most technical and difficult to recognize. The essence of holding attention is delivering sufficient stimuli to the listener to keep him from becoming aware of the passage of time. When stimuli drop low enough for the auditor to become aware of time's movement he is apt to become bored.[18] The essence of keeping stimuli impinging on the consciousness of the auditor is change. An unbroken shout will lose attention as quickly as the unbroken, soft monotone. Attention is seized by change when one sentence is vigorous and the next a whisper. So this person is monitoring *changes: changes* in content—let him list the persons, activities, conflicts, basic wants, curiosity items, suspense moments, unusual things, and very familiar items you mention; *changes* in direct appeal to the senses—the ears through silence, rate changes, volume changes, tone changes, and the eyes through visual aids (someone else is already checking the gestures); *changes* through indirect appeal to the senses— remembered things seen, heard, smelled, tasted, felt; *changes* in types of material—solemn, grim, earnest, shocking, surprising, amusing, ludicrous, satirical; *changes* in emotional tenor—anger, anxiety, contempt, disappointment, fear, gratitude, grief, hate, hope, jealousy, joy, love, pity, pride, regret, relief, remorse, shame; and *changes* in type of sentence structure—long, short, declarative, exclamatory, interrogative.[19] One can simply place these areas of change down the left side of a sheet of paper and the main points of the message across the top of the sheet and have the monitoring individual put a mark down in the proper area every time he detects a change. Three monitors ought to be able unobtrusively to check the *charisma* of your delivery—its gestures, supporting material, and attention-holding factors—without disrupting an ordinary-sized service of worship.

Such are the areas of human skill the preacher can train in, practice, increase: *relevance, structure, style,* and *charisma.* Admittedly these are secondary and minor compared to matters of other-worldly givens and a theologically informed biblical content. Should the busy pastor spend the energy and time to improve his performance in these secondary areas? Let this question be answered by a second: given the One who called us, God, and the sublime level of the task, preaching, should we not strive to be unashamed workmen in technique as well as in content?

VI. A CHALLENGE TO US AS PASTORS

Well does this author know the busy comings and goings, the demands and privileges of the parish! If this book is something other than a respectable library decoration, if it is read, if this chapter should be read to this point, and if you feel as the author does in regard to his own preaching, that sometimes it falls into the gray-flannel area of dullness, the final question becomes: Will we do anything about improving the preaching we deliver? Might it be suggested that we trap ourselves into action? Obtain two or three copies of this book. Muster the pastoral fortitude to urge your people to candor. Invite all who sometimes find your preaching dull to meet with you after service. Pass out those book copies and let them study this chapter at their leisure, making a list of its suggestions. Let them then join us in praying and monitoring us toward more vital proclamation. Then the chips will be down and we will be under some obligation to improve, to grow in our preaching ability. "Great idea, but we might lose our jobs," the heart responds. Well . . . perhaps if we do not care enough to continually improve our preaching we should lose those jobs of ours. . . .

> Let me be as candid as possible, and address the reverend clergy directly. As a preacher in an age when preaching is widely regarded as the bogus currency of a bankrupt ministry, the best thing you can do, for yourself and your ministry, is to set the business of preaching at the very center of your life and work, and give it first claim on your time and energy.[20]

CHAPTER THIRTEEN

PREACHING AS WORSHIP: MEDITATIONS ON EXPOSITORY EXULTATION

John Piper

I. THE WORSHIP THAT COMES BY THE WORD: SATISFACTION IN THE GREATNESS OF GOD

I want to begin by posing a question about the relationship between contemporary worship songs and preaching. I think most of us would agree that the last twenty years have seen a phenomenal explosion of "contemporary worship music"; songs like Jack Hayford's *Majesty* and Graham Kendrick's *Shine, Jesus, Shine* and dozens of others—*Thou Art Worthy; Father I Adore You; Open Our Eyes Lord; We Worship and Adore You; Thou, O Lord, Art a Shield about Me; You are Lord;* and on and on. The common vocabulary of contemporary worship songs today is astonishing in evangelicalism and beyond.

Some of them are grammatically, poetically, and musically deplorable (which we shouldn't make too much of if we grew up on the likes of *Do Lord, Oh, Do Lord . . .*). Every explosion has its fluff. But one thing is unmistakable as a trend in these songs: they are, by and large, and in a new way, *God-ward*. All the ones I mentioned address God in the second person. They are sung to God directly, not merely to each other about God. Therefore they force the issue of worship as a God-ward act—an engagement of the heart with the living God as the song is sung. Add to this that these contemporary tunes are emotionally moving. They are composed in such a way as to awaken and carry affections. They are not excessively complex or intellectual or demanding but catch the heart up into their mood.

So two things happen in the best contemporary worship songs: the mind is brought to focus on God with words that are usually biblical (much more so than the spiritual choruses of previous generations); and the heart is moved by the music with a mood of tenderness or devotion or enjoyment (at least this is true for millions of ordinary Christians).

So as we look at the "worship awakening" over the last twenty years or so, what stands out to me as astonishing is that its content is so God-centered and God-exalting. "He is Lord, risen from the dead"; "He is majestic"; "He is mighty"; "He is holy"; "He has conquered the power of death"; "He is a shield about us, our glory, the lifter of our heads"; "He is King of kings, Lord of lords, Emmanuel, great and wonderful, our Rock, our Fortress, our Deliverer, the coming King, Redeemer, Name above all names, precious Lamb of God, Messiah, Holy One"; "he is our God"; and "our God reigns."

Whatever you think of the drums, the electric guitar and bass and amplification and T-shirts and platforms cluttered with wires and mikes and speakers, it is unmistakable—the dominant theme of these songs is God—the character of God, the power of God, the mercy of God, the authority of God, and the fatherhood of God. And the hoped-for effect of relentlessly addressing God directly in the second person is engagement—genuine, real, spiritual engagement—of the heart with God.

But there is another remarkable fact of the last twenty years or so, and it has to do with preaching. My observation is that the preaching that follows this music in most churches has moved in exactly the opposite direction from the musical worship awakening. While the worship songs have moved God-ward, preaching has moved man-ward. While the worship songs focus our attention again and again on the character of God and the great works of God, preaching focuses on contemporary issues, personal problems, relationships. While the worship songs lift us into the presence of God, preaching gives advice on how to get along better on earth. No one would say today the same thing about preaching that we have seen in the "worship awakening"—namely, that there has been a great resurgence of God-centeredness, or a great moving of the spirit of God-wardness in the pulpit, or a focus on God's character and mighty acts in the preaching of evangelicalism. Rather, I think most would agree that preaching has moved in the other direction: relational, anecdotal, humorous, casual, laid-back, absorbed in human need, fixed on relational dynamics, heavily saturated with psychological categories, wrapped up in strategies for emotional healing.

This very different development in singing and preaching begs for an explanation. I'm sure the answer is more complex than I can presently understand or explain. But I want to suggest one possible answer that highlights the need for my focus in this chapter. Why have we preachers not followed the lead of worship music into a sustained focus on the greatness of God and the majesty of His name and the glory of His works? Why is the subject matter and the focus of preaching so different from that of contemporary worship songs?

One aspect of the explanation is that the God-centered lyrics of the worship songs have one great advantage over preaching—they are accompanied by heart-engaging music. The words would never in themselves hold the interest of the worshipers and never release the affections for God as they do in connection with the music. Therefore, one might say, the music is what makes God-centered lyrics palatable to contemporary evangelicals, who are basically a-theological and who would not be stirred by them without the moving music. Without the music the words would be considered dry, irrelevant, distant, unengaging. Or we can put it more generously than that. We could say to the degree that the tunes are pleasing and stirring and heart-engaging, the worshiper is genuinely opened to at least some of the significance of the truth about God Himself and indeed brought to experience the reality of that very God.

However you put it—negatively: the music makes God-centeredness palatable; or positively: the music opens the heart to the true joy of God-centeredness—we preachers know that our words have to stand or fall without the help of music.

And yet almost every preacher—and rightly so!—wants to accomplish what music accomplishes. We want to move the heart. We want to stir the emotions as well as stock the mind. We want to awaken heartfelt affections as well as win intellectual assent.

And right here many preachers, I fear, make a fateful, mistaken judgment. They reason: since I do not have music to accompany me in my preaching, I cannot, with a God-centered message, hold or move the hearts of my people and engage their emotions. Doctrine and theological portraits of God, a focus on His supremacy and a spirit of transcendence will simply not hold and move a contemporary audience—not without music to sustain the mood. What holds a contemporary audience *verbally* is not a message about God but a message about divorce or drugs or parenting or anger or success or abuse or intimacy or depression.

In other words, the common strategy of preachers today for awakening people's emotions and engaging their hearts is to find the areas of human life where the emotions are already running high and where the hearts are already engaged; and then we root the sermon there—the pain in the marriage; the anguish of wayward teenagers; the stress at work; the power of sexual temptation; the breakdown of community; the woundedness of past abuses; the absence of intimacy and vulnerability. We preachers know that if we plant our sermons here—if we tend this garden with modest skill in anecdote and illustration and personal vulnerability—we will move the hearts of our hearers; we will accomplish what the worship tunes accomplish. Our listeners will experience the good feelings of empathy, and we will feel the satisfaction of attentive, resonating faces.

Now at this point I could put either a positive or a negative spin on this development in preaching. Positively, I could say: a lot of preaching is in touch with where people are and where they feel pain, and that is certainly not a bad thing. Preaching that is ignorant of people and unempathetic with their pain will not bear biblical fruit.

But there is also a negative spin that we can put on this development—one that I do indeed put on it, and one that helps explain my burden in this chapter. It is this: the reason we preachers do not believe that the greatness of God, the spirit of transcendence, the glory and majesty of Christ, the deep things of the Spirit, will move the hearts of our people and awaken profound affections is that these things do not move us; they don't awaken our affections. We preachers prefer to read books about anger and intimacy and marriage and success and all manner of how-to strategies for home and work and church than to read books about God. Ask any publisher what sells—even to pastors.

What gets preachers' juices flowing is a new psychological angle on family dysfunction; a new strategy for mobilizing lay people; a new tactic for time management; a fresh approach to dealing with depression; an empathetic focus on his own resentments and pain and anger after years of being beat up by carnal Christians. But not a book about God. Not the infinite expanse of God's character. Not the inexhaustible riches of the glory of God in Christ.

So this is why I think there is a cleavage between worship music and preaching. I would say, paradoxically, that preachers are not really trying to go in a different direction from contemporary worship music. In fact, we preachers want desperately to sustain some of the same interest and enjoyment and engagement in our preaching. We want the same thing to happen emotionally in our preaching that happens in emotionally charged times of worship. And since we are persuaded that it just won't happen with God-centeredness, we seek it with empathetic human pain-centeredness. We find the engaging itch and we scratch it.

I don't think that this tension between God-focused worship lyrics and human-focused preaching can go on indefinitely. Either the God-centered worship singing will be pulled down or the human-saturated preaching will be pulled up. My aim is to plead for preaching to be pulled up—not away from the pain of the people, but, along with the pain of the people, into the presence of God, whose presence and reality alone is the final answer. My conviction is that the aim of preaching—no less than singing—is God-exalting worship. And not only that, my conviction is—hence the title of this chapter—that true biblical preaching *is* worship.

In other words, in the same way that a melody can awaken us to the true beauty of God in the lyrics of a worship song, so the spiritual music of the preacher's soul can awaken the people to the glory of the preached truth of God. When the Word comes worshiping, it will beget worship. When preaching is not just expository but *expository exultation*—that's my definition of preaching—it will move the hearers, and it will engage the heart with the presence and glory of God.

Now it may be that someone would say, "Well, what's wrong with having a God-centered worship time in song followed by an empathetic human-centered word from God about our problems?" What's wrong with it is that preaching is meant by God to catch people up into worship, not to be a practical human application after worship. The aim of preaching is to deal with divorce worshipfully, and to deal with teenagers worshipfully, and to deal with anger worshipfully. Preaching exalts the centrality of God in all of life or it is not Christian preaching.

Let me point to three biblical reasons for believing this—that preaching is meant to be and to kindle God-exalting worship.

First, I believe it because the Word of God says that everything is to be done in a worshipful, God-centered way: "Whether, then, you eat or drink or whatever you do, do all to the glory of God" (1 Cor. 10:31); "Whatever you do in word or deed, do all in the name of the Lord Jesus" (Col. 3:17). If everything is to be radically oriented on magnifying the glory of God and exalting the name of Jesus, how much more preaching. Whatever preaching deals with—and it is to deal with everything—it must be done with a view to begetting and sustaining worship—the valuing and cherishing and displaying of the glory of God.

Second, I believe that preaching is meant to exalt the centrality of God because the Word says that God Himself exalts His own centrality in all that He does. And preaching is one of the great things that God does. God's Word in Isaiah 48:11 is like a great banner flying over all His acts from creation to consummation: "For My own sake, for My own sake, I will act; For how can My name be profaned? And My glory I will not give to another." He chose us and predestined us for His glory (Eph. 1:6), He created us for His glory (Isa. 43:7), He saved us for His glory (Eph. 1:14), He sanctifies us for His glory (2 Thess.

1:12). All God does He does to magnify His glory in the earth. Preaching is one of the great things that God does. It is God's work. And therefore the mission of preaching is the mission of God: "I will be exalted among the nations, I will be exalted in the earth" (Ps. 46:10). Our aim is worship—the valuing and cherishing and displaying of the greatness and the glory of God.

Finally, I believe that preaching is meant to exalt the centrality of God because the NT teaches that the appointed end of preaching is faith, and faith is the primary covenant requirement of God, precisely because it humbles us and amplifies the trustworthiness and all-sufficiency of God. Repeatedly Paul lines up preaching with faith as its goal: "How shall they *believe* in Him whom they have not heard? And how shall they hear without a *preacher?* . . . So *faith* comes from hearing, and hearing by the *word of Christ*" (Rom. 10:14, 17). "Since in the wisdom of God the world did not know God through its wisdom, God was pleased through the foolishness of *preaching* to save those who *believe*" (1 Cor. 1:21). "My message and my *preaching* were not in persuasive words of wisdom, but in demonstration of the Spirit and of power, that your *faith* should not rest on the wisdom of men, but on the power of God" (1 Cor. 2:4–5; see also Rom. 16:25–26; 1 Cor. 15:11, 14). The aim of preaching is to beget and sustain faith. Why? Because faith magnifies the power and trustworthiness of God. This is why Paul loves the model of Abraham: Abraham "grew strong in his *faith,* giving *glory to God,* fully convinced that God was able to do what he had promised" (Rom. 4:20). The heart of saving faith is a spiritual apprehension of the glorious trustworthiness of God in Christ and an earnest embracing of all that God is for us in Christ to satisfy the hunger of the soul.

That is the way Jesus described faith in John 6:35: "I am the bread of life; he who comes to me shall not hunger, and he who *believes* in me shall *never thirst.*" Believing in Jesus means coming to Him for the quenching of our souls' thirst. Faith in Christ is being satisfied with all that God is for us in Jesus. When we experience that, we magnify the preciousness and worth of God, because God is most glorified in us when we are most satisfied in Him—which means we worship.

The aim of preaching, whatever the topic, whatever the text, is this kind of faith—to quicken in the soul a satisfaction with all that God is for us in Jesus, because this satisfaction magnifies God's all-sufficient glory; and that is worship. Therefore the mission of all preaching is soul-satisfying, God-exalting worship.

II. THE WORD THAT KINDLES WORSHIP: SHOWING THE GLORIES OF GOD

Worship, we have argued, is implicit in saving faith because God is most glorified in us when we are most satisfied in Him. So biblical preaching always aims to quicken and sustain God-exalting satisfaction in God. James Henry Thornwell expresses this thought in a letter he wrote about beginning his ministry in South Carolina in 1834. Henry Ward Beecher called Thornwell "the most brilliant minister in the Old School Presbyterian Church."[1] Thornwell said,

> I felt that a new era had commenced in my life in that I was no longer a citizen
> of the world, but an ambassador of God, standing in the stead of Jesus Christ

and beseeching men to turn from the *unsatisfying* vanities of a fleeting life and to fix their hopes on the enduring sources of *beatitude* which surrounds the throne of God.[2]

In other words, the task of preaching is to warn people about the futility of the broken cisterns of sin that hold no water (Jer. 2:13) and to compel them with truth and power to come to the fountain of living water that satisfies forever.

> Ho! Every one who thirsts, come to the waters;
> And you who have no money come, buy and eat.
> Come, buy wine and milk
> Without money and without cost.
> Why do you spend money for what is not bread,
> And your wages for what does not satisfy?
> Listen carefully to Me, and eat what is good,
> And delight yourself in abundance (Isa. 55:1–2).

That's the essence of preaching. The best way to glorify an inexhaustible fountain is to keep on drinking and to keep on being so satisfied with that fountain that nothing can draw you away. And therefore the task of preaching is to display the all-satisfying glories of God in such a way that the power of all competing pleasures is broken, and God Himself holds people captive. For in His presence is fullness of joy and at His right hand are pleasures forevermore (Ps. 16:11).

I have also argued that preaching can make its own music. It doesn't need to domesticate its message and to be limited to scratching where people itch. And it doesn't need the music of organ or piano or synthesizer or guitar to make its God-exalting theme palatable. What it needs is the Spirit-given singing of the soul of the preacher. When the worship-seeking Word comes, it must come worshiping. When preaching is worship, the people will be moved.

James Stewart, the great Scottish preacher, has a section on this in his book, *Heralds of God,* where he says,

> If in a congregation one soul here and another there may be receiving, as the sermon proceeds, some vision of the majesty of God, some glimpse of the loveliness of Christ, some revelation of personal need beneath the searchlight of the Spirit, is the ministry of the Word to be minimized, or regarded as less divine . . . than other parts of the service? *Is not such preaching worship?*[3]

And I would stress that it is worship—not just because it awakens a satisfying sense of God's glory in the people but also because it exhibits a satisfying sense of God's glory in the preacher.

Now we must make clear that preaching pursues its aim of worship not merely through the preaching exultation but through expository exultation. The song of His heart has power, but it is God's power only when He is singing over the Truth. Therefore I have defined preaching as expository exultation. Not just exultation but expository exultation. By exposition I mean exactly what John Stott means, as he puts it in his book, *Between Two Worlds:*

> It is my contention that all true Christian preaching is expository preaching. Of course, if by an "expository" sermon is meant a verse-by-verse explanation of a lengthy passage of Scripture, then indeed it is only one possible way of preaching, but this would be a misuse of the word. Properly speaking, "exposition" has a much broader meaning. It refers to the content of the sermon (biblical truth) rather than its style (a running commentary). To expound Scripture is to bring out of the text what is there and expose it to view. The expositor pries open what appears to be closed, makes plain what is obscure, unravels what is knotted and unfolds what is tightly packed. The opposite of exposition is "imposition," which is to impose on the text what is not there. But the "text" in question could be a verse, or a sentence, or even a single word. It could equally be a paragraph, or a chapter, or a whole book. The size of the text is immaterial, so long as it is biblical. What matters is what we do with it. Whether it is long or short, our responsibility as expositors is to open it up in such a way that it speaks its message clearly, plainly, accurately, relevantly.[4]

When I call preaching "expository exultation" that's what I mean by "expository." "To expound Scripture," Stott says, "is to bring out of the text what is there and expose it to view." And what is there in Scripture mainly is God. The all-pervasive, all-important, all-surpassing reality in every text is God. Whether He is commanding or warning or promising or teaching, He is there. And where He is, He is always supreme. And where He is supreme, He will be worshiped. Therefore the overarching, pervasive, relentless subject of preaching is God Himself with a view to being worshiped.

Therefore we ask—as every preacher must ask who knows this aim of preaching—how can I awaken the slumbering passions of God's people for the surpassing worth of knowing God and His Son, Jesus Christ? How can I kindle the flame of knowledge and faith that says, there is none like Christ, there is no treasure, no pleasure, no perk, no profit, no prize, no reward, no wife, no child, like Christ; that says, "for me to live is Christ and to die is gain"? How shall we preach to beget and sustain such a passion for God?

The answer is at least this: in our preaching we must display from Scripture, week in and week out, the glories of God in Christ. It won't do briefly to say that Christ is great or that our mission is to glorify God and then hasten on to speak of other things. Oh how many preachers in pulpits, and teachers in Christian colleges and seminaries, and Christian counselors account for their God-neglecting sermons and syllabi and sessions by saying: well, God is the foundation of all we say, we assume that; we take that for granted. But more and more I have come to believe that God does not like being taken for granted. The whole point of the creation of the universe is to display God. The heavens are telling the glory of God; day unto day pours forth speech. The point of the Incarnation is to display God. The point of preaching is to display God. The analogy of God as a foundation is an utterly inadequate analogy to account for how God relates to our work. Cement-block foundations are indispensable—but who thinks about them, talks about them, loves them, worships them? They are forgotten.

God did not put His glory on display in creation and redemption in order that it might be taken for granted as a foundation beneath the building of our church activity, or the school of our academic enterprise, or the clinic of our psychological techniques, or the house of our leisure. Woe to us if we get our satisfaction from the food in the kitchen and the TV in the den and the sex in the bedroom with an occasional tribute to the cement blocks in the basement! God wills to be displayed and known and loved and cherished and worshiped always and everywhere and in every act—especially preaching.

We will awaken worship in our people when we stop treating God as an out-of-sight foundation for all the other things we like to talk about and instead start talking about the glories—glories, plural—of God Himself and His Son, Jesus:

- His value and worth;
- His triumphs past, present, and future, over sin and death and hell and Satan;
- His knowledge, which makes the Library of Congress look like a matchbox and quantum physics like a first-grade reader;
- His wisdom, which has never been and never can be counseled by men;
- His authority over heaven and earth—without His permission no demon can move an inch;
- His providence, without which not a bird falls to the ground or a single hair turns gray;
- His word, which upholds the universe and keeps all the atoms and molecules together;
- His power to walk on water, and cleanse lepers, and heal the lame, and open the eyes of the blind, and cause the deaf to hear, and to still storms with a word, and raise the dead;
- His purity never to sin;
- His trustworthiness never to break His word or let one promise fall to the ground;
- His justice, to render all accounts settled either in hell or on the cross;
- His patience, to endure our dullness for decades;
- His endurance, to embrace the excruciating pain of the cross willingly;
- His wrath, that will one day cause people to call out for the rocks and the mountains to fall on them;
- His grace, that justifies the ungodly; and
- His love, that led Him to die for us even while we were sinners.

If we want to beget worship through preaching we have to bring the glory of God up out of the basement and put it in the window. We have to stop speaking in vague, passing generalizations about God's glory and begin to describe the specific contours of His perfections. The task of the sermon week in and week out is to help our people bring into sharp focus a fresh picture of why God is the all-satisfying Treasure of their lives. People are seldom moved by vague allusions to the greatness of God. They need to see some particular, concrete, stunning representation of His greatness—some fresh angle on an old glory that makes people say with Paul: I count everything as loss for the surpassing value of knowing this Christ.

For example, last week I was reading my devotions in John 8, and this word bolted off the page: "Truly, truly, I say to you, if anyone keeps my word, he shall never see death." Now there's a text for the glory of the authority and power of Jesus. Who today could stand before a TV camera and look out over the world of humankind and say, "If anyone keeps my word, he will never see death"? In other words, "I have absolute power over death and I have absolute authority over the life of every human being. If you keep my word, just when death raises its ugly face and reaches out its horrid claws, in the last split second of your life I will come and take you. You will not even see its grisly face." You either put that man behind bars or you bow down and worship. But you don't trifle with him. If our people are going to worship, they must see the glories of Christ and be satisfied with all that God is for them in Jesus. That is the task of preaching: show them the glories.

A final point on this matter. Just as there is a tendency today to take the glory of God for granted and to keep it in the basement as the assumed foundation for other topics, in the same way there is a similar tendency to hide the actual wording of the biblical text as the unseen foundation of the sermon. There seems to exist the idea that to tell people to look with you at the words and phrases of the text as you make your points is academic or pedantic—that it smacks of school and lectures that have boring connotations and so don't hold the attention or stir affections, let alone assist worship.

I want to plead otherwise. Our people need to see that what we say about God comes from the Word of God. We should not ask them to take our word for it. We should show it. Our aim is to show the glories of Christ with the authority of God's words, not ours. Our ideas about the glories of Christ are of no great importance. What matters is what God says about the glory of God. And it matters that the people see that it is God who says it and not us. And showing them the very words and phrases and clauses that display the glory of Christ does not have to be pedantic or boring. I am pleading not merely that what you show of Christ really be from the text but that you demonstrate to your people that it is from the text, that you deflect the authority away from yourself to the text, and that you enable them to see it and hold it from the text for themselves.

I close this section with an example. My aim in preaching is that God be glorified through the people's being satisfied in Him, that God become so gloriously all-satisfying in their lives that nothing can lure them away from Him. I open to them Matthew 13:44 and read, "The kingdom of heaven is like a treasure hidden in the field, which a man found and hid; and from joy over it he goes and sells all that he has, and buys that field." And I say to them, "Look at this. How valuable, how precious is the kingdom of heaven? Is it valuable enough to lose everything you have in order to get it—your house, your wedding ring, your car, and stocks and retirement portfolio and books and computer and clothes and health insurance?" And they say, "Yes, it says that here: he sold all he has to get that field—to have the kingdom." And I say, "Yes, so far so good. But how valuable is it really? Is that all Jesus wanted us to feel—that the kingdom is worth losing everything for? That we can count everything as rubbish for the surpassing value of having the kingdom of heaven? No, there's another phrase here. Don't miss it. It makes all the difference in the world. It has made all the difference in my life. It makes all the difference in my preaching. Do you see it?

Do you see it in God's Word and not my word? 'And from joy over it, he goes and sells all that he has, and buys that field.' It's the joy that drives him. The power to 'let goods and kindred go,' the power that overcomes the health, wealth, and prosperity 'gospel,' the power that severs us from all the fleeting pleasures of sin, the power that binds us to God and holds us there enthralled is the joy of the all-satisfying glory of the kingdom of God. Read it. Read the very words. 'And from joy over it—from joy, he sold all that he had.' All sacrifice, all obedience, all worship is the impulse of this joy in God." This is the goal of God, the goal of life, the goal of preaching: God-exalting joy in the kingdom of God.

III. THE WORD THAT COMES WORSHIPING: SAVORING WHAT WE SAY ABOUT GOD

The aim of preaching is worship. That is, all preaching should aim to wean the human heart off the breast of sin and bring it to satisfaction in God as the Fountain of Life. The assumption here is this: God is most glorified in our people when our people are most satisfied in Him. That is, the essence and heart of worship is being satisfied with all that God is for us in Christ. And, if the mission of preaching is to beget and sustain a satisfying, liberating sense of the glory of God in the human heart, then the matter of preaching must be the glories of God and of His Son, Jesus. The people can't savor what they don't see. Our task is to show the glories of God—concretely, specifically, compellingly, and not from our own imagination but from the revelation of that glory in God's Word. Therefore, all Christian preaching is expository. It "exposes" the all-satisfying God as He speaks and reveals Himself in Scripture.

And the *mission* of preaching is worship, and the *matter* of preaching is the manifold glories of God revealed in Scripture. Now what about the *manner* of the preaching? I have agreed with James Stewart that preaching not only aims at worship but is worship. Therefore I have defined it as expository exultation. Preaching should not only awaken a satisfying sense of God's glory in the people; it should also exhibit a satisfying sense of God's glory in the preacher. It exposits the perfections of God, and it exults in those perfections in the process.

It is for this reason that the preacher does not need the music of piano or guitar or synthesizer to make his God-exalting sermon palatable, the way contemporary worship songs are assisted by the music to draw people into their God-exalting lyrics. The preacher does not need to forsake the centrality of God, nor does he need the support of any music but the music of his own soul. When the preacher's own soul exults and sings and worships over the truth that he preaches he makes his own music, and the hearts of the people are engaged with the value of his God.

I will try now to root these points more deeply in Scripture. I would like to focus first on Philippians 1:18–21. Paul writes from imprisonment in Rome. Those who don't like him are gloating over the fact that they are free to preach and he is not. Paul is not discouraged by this but says,

> What then? Only that in every way, whether in pretense or in truth, Christ is proclaimed; and in this I rejoice, yes, and I will rejoice. For I know that this shall turn out for my deliverance through your prayers and the provision of the

Spirit of Jesus Christ, according to my earnest expectation and hope *that I shall not be put to shame in anything,* but that with all boldness, *Christ shall even now, as always, be exalted in my body, whether by life or by death.*

Notice what Paul's mission is: above life and death his mission is to magnify Christ, to show that Christ is magnificent, to exalt Christ and demonstrate that He is great—"that Christ shall be exalted in my body, whether by life or death." Now comes a tremendously important verse to explain how it is that Christ could be exalted in life and death. Notice the reference to "life" and "death" in verse 20 and then the link up with the words "live" and "die" in verse 21: "For to me, to live is Christ, and to die is gain." What I want you to see here is the connection between magnifying Christ and treasuring Christ. What this text teaches is that if you want to exalt and magnify Christ (for example, in your preaching), then you have to treasure Christ above all things. If Christ is to be proclaimed for the praise of our people, He must be preached as the prize of the preacher. We can't declare Him worthy of praise if we don't delight in Him as our prize. Paul makes this explicit in the connection between verses 20 and 21. In verse 20 he says that his expectation and hope is to magnify, exalt, glorify Christ in life or death. Then in verse 21 he shows how Christ can be magnified in life or death. He says, "For to me to live is Christ and to die is gain." So the way that Christ is magnified in death is to experience death as gain. And the reason death is gain is given in verse 23: "My desire is to depart [i.e., die] and be with Christ." Death takes us into more intimacy with Christ. Therefore death is gain. And when you experience death this way, you show that Christ is a greater treasure to you than anything on earth. And that is magnifying Christ.

The key to praising is prizing.

If you want to glorify Christ in your dying, you must experience death as gain—which means Christ must be gain to you. He must be your prize, your treasure, your joy. He must be a satisfaction so deep that when death takes away everything you love, but gives you more of Christ, you feel it as gain. It's the same with life. We magnify Christ in life, Paul says, by experiencing Christ in life as our all-surpassing treasure. That's what he means in verse 21 when he says "For me to live is Christ." We know this because of Philippians 3:8, where Paul says, "I count all things to be loss in view of the surpassing value of knowing Christ Jesus my Lord, for whom I have suffered the loss of all things, and count them but rubbish in order that I may gain Christ."

So "to die is gain" because it means greater intimacy with Christ—He is our treasure and what we long for more than anything. And "to live is Christ" because living means counting everything as loss for the sake of gaining Christ. The common denominator between living and dying is that Christ is the all-satisfying treasure that we embrace. And this truth in verse 21 is given as the explanation and ground of verse 20 (see the "for" in v. 21), namely, that for this reason Paul knows that Christ will be exalted, magnified, praised in his living and in his dying.

Christ is praised by being prized. He is magnified as a glorious treasure when He becomes our unrivaled pleasure. Christ is most glorified in us when we are most satisfied in Him. This is the biblical foundation for that all-important sentence.[5] This is the music the preacher must make. The preacher's song is this: Christ is my treasure in life; Christ is my gain in death; Christ is the all-satisfying fountain of my hope and peace and joy; I count everything as loss for the surpassing worth of knowing Christ Jesus my Lord. And when the thread of that song is woven through the fabric of all your God-exalting sermons, it will awaken and engage the hearts of your people more deeply than all the best tunes of contemporary worship songs put together. If you would draw them into praising Christ, they must see you prizing Christ.

This is why the ministry of preaching, with all its pain and pressure, is a great and happy work. James W. Alexander gets it exactly right when he says in his *Thoughts on Preaching*, "There is happiness in preaching. . . . The declaration of what one believes, and the praise of what one loves, always give delight: and what but this is the minister's work?"[6] Preaching is the declaration of what one believes, in a way that praises what one loves. It is expository exultation.

About a year ago I began to spend a good bit of time with John Owen, the seventeenth-century pastor whom J. I. Packer calls "the greatest among the Puritan theologians." And I found in him a magnificent model of what I am trying to get across in this final message.

Owen warned against the danger of preaching without penetrating into the things we say and making them real to our own souls. Over the years words begin to come easy for preachers, and we find we can speak of mysteries without standing in awe; we can speak of purity without feeling pure; we can speak of zeal without spiritual passion; of God's holiness without trembling; of sin without sorrow; of heaven without eagerness. And the result is a terrible deadening of the spiritual life and depletion of preaching power. Words came easy for Owen, but he set himself against this terrible disease of inauthenticity by laboring to experience every truth he preached. In my words, he aimed not just at exposition but at exultation. He said,

> I hold myself bound in conscience and in honor, not even to imagine that I have attained a proper knowledge of any one article of truth, much less to publish [i.e., preach] it, unless through the Holy Spirit I have had such a taste of it, in its spiritual sense, that I may be able, from the heart, to say with the psalmist, "I have believed, and therefore I have spoken." (*Works,* 10:488)

So, for example, his *Exposition of Psalm 130* (320 pages on eight verses) is the laying open not only of the psalm, but of his own heart. One of his biographers, Andrew Thomson, says,

> When Owen . . . laid open the book of God, he laid open at the same time the book of his own heart and of his own history. . . . [It] is rich in golden thoughts, and instinct with the living experience of "one who spake what he knew, and testified what he had seen." (*Works,* 1:lxxxiv)

The conviction that controlled Owen was this:

> A man preacheth that sermon only well unto others which preacheth itself in his

own soul. And he that doth not feed on and thrive in the digestion of the food which he provides for others will scarce make it savoury unto them; yea, he knows not but the food he hath provided may be poison, unless he have really tasted of it himself. If the word do not dwell with power *in* us, it will not pass with power *from* us. (*Works*, 16:76)

Owen's life was full of controversy and upheaval. He was an incredibly busy and embattled man. Richard Baxter called him "the great doer." What kept him steady in the battle was this commitment first to experience the reality of God and then preach it. Here is the way he put it in the Preface to *The Mystery of the Gospel Vindicated* (1655):

When the heart is cast indeed into the mould of the doctrine that the mind embraceth,—when the evidence and necessity of the truth abides in us,—when not the sense of the words only is in our heads, but the sense of the thing abides in our hearts—when we have communion with God in the doctrine we contend for—then shall we be garrisoned by the grace of God against all the assaults of men. (*Works*, 1:lxiii-lxiv)

There's the key: living, heartfelt "communion with God in the doctrine we contend for"—exultation in God through our exposition of God.

At the end of his life in 1683 at the age of seventy-seven, as a kind of fugitive pastor in London, Owen was working on a book called *Meditations on the Glory of Christ*. It was the last thing he chose to think about. His friend William Payne was helping him edit the work. Near the end Owen said, "O, brother Payne, the long-wished for day is come at last, in which I shall see the glory in another manner than I have ever done or was capable of doing in this world."[7] In other words, "to die is gain!" But Owen saw more glory in this world than most of us see, and that is why he was known for his holiness, and that's why, even three hundred years later, his preaching has a God-exalting power that most contemporary preaching does not even aspire to. He saw and experienced the glory of Christ before he preached it. So his preaching was real and powerful because its mission was worship, its matter was the glory of Christ, and its manner was exultation.

I could well add one more topic to this discussion. I have talked about the mission of preaching—awakening in the people a heartfelt satisfaction in all that God is for us in Christ; the matter of preaching—proclaiming the all-satisfying glories of God; and the manner of preaching—exhibiting that very satisfaction in God by exulting over what we preach. But I could go on and speak also about the means of preaching—how do you become that kind of preacher and sustain a heartfelt exultation in the great things of God?

But I content myself with an outline of what I would want to say.

1. You must be born again.

"Unless one is born again, he cannot see the kingdom of God" (John 3:3). I do not doubt that there are preachers who have no life in the pulpit because there is no life in the soul. The natural person cannot receive, let alone exult in, the things of the Spirit. If you do not delight in the things of God, search your heart to see if you are born of God.

2. Turn off the television.

It is not necessary for relevance. And it is a deadly place to rest the mind. Its pervasive banality, sexual innuendo, and God-ignoring values have no ennobling effects on the preacher's soul. It kills the spirit. It drives God away. It quenches prayer. It blanks out the Bible. It cheapens the soul. It destroys spiritual power. It defiles almost everything. I have taught and preached for twenty years now and never owned a television. It is unnecessary for most of you, and it is spiritually deadly for all of you.

3. Meditate on the Word of God day and night.

Paul said, "Do not get drunk with wine . . . but be filled with the Spirit" (Eph. 5:18). How do you get filled with the Spirit? The same way you get drunk with wine: you drink a lot of it. And Paul is pretty clear about how we drink the Spirit. In 1 Corinthians 2:14 it is by welcoming the things of the Spirit of God; and in Romans 8:5 it is by setting the mind on the things of the Spirit. And in both cases the "things of the Spirit" refers mainly to the words taught by the Spirit (1 Cor. 2:13). This means simply that if you want to be filled with the Spirit of passion and exultation over the great things of God, you must fill your mind day and night with the Word of God. Pore over it. Memorize it. Chew it. Put it like a lozenge under the tongue of your soul and let it flavor your affections day and night.

4. Plead with God unceasingly for passions that match his reality.

When you meditate on a passage of Scripture ask yourself this question: Am I experiencing affections in my heart that accord with the reality revealed in the text? Is my exposition creating in my own heart a corresponding exultation? And if not, then repent for your hardheartedness and plead with God for your heart to be stirred with emotions as terrible as hell and as wonderful as heaven.

John Stott said,

> I have always found it helpful to do as much of my sermon preparation as possible on my knees, with the Bible open before me, in prayerful study. This is not because I am a bibliolater and worship the Bible; but because I worship the God of the Bible and desire . . . to pray earnestly that the eyes of my heart may be enlightened.[8]

5. Linger in the presence of God-besotted saints.

Hebrews 13:7 says, "Remember those who led you, who spoke the Word of God to you; and considering the result of their conduct, imitate their faith." It is a biblical value to have God-besotted heroes. I fear that many contemporary pastors read more Barna and Shaller and Drucker than they do Owen and Edwards and Spurgeon (to name my heroes).

Judge for yourselves: what writers are so saturated with God that you come away with your mind rich and your heart exulting? Find your God-besotted heroes and live with them.

6. Finally, leave your study, go to a hard place, take a risk for the kingdom, and prove to your own soul that you treasure the promises of God more than the pleasures of this world.

". . . like a treasure hidden in a field, which a man finds and from joy over it sells everything he has to buy that field."

ENDNOTES

Chapter 1

1. William Lawrence, "The Relation of Wealth to Morals," *Christian Social Teachings*, Ed. G. W. Forell (Garden City, N.Y.: Doubleday, 1966), 331.
2. Bruce Barron, *The Health and Wealth Gospel* (Downers Grove, Ill.: InterVarsity, 1987), 9.
3. Letter from Kenneth Hagin, Jr., Executive Vice-President of the Kenneth Hagin Ministries, Tulsa, Oklahoma, August 19, 1988.
4. Kenneth Copeland, *Welcome to the Family* (Fort Worth: KCP Publications, 1979), 22.
5. Fred Price, *Is Healing for All?* (Tulsa: Harrison House, 1976), 113.
6. See Barron, *Gospel,* chap. 2, for a detailed account of the Hobart Freeman story. The Indiana-based preacher died in December of 1984 of bronchopneumonia and heart failure for which he received no medical treatment.
7. Kenneth Copeland, *You Are Healed* (Fort Worth: KCP Publications, 1979), 7.
8. Jerry Savelle, *God's Provision for Healing* (Tulsa: Harrison House, 1981), 8.
9. Elbert Willis, *God's Plan for Financial Prosperity* (Lafayette, La.: Fill the Gap Publications, n.d.), 15.
10. Fred Price, *Faith, Foolishness or Presumption?* (Tulsa: Harrison House, 1979), 34.
11. Kenneth Hagin, "The Law of Faith," *Word of Faith* (November, 1974), 2.
12. Gordon Lindsay, *God's Master Key to Success and Prosperity* (Dallas: Voice of Healing, 1959), 46.
13. Kenneth Copeland, *The Laws of Prosperity* (Fort Worth: KCP Publications, 1974), 67.
14. Kenneth Hagin, Jr., "Victory Words for Front-Line Battles," *The Word of Faith* (November, 1980), 7.
15. Noted in Barron, *Gospel,* 97.
16. Jerry Savelle, *Living in Divine Prosperity* (Tulsa: Harrison House, 1982), 77.
17. Kenneth Hagin, *You Can Have What You Say!* (Tulsa: Kenneth Hagin Ministries, 1979), 6.
18. Hagin, *Exceedingly Growing Faith* (Tulsa: Kenneth Hagin Ministries, 1983), 76.
19. Copeland, *Our Covenant with God* (Fort Worth: KCP Publications, 1976), 32.
20. Charles Capps, *The Tongue: A Creative Force* (Tulsa: Harrison House, 1976), 24.
21. D. L. McConnell, *A Different Gospel: A Historical and Biblical Analysis of the Modern Faith Movement* (Peabody, Mass.: Hendrickson, 1988), 3. McConnell gives an in-depth overview of Hagin's life and ministry. Much of the following material on Hagin and the other faith teachers is drawn from McConnell and Barron, *Gospel,* unless otherwise noted.
22. David Harrell, *All Things Are Possible: The Healing and Charismatic Revivals in Modern America* (Bloomington: Indiana University Press, 1975), 185–86.

23. Quoted from a publicity pamphlet, "Kenneth Copeland Ministries: Living to Give."
24. McConnell, *Different Gospel*, 4.
25. Noted in a public-relations resume, "Dr. Jerry Savelle," sent to me by his ministries headquarters.
26. Quoted in McConnell, *Different Gospel*, 4, from his taped correspondence with Price.
27. Quoted in Harrell, *All Things Are Possible*, 235. For a brief overview of Rev. Ike see David Broersma, "A Definition and Analysis of Prosperity Theology," (M.Th. thesis; Dallas Theological Seminary, 1985), 39.
28. Harrell, *All Things Are Possible*, 4.
29. Ibid., 229.
30. A. A. Allen, *Power to Get Wealth* (Miracle Valley, Ariz.: A. A. Allen Revivals, 1963), i–ii.
31. David Harrell, *Oral Roberts: An American Life* (Bloomington, Ind.: Indiana University Press, 1985), 66.
32. See Harrell, *All Things Are Possible*, 108–9.
33. Barron, *Gospel*, 11.
34. For description of this and surrounding events see Harrell, *Oral Roberts*, 423–27.
35. Rodney Clapp, "Faith Healing: A Look at What's Happening," *Christianity Today* (December 16, 1983), 13.
36. McConnell, *Different Gospel*, 19.
37. Ibid., 39.
38. Ibid., 49.
39. E. W. Kenyon, *The Hidden Man: An Unveiling of the Subconscious Mind* (Seattle: Kenyon's Gospel Publication Society, 1970), 98.
40. Ibid., 99.
41. See, for example, the preface of Hagin's *The Name of Jesus* (1979), in which he shows his indebtedness to Kenyon's *The Wonderful Name of Jesus* and even calls it revelation knowledge.
42. McConnell, *Different Gospel*, 8–12.
43. From a taped phone conversation McConnell had with Houseworth, in McConnell, *Different Gospel*, 5.
44. Quoted in McConnell, *Different Gospel*, 5, from an unpublished statement by Kennington.
45. Gary Schwartz, *Sect Ideologies and Social Status* (Chicago: University of Chicago Press, 1970), 40–41.
46. Hagin, *New Thresholds of Faith* (Tulsa: Faith Library, 1980), 54–55.
47. R. O. Corvin, "Pentecost in Three Dimensions," *World Pentecost* (first issue, 1971), 12.
48. Quoted in "A Nation of Healthy Worrywarts?" *Time* (July 25, 1988), 66.
49. Quoted in David M. Potter, *People of Plenty: Economic Abundance and the American Character* (Chicago: University of Chicago Press, 1954), 78.
50. Ibid., 141.
51. Robert N. Bellah et al., *Habits of the Heart: Individualism and Commitment in American Life* (New York: Harper & Row, 1985), 22.
52. Ibid., 221.
53. Barron, *Gospel*, 139.
54. Harold Woodson preaching in Cincinnati, Ohio, July 7, 1972. Quoted in Harrell, *All Things Are Possible*, 229.

Chapter 2

1. Richard Quebedeaux, *The Worldly Evangelicals: Has Success Spoiled America's Born Again Christians?* (San Francisco: Harper and Row, 1977).
2. For some of the key bibliography, see Kenneth E. Hagin, *How to Turn Your Faith Loose* (Tulsa: Faith Library, 1983); Gloria Copeland, *God's Will Is Prosperity* (Tulsa: Harrison House, 1978); Kenneth Copeland, *The Laws of Prosperity* (Fort Worth: KCP Publications, 1974); Charles Capps, *The Tongue—A Creative Force* (Tulsa: Harrison House, 1976); Kenneth E. Hagin, *Redeemed From Poverty, Sickness, and Death* (Tulsa: Faith Library, 1983); Charles Hunter, *God's Condition for Prosperity* (Kingwood, Tex · Hunter, 1984); Jerry Savelle, "True Prosperity—What Is It?" *Christian Life* 45 (1983–84): 47, 49.
3. Robert Schuller, *Self-Esteem: The New Reformation* (Waco, Tex.: Word, 1982), 14.
4. Walter C. Kaiser, Jr., "Holiness in Motive and Heart," in *Toward Old Testament Ethics* (Grand Rapids: Zondervan, 1983), 235–44.
5. Berend Gemser, "The Importance of the Motive Clause in Old Testament Law," *VT Sup* 1 (1953): 50–66; reprinted in *Adhuc Loquitur: Collected Essays by B. Gemser,* ed. A. van Selms and A. S. van der Woude, Pretoria Orientalia Series, 7 (Leiden: Brill, 1968), 96–115. See also Rifat Sonsino, *Motive Clauses in Hebrew Law: Biblical Forms and Near Eastern Parallels* (Chico, Calif.: Scholars, 1980), 65; and R. W. Uitti, "The Motive Cause in Old Testament Law" (Dissertation, Chicago Lutheran School of Theology, 1973), 6–8; and Henry John Postel, 'The Form and Function of the Motive Cause in Proverbs 10–29" (Dissertation, University of Iowa, 1976), 22.
6. For a fuller discussion and complete bibliography, see Kaiser, *Toward Old Testament Ethics,* 7–10, 243–44.
7. R. N. Gordon, "Motivation in Proverbs," *Biblical Theology* 25 (1975): 49–56.
8. Kenneth E. Hagin, *How to Write Your Own Ticket with God* (Tulsa: Rhema Bible Church, 1979), 8.
9. Kenneth E. Hagin, *Understanding Our Confession* (Tulsa: Rhema Bible (Church, n.d.), 10. See the critique of Hagin in D. R. McConnell, *A Different Gospel: A Historical and Biblical Analysis of the Modern Faith Movement* (Peabody, Mass.: Hendrickson, 1988), 58–99.
10. Sid Roth, *Why God?* (Bethesda, Md.: Messianic Vision, 1984), 3. The above three references were called to my attention by Jim Kennebrew, "The Gospel of Affluence," *Mid-America Theological Journal* 9 (1985): 49–68.
11. Edmond Jacob, *Theology of the Old Testament* (New York: Harper, 1958), 127.
12. These similes are quoted in the article, which has been most helpful to me in responding to the charge in this section: Anthony C. Thiselton, "The Supposed Power of Words in Biblical Writings," 25 (1974), 283–99. Thiselton refers to Walther Eichrodt, *Theology of the Old Testament,* 2 vols. (Philadelphia: Westminster, 1967), 2:69. Similar statements are quoted from Walther Zimmerli, Gerhard von Rad, G. A. F. Knight, and Otto Procksch.
13. Thiselton, "Supposed Power," 283–84; especially nn. 1–8 on p. 283.
14. Thiselton, "Supposed Power," 289–99. Notice that the same argument for the power of the spoken word appears in Gary Smalley and John Trent, *The Blessing* (Nashville: Thomas Nelson, 1986), 49–64.
15. Robert Sabath, "The Bible and the Poor," *Post-American* (February/March, 1974): 5. Contrast H. G. M. Williamson, "The Old Testament and the Material World," *EvQ* 57 (1985): 5–22.

16. For more discussion on this topic, see Reginald H. Fuller, "The Old Testament Background [of Wealth in the Bible]," *Christianity and the Affluent Society,* Reginald H. Fuller and Brian K. Rice (Grand Rapids: Eerdmans, 1966), 11–22; John Jefferson Davis, *Your Wealth in God's World* (Phillipsburg, N.J.: Presbyterian and Reformed, 1984), 12–25.
17. See the perceptive insights of Dennis W. Roberts, "Christian Prosperity: Is It Really God's Will for You?" *Logos Journal* 10 (1980): 42–46. Also, Gordon A. Chutter, "'Riches and Poverty' in the Book of Proverbs," *Crux* 18 (1982): 23–28.
18. G. W. Wittenberg, "The Situational Context of Statements Concerning Poverty and Wealth in the Book of Proverbs," *Scriptura* 21 (1987): 1–23. Also G. W. Wittenberg, "The Message of the Old Testament Prophets During the Eighth Century BC Concerning Affluence and Poverty," in *Affluence and Poverty and the Word of God,* ed. K. Nurnberger (Durban: Lutheran Publishing House, 1978), 141–52.
19. Milton S. Terry, *Biblical Hermeneutics* (Grand Rapids: Zondervan, n.d.), 223.
20. David Harrell, *All Things Are Possible: The Healing and Charismatic Revivals in Modern America* (Bloomington, Ind.: Indiana University Press, 1975), 229.
21. McConnell, *A Different Gospel,* 3–56.
22. Ibid., 171.
23. Ralph Waldo Trine, *In Tune With the Infinite* (New York: Bobbs-Merrill Co., 1970), 138.
24. McConnell, *A Different Gospel,* 173–74 (italics his).
25. Chutter, "Riches and Poverty," 23–24.
26. Davis, "Poverty, Justice, Compassion, and Personal Responsibility," in *Your Wealth,* 26–37.
27. Kenneth S. Kantzer, "The Cut-rate Grace of a Health and Wealth Gospel," *Christianity Today* (June 14, 1985): 14–15. Cf., however, Kenneth E. Hagin, *Redeemed From Poverty, Sickness, and Death,* 2d ed. (Tulsa: Rhema Bible Church, 1983), 11–23. Note also the discussion of Gerhard F. Hasel, "Health and Healing in the OT," *Andrews University Seminary Studies* 21 (1983): 191–202.

Chapter 3

1. A more thorough discussion of the context and references to the secondary literature are contained in my *Hostility to Wealth in the Synoptic Gospels* (Sheffield: JSOT, 1987). Limitation of space requires that I pass over such interesting points as the relation of chap. 6 to the Lord's Prayer and the economic connotations of vv. 22–23.
2. Interestingly, the same introduction occurs in Luke, but following the parable of the rich fool, which ends, "So is he who lays up treasure for himself, and is not rich toward God" (Luke 12:21). Thus the Trust or Anxiety teaching in Luke is grounded in a virtually identical command, but the actual texts employed by Matthew occur elsewhere: 6:19–21 = Luke 12:33–34; 6:22–23 = Luke 11:34–36; 6:24 = Luke 16:13.
3. Significantly, this is the form in Luke 12:29.
4. μεριμνάω is employed with negative connotations in 1 Cor. 7:32–34; 12:25; Phil. 2:20; 4:6; LXX Isa. 57:11; Jer. 17:8; 42:16; Ezek. 12:18; Sir. 30:24–31:2; 42:9.
5. Matt. 7:7–8 is especially important as the most proximal reference (where ζητέω denotes prayer).
6. See also Prov. 12:25; Jer. 17:8; Ezek. 4:16 for ראג as anxiety over possessions.

Commentators have overlooked this connection because the LXX only once translates ראה as μεριμνάω (Ps. 37:18).

7. For the latter reference and for stimulation of my thought in this direction I am indebted to Mr. David Harbeson, an insightful undergraduate student. I hope to develop further the relation between the wilderness wanderings, the Sabbath year legislation, and the radical demands of Jesus. Were these demands understood as *illustrative* rather than *normative* with respect to the kingdom by Jesus' audiences?
8. LXX Ex. 5:9; Prov. 14:23; Bar. 3:18.
9. For J. Jeremias (*The Parables of the Kingdom,* 2d ed. [New York; Scribner, 1972], 214–15), this is the compelling argument for an active connotation.
10. See, e.g., Pss. 9:8; 72:2; Isa. 16:5; 51:5; 62:1.
11. Contra R. H. Gundry, *Matthew: A Commentary on His Literary and Theological Art* (Grand Rapids: Eerdmans, 1982), 106–7. Gundry builds a strong argument for "realized eschatology" in this petition. If he is correct, the apparent allusion to the Lord's Prayer in 6:33 must be coincidental.
12. R. Guelich, *The Sermon on the Mount* (Waco, Tex.: Word, 1982), 346 (cf. 84–87). Guelich lists the scholars who take sides on this question. He does not think that Matthew would shift from conduct to vindication in using the word, and he opts for a consistent "conduct" connotation. He also draws into the discussion the ethical focus of reference to God's will (7:21; 12:50; 21:31; 26:42; cf. 6:10 and its relation to 6:33).
13. Ibid., 341–42.
14. Gundry, *Matthew,* 118.
15. Jeremias, *Parables,* 196; I. H. Marshall, *The Gospel of Luke,* NIGTC (Grand Rapids: Eerdmans, 1978), 591; J. Fitzmyer, *The Gospel According to Luke X–XXIV,* AB (Garden City, N.Y.: Doubleday, 1985), 1062.
16. A. Jülicher, *Die Gleichnisreden Jesu,* 2 vols. (Tübingen: Mohr, 1910), 2:208.
17. J. Wellhausen, *Das Evangelium Lucae* (Berlin: Reimer, 1904), 80.
18. Mark 10:21 and parallels; Luke 12:33; 19:8; cf. Matt. 5:42; 13:44–46; Luke 6:30.
19. Mark 1:16–20; 2:14; 10:28 and parallels.
20. Mark 6:46; Luke 9:61; Acts 18:18, 21; 2 Cor. 2:13.
21. See also Philo, *Leg. All.* 2.25, 3.41, 238; *Sobr.,* 51; *Mig.,* 92; *Leg.,* 325; Josephus, *Ant.* 8.354, 11.232, 11.344; LXX Eccl. 2:20.
22. Marshall, *Luke,* 594.
23. N. Geldenhuys, *Commentary on the Gospel of Luke,* NICNT (Grand Rapids: Eerdmans, 1951), 399.
24. G. Delling, "τάσσω, κτλ." *TDNT* 8:33 n. 3.
25. E.g., 4:28–30; 11:53–54; 13:17; 20:19, 26, 39–40. 19:9–10 is similar in that it includes Jesus' comment on the reaction of the audience.
26. See Schmidt, *Hostility,* esp. 84–90.
27. So, e.g., T. W. Manson, *The Sayings of Jesus* (London: SCM, 1937); Marshall, *Luke* 682; Fitzmyer, *Luke,* 1113.
28. Cf., e.g., Deut. 7:25–26; 1 Kings 14:24; Ezra 9:11; Isa. 44:19; see also Mark 13:14; Matt. 24:15; Rom. 2:22.

Chapter 4

1. Brief surveys of this history are found in Paul G. Chappell, "The Birth of the Divine Healing Movement in America," *Healing in the Name of God,* ed. Pieter G. R. de Villiers (Pretoria, South Africa: C. B. Powell Bible Centre, 1986), 60–78; and in Bruce Barron, *The Health and Wealth Gospel* (Downers Grove: InterVarsity, 1987), 35–60.

2. See, e.g., Ken Blue, *Authority to Heal* (Downers Grove: InterVarsity, 1987).
3. Ibid., 37–38.
4. Barron claims that the teaching of "positive confession" is the third key belief—after "health" and "wealth"—of the HWG (*Health and Wealth Gospel*, 71–73).
5. See, e.g., Edwin Howard Cobb, *Christ Healing* (London: Marshall, Morgan & Scott, 1933), 1–7.
6. Despite recent arguments to the contrary, the textual evidence is decisively against the inclusion of 16:9–20 in the original text of Mark's gospel.
7. E.g., Leon Morris, *The Gospel According to John*, NICNT (Grand Rapids: Eerdmans, 1971), 645–46; C. K. Barrett, *The Gospel According to St. John*, 2d ed. (Philadelphia: Westminster, 1978), 460.
8. E.g., Calvin, *Institutes* 4.19.18.
9. London: Banner of Truth, 1972 (=1918).
10. Cf. Richard Mayhue, *Divine Healing Today* (Chicago: Moody, 1983), 77–79.
11. Warfield, *Counterfeit Miracles*, 193.
12. Ibid., 169–73.
13. "Healing As an Integral Part of Salvation," *Healing in the Name of God*, 92.
14. Cf. D. A. Carson, *Divine Sovereignty and Human Responsibility* (Atlanta: John Knox, 1981), 201–22 for some suggestions toward a biblically balanced statement of the issue.
15. E.g., Blue, *Authority to Heal*, 21–40.
16. Murray J. Harris, "2 Corinthians," in *The Expositor's Bible Commentary*, vol. 10, ed. Frank E. Gaebelein (Grand Rapids: Zondervan, 1976), 322.
17. E.g., R. V. G. Tasker, *The Second Epistle of Paul to the Corinthians*, TNTC (Grand Rapids: Eerdmans, 1958), 173–77.
18. Victor Paul Furnish, *II Corinthians*, AnBib (Garden City, N.Y.: Doubleday, 1984), 548–50.
19. Harris, "2 Corinthians," 396.
20. J. Wilkinson provides a full discussion of the medical alternatives; he leans toward malaria (*Health and Healing: Studies in New Testament Principles Practices* [Edinburgh: Handsel, 1980], 112–42).
21. Some divine healing advocates appear to think that Peter is speaking here of physical healing, but this is manifestly not the case.
22. Cobb, *Christ Healing*, 23; T. L. Osborn, *Healing the Sick* (Tulsa: T. L. Osborn Evangelistic Association, 1961), 27–28.
23. Alan Hugh McNeile, *The Gospel According to St. Matthew* (London: Macmillan, 1928), 107–8.
24. See, e.g., D. A. Carson, "Matthew," in *Expositor's Bible Commentary*, vol. 8, ed. Frank E. Gaebelein (Grand Rapids: Zondervan, 1984), 205–7.
25. Warfield, *Counterfeit Miracles*, 175–76.
26. "Petitionary Prayer: A Problem Without an Answer," most conveniently found in *Christian Reflections* (Grand Rapids: Eerdmans, 1967), 142–51.
27. Cf. Barron, *Health and Wealth Gospel*, 107–8.
28. E.g., M. Meinertz, "Die Krankensalbung Jak. 5,14f," *BibZeit* 20 (1932), 23–36; C. Amerding," Is any among you afflicted? A Study of James 5:13–20," *Bibliotheca Sacra* 95 (1938): 195–201; D. R. Hayden, "Calling the Elder to Pray," *Bibliotheca Sacra* 138 (1981): 258–86.
29. The Roman Catholic sacrament of extreme unction is based on this view.
30. Cf. Barron, *Health and Wealth Gospel*, 83–86.
31. For substantiation and more detail, see Douglas J. Moo, *The Letter of James*, TNTC (Grand Rapids: Eerdmans, 1985), 177–81.
32. *The Miracles of Jesus*, NovTSup 9 (Leiden: Briil, 1965), 263.

33. Again, see Moo, *James,* 183–87 for more detail.
34. Barron, *Health and Wealth Gospel,* 83.
35. See the surveys in Johann Engelbrecht, "'The Blind can see, the lame can walk, the deaf hear . . .': Miracle Workers and their Miracles in the New Testament," *Healing in the Name of God,* 40; König, "Healing," *Healing in the Name of God,* 91.
36. Henry Lederle, "Models of Old Testament Healing: A Denominational Charismatic Perspective," *Healing in the Name of God,* 131.
37. Two other texts are sometimes cited by the HWG in support of this universal promise, but neither is applicable. Third John 2—"I pray that all may go well with you and that you may be in health" (ὑγιαίνειν)—is not a promise from God, but a prayer, or "wish," of John. And Romans 8:11—"the Spirit . . . will give life to your mortal bodies"—plainly refers to eschatological transformation, not to physical well-being in this life.

Chapter 5

1. *The Wall Street Journal,* Thursday, August 23, 1984, 5–6.
2. Robert W. Glasgow, "The Obsessive Concern with Self," an interview with Robert Nisbet, *Psychology Today* (December 1973), 43ff.
3. Allan Bloom, *The Closing of the American Mind* (New York: Simon and Shuster, 1987), 173.
4. Eugene H. Peterson, *Earth and Altar: The Community of Prayer in a Self-Bound Society* (Downers Grove: InterVarsity, 1985), 13.
5. Ibid., 65.
6. Amitai Etzioni, *An Immodest Agenda: Rebuilding America Before the Twenty-First Century* (New York: McGraw-Hill, 1982).
7. *World Press Review,* January 1987, 49.
8. "Changing Values of Young People," *Minneapolis Star and Tribune,* February 8, 1988.
9. James Davison Hunter, *Evangelicalism: The Coming Generation* (Chicago: University of Chicago Press, 1987).

Chapter 6

1. By "truth-claim" I mean any explicit or implicit claim to truth; that is, any statement that explicitly or implicitly affirms that a particular state of affairs obtains. Thus, "Today is Friday," "My wife loves me," "There is no God but Allah and Muhammed is his prophet," whatever else they may be, are examples of truth-claims.
2. We should note that the exclusivist view, as defined here, does not entail that if the claims of one religion are true then all of the claims of the other religions must be false. It simply maintains that if there are two or more incompatible beliefs advanced by various religions they cannot all be true.
3. Arthur Glasser, "A Paradigm Shift? Evangelicals and Inter-religious Dialogue," in *Contemporary Theologies of Mission,* ed. A. Glasser and D. McGavran (Grand Rapids: Baker, 1983), 210.
4. It is, of course, quite a separate (and enormously complex) question as to how we are to determine whether they are true or false.
5. On this point see the comments of Paul Griffiths and Delmas Lewis in "On Grading Religions, Seeking Truth, and Being Nice to People—A Reply to Professor Nick," in *RelS* 19 (1983): 77.
6. W. Cantwell Smith, *Questions of Religious Truth* (London: V. Gollancz, 1937), 73.

7. W. Cantwell Smith, *The Meaning and End of Religion* (New York: Harper and Row, 1962, 1978), 322 n. 14.
8. W. Cantwell Smith, *Questions,* 67–68.
9. Strictly speaking, truth is a property or quality of propositions such that a proposition is true if and only if the state of affairs to which it refers obtains; otherwise it is false. But there is an extended sense in which we can also think of religions as true or false. Let us think of a "defining belief" of a religion as a belief that one must accept if one is to be an active participant in good standing within that particular religion. It seems clear that each religious tradition has a set of defining beliefs (there may, of course, be considerable dispute over just what is to be included in this set). We can speak of a religion R as true if its defining beliefs are all true, and conversely, R can be said to be false if its defining beliefs are all false. And in the case of mixed truth value among defining beliefs, R will be true to the extent that its defining beliefs are true and false to the extent that its defining beliefs are false.
10. W. Cantwell Smith, *Faith and Belief* (Princeton, N.J.: Princeton University Press, 1979), 142.
11. An incisive critique of Cantwell Smith's suggestion that the concept of "a religion" is confused is found in Ninian Smart, "Truth and Religions" in *Truth and Dialogue in World Religions: Conflicting Truth-Claims,* ed. John Hick (Philadelphia: Westminster, 1974), 45–47. See also J. Nick, "The Outcome: Dialogue into Truth," 143–48, in the same volume.
12. Most philosophers make an important distinction between statements or sentences and propositions. A proposition is the meaning expressed by a declarative sentence. As such, propositions are translinguistic: the same proposition can be expressed in a variety of sentences in a variety of languages. All propositions are either true or false. A helpful introductory discussion can be found in S. Gorovitz et al., *Philosophical Analysis: An Introduction to Its Language and Techniques,* 3d ed. (New York: Random House, 1979), 85–98. For the relation between propositions and truth see Roderick Chisholm, *Theory of Knowledge,* 2d ed. (Englewood Cliffs, N.J.: Prentice-Hall, 1977), 87–89.
13. W. Cantwell Smith, "A Human View of Truth," in *Truth and Dialogue in World Religions,* 20, 29, 31. See also his *Faith and Belief,* 150–58, 333 n. 12, for an attack upon the notion of propositional truth.
14. "A Human View of Truth," 20, 26.
15. Ibid., 26.
16. Ibid., 37.
17. Ibid., 35.
18. *Questions of Religious Truth,* 68.
19. He seems ambivalent on the question whether propositional truth has any place in religion. On the one hand, he repeatedly emphasizes that religious truth is not propositional and that the "impersonal, amoral" notion of propositional truth is responsible for many of the ills in western society (see "A Human View of Truth," 26, 29, 30–31). And yet elsewhere he seems to allow for a limited role for propositional truth in religion:
    Perhaps a sober position might be that truth or falsity in this realm is a function not of propositions only but of it and the person who makes it, but that there is perhaps a range of types of proposition, with the personalist element being lowest (or merely: most universal?) when the proposition refers to natural science matters, higher when it refers to social science matters, very high in various special cases, and highest in the religious realm [ibid., 40–41 n. 5].

It seems clear, however, that in some sense priority is to be given the notion of personalistic truth; propositional truth, if applicable in religion at all, seems to be very much in a subordinate position. "The important matter in the life of any religious community is what their religious tradition does to them" (*The Meaning and End of Religion*, 136).

20. For a helpful introductory discussion of the relation between propositions and belief see W. V. O. Quine and J. S. Ullian, *The Web of Belief*, 2d ed. (New York: Random House, 1978), 9–19; and R. Chisholm, *Theory of Knowledge*, 5–15.

21. Three levels of such conflict among truth-claims are distinguished. First, there are differences in claims about certain historical facts that carry significant theological implications: Did Jesus have a human father or not? Did Jesus actually die on the cross or did He just appear to die? Second, there are what can be called "quasihistorical" or "transhistorical" differences in claims, of which the acceptance or rejection of the doctrine of reincarnation is given as a prime example. However, the most significant differences are on the third level, for it is here that we encounter ". . . differences in the ways of conceiving and experiencing, and hence also of responding to, the divine Reality" (John Hick, "On Conflicting Religious Truth-Claims," *RelS* 19 [1983]: 487). The major difference here is between those who conceive of the divine as personal and those who regard it as nonpersonal. Differences on each of these three levels are over questions of "fact," of the way reality actually is, and although in practice it may prove difficult or even impossible to resolve such disputes, in principle it should be possible to do so.

22. J. Hick, *God Has Many Names* (Philadelphia: Westminster, 1982), 36.

23. "The Outcome: Dialogue into Truth," 151.

24. *God Has Many Names*, 83, 11, 53.

25. For Nick's religious epistemology see his *Faith and Knowledge*, 2d ed. (Ithaca, N.Y.: Cornell University Press, 1966); "Religious Faith as Experiencing-As," in *Talk of God*, ed. G. N. A. Vesey (New York: Macmillan, 1969); and M. Goulder and J. Nick, *Why Believe in God?* (London: SCM, 1983).

26. *God Has Many Names*, 52–53.

27. Ibid., 53, 83.

28. H. Netland, "Professor Hick on Religious Pluralism," *RelS* 22 (1986): 249–61.

29. Thus Hick states,
    The Eternal One is thus the divine noumenon which is experienced and thought within different religious traditions as the range of divine phenomena witnessed to by the religious history of mankind. . . . When I say in a summarizing slogan that God has many names, I mean that the Eternal One is perceived within different human cultures under different forms, both personal and nonpersonal, and that from these different perceptions arise the religious ways of life which we call the great world faiths [*God Has Many Names*, 83, 59].

30. Ibid., 24–25, 52, 78.

31. Ibid., 38.

Chapter 7

1. See Bryan Magee, *Men of Ideas* (London: Jolly & Barber, Ltd., Rugby, 1978), 171. Compare Quine's views with those of Edmund Husserl in *The Crisis of European Sciences* (Evanston, Ill.: Northwestern University Press, 1970), 3–7.

2. Cited in E. D. Klemke, ed., *The Meaning of Life* (New York: Oxford University Press, 1981), 4.

3. See A. J. Ayer, *The Central Questions of Philosophy* (New York: Holt, Reinhart, and Winston, 1973), 233–35; Paul Kurtz, *In Defense of Secular Humanism* (Buffalo, N.Y.: Prometheus Books, 1983), 153–68
4. Ayer, ibid., 235. Cf. James Rachels, *The End of Life* (Oxford: Oxford University Press, 1986), 39–59.
5. Kurtz, *Secular Humanism,* 156–57.
6. See William Frankena, *Ethics* (Englewood Cliffs, N.J.: Prentice-Hall, 1963), 113–16; Ronald M. Green, *Religious Reason: The Rational and Moral Basis of Religious Belief* (New York: Oxford University Press, 1978), 13–79; and the articles by John Hospers and Kai Nielsen in Wilfrid Sellars and John Hospers, eds., *Readings in Ethical Theory* (Englewood Cliffs, N.J.: Prentice-Hall, 1970).
7. See Karl Britton, *Philosophy and the Meaning of Life* (Cambridge: Cambridge University Press, 1969); Robert Nozick, *Philosophical Explanations* (Cambridge, Mass.: Harvard University Press, 1981), 571–647.
8. Britton, ibid., 189.
9. William H. Halverson, *A Concise Introduction to Philosophy,* 4th ed. (New York: Random House, 1981), 429–34, 463–69.
10. J. L. Mackie, *The Miracle of Theism* (Oxford: Clarendon Press, 1982), 111–18; cf. 254–62. Mackie rejects the objective existence of values for two primary reasons: (1) moral properties are queer entities and if they exist they lend some support to the existence of God, but it is more rational to be a subjectivist about morality; and (2) moral intuitionism is an unclear epistemological doctrine.
11. Britton does not treat the metaphysical aspects of his theory of the meaning of life, and thus it is not entirely clear that he should be classified as an advocate of the Immanent Purpose view. But he does hold that we must formulate our views of the meaning of life in terms of what we find in the world and he takes it to be the case that several aspects, e.g., human relationships, have value in and of themselves without some transcendent ground of meaning. So he appears to be promoting a version of the Immanent Purpose view as I have defined it (see *Philosophy,* 1–20, 172– 91).
12. I am not denying that some values may presuppose a specifically Christian framework. In this regard, some have argued that, in addition to utilitarian reasons, fidelity in marriage should be kept because marriage presupposes a covenant before God. Further, it is also the case that Christianity offers extra justification for opposing some practices. For example, advocates of the Immanent Purpose view could rightly oppose suicide because such an act treats the subject as a means to an end and not as an end. But a Christian worldview could offer more arguments against suicide, e.g., the possibility of a large harm (hell) for an unbeliever, the ownership of life by God, the need to teach the community how to endure suffering, etc. See Stanley Hauerwas, *Suffering Presence* (Notre Dame, Ind.: University of Notre Dame Press, 1986) for more on the Christian contribution to the specific content of morality. Finally, I do not mean to imply that special revelation does not aid and specify our moral knowledge over that available in moral intuition of moral values and properties. In this regard, see John Warwick Montgomery, *Human Rights & Human Dignity* (Grand Rapids: Zondervan, 1986), 105–88. My main point here is to argue that Christianity and advocates of the Immanent Purpose view can agree about some of the nature and content of an absolute moral law. Their primary area of disagreement is over the explanation of how that moral law came about in the universe.

13. J. P. Moreland, *Scaling the Secular City* (Grand Rapids: Baker, 1987), 77–103.
14. H. P. Owen, *The Moral Argument for Christian Theism* (London: Allen and Unwin, 1965), 49–50. See also A. C. Ewing, *Value and Reality* (London: Allen and Unwin, 1973), 189–91.
15. Nozick, *Philosophical Explanation*, 370–74.
16. See Dom Illtyd Trethowan, *Absolute Value* (London: George Allen and Unwin, 1970), 80–107; Robert Adams, "Moral Arguments for Theistic Belief," *Rationality and Religious Belief*, ed. C. F. Delaney (Notre Dame, Ind.: University of Notre Dame Press, 1979), 116–40.
17. Mackie, *Theism*, 115.
18. Michael Russ, "Evolutionary Ethics: A Phoenix Arisen," *Zygon* 21 (March 1986): 95–111; Jeffrie G. Murphy, *Evolution, Morality, and the Meaning of Life* (Totowa, N.J.: Rowman and Littlefield, 1982), 9–29, 91–113.
19. John Barrow and Frank Tipler, *The Anthropic Cosmological Principle* (Oxford: Clarendon Press, 1986), 658–77.
20. J. L. Mackie, *Ethics: Inventing Right and Wrong* (New York: Penguin, 1977), 38.
21. See Tom L. Beauchamp, *Philosophical Ethics* (New York: McGraw-Hill, 1982), 170–73.

Chapter 8

1. John Hick, *Death and Eternal Life* (London: Macmillan, 1976), 247.
2. Ibid., 248–49.
3. And also between what might be called "soft" and "hard" negativism, the views, respectively, that no one is saved due to the contingent fact that all men refuse salvation and that no one is saved due to the divine will not to save anyone. But as no one has seriously entertained these two views in the history of Christianity they can be safely ignored. "Soft" and "hard" universalism, particularism, and negativism exhaust all the possibilities, though it is possible to hold a combination of views: e.g., that God will ensure the salvation of some while leaving the salvation of others solely to human free will.
4. See the views of Twisse discussed by John Owen in *A Dissertation on Divine Justice* (*Works*, ed. W. N. Goold [London: Johnstone and Hunter, 1850–53]), 10, pt. 2, chaps. 12–15. The quotation from Twisse (for which I am indebted to William Young) is from *Animadversiones . . . in Corvini Defensionem* (Amsterdam: Joannem Janassonium, 1649), 72.
5. Owen, 10:596–97.
6. *The Plan of Salvation*, rev. ed. (Grand Rapids: Eerdmans, 1942), 97–98. See 74: "God in his love saves as many of the guilty race of man as he can get the consent of his whole nature to save." See also *Select Shorter Writings* of B. B. Warfield, ed. John Meeter (Philadelphia: Presbyterian and Reformed, 1970), 1:297.
7. Hick, *Death*, 242.
8. J. A. T. Robinson, *In The End, God . . .* (London: James Clarke, 1950), 119.
9. Hick, *Death*, 251.
10. I am grateful to Dr. Richard Bauckham and Professor William Young for help with an earlier draft of this paper.

Chapter 9

1. J. Baille, *Our Knowledge of God* (New York: Scribner's Sons, n.d.), 126.
2. Thomas Aquinas, *Summa Theologica* 1.1.8.

3. For a fine comparison of apologetic systems according to these five criteria see G. R. Lewis, *Testing Christianity's Truth Claims* (Lanham, Md.: University Press of America, 1990).
4. See J. P. Moreland, *Scaling the Secular City: A Defense of Christianity* (Grand Rapids: Baker, 1987).
5. See W. L. Craig, *Apologetics: An Introduction* (Chicago: Moody, 1984). A revised version of this text is due out from Crossway Books but had not been published at the time of this writing.
6. For an example of this strategy in a philosophical debate see J. P. Moreland and K. Nielsen, *Does God Exist?* (Nashville: Thomas Nelson, 1990), 33–47. This has been republished by Prometheus Books. The cumulative case approach is also used in W. Corduan, *Reasonable Faith: Basic Christian Apologetics* (Nashville: Broadman, 1993).
7. See R. Nash, ed., *The Philosophy of Gordon Clark* (Nutley, N.J.: Presbyterian and Reformed, 1968).
8. See C. F. H. Henry, *God, Revelation, and Authority*, 6 vols. (Waco, Tex.: Word, 1976–83).
9. See E. R. Geehan, ed., *Jerusalem and Athens: Critical Discussions of the Theology and Apologetics of Cornelius Van Til* (Nutley, N.J.: Presbyterian and Reformed, 1971).
10. See J. Frame, *The Doctrine of the Knowledge of God* (Grand Rapids: Baker, 1987).
11. See G. L. Bahnsen, "Socrates or Christ: The Reformation of Christian Apologetics," in *Foundations of Christian Scholarship: Essays in the Van Til Perspective* (Vallecito, Calif.: Ross House Books, 1976), 191–239.
12. See A. Plantinga and N. Wolterstorff, eds., *Faith and Rationality* (Notre Dame, Ind.: University of Notre Dame Press, 1983). For an introductory summary of this viewpoint see K. J. Clark, *Return to Reason: A Critique of Enlightenment Evidentialism and a Defense of Reason and Belief in God* (Grand Rapids: Eerdmans, 1990).
13. Plantinga does think that some theistic arguments are helpful. Yet he would not grant them the same epistemic function as would someone in the Thomistic tradition. See Clark, *Return to Reason*, 156.
14. See E. J. Carnell, *An Introduction to Christian Apologetics* (Grand Rapids: Eerdmans, 1948).
15. See Lewis, *Truth Claims*. A Carnellian approach is also used in G. R. Lewis and B. A. Demerest, *Integrative Theology: Historical, Biblical, Systematic, Practical*, 3 vols. (Grand Rapids: Zondervan, 1987–94).
16. Blaise Pascal, *Pensées,* trans. with an introduction by A. J. Krailsheimer (New York: Penguin, 1985), 190/543 (the first number refers to the Lafuma enumeration; the second number refers to the older Brunschvicg system).
17. See *Pensées*, 913.
18. One seldom if ever hears the ontological argument presented in miniature (unless one is already in philosophical circles), although one might so hear it.
19. A. Kenny, *The Five Ways* (Notre Dame, Ind.: University of Notre Dame Press, 1980).
20. Although Pascal uses the ontological language of faculty psychology when speaking of the heart as an organ of knowledge, one can recast (and deontologize) his terms by saying that the "heart" simply refers to a capacity to know intuitively or nondiscursively.
21. C. S. Lewis, *Surprised by Joy* (New York: Harcourt Brace Jovanovich, 1955), 233–34.

22. Pascal, *Pensées*, 190/543.
23. For an illuminating discussion of the nature of religious faith see S. MacDonald, "Christian Faith," in *Reasoned Faith*, ed. E. Stump (Ithaca, N.Y.: Cornell University Press, 1993), 42–69.
24. See Mark 9:1–32 for the entire account.
25. One should consider here the many arguments from religious experience, as distinct from the kind of metaphysical proofs Pascal was addressing. Pascal himself gives a kind of argument from religious experience (although in a different epistemic atmosphere) in the wager, when he urges the skeptic to participate in religious activities in order to find faith.
26. *Pensées*, 821/252; emphasis mine.
27. Ibid., 99/536.
28. Ibid., 418/233; See D. Groothuis, "Wagering Faith: Examining Two Objections to Pascal's Wager," *RelS* 30 (1994): 479–86.
29. My thanks go to Professor Robert T. Herbert, David Werther, and to referees at *Trinity Journal* for their comments on earlier versions of this paper.

Chapter 10

1. Acts 16:9–10.
2. *Light from the Ancient Near East* (New York: H. Doran, 1927), 384.
3. Ibid.
4. *St. Paul the Traveller and the Roman Citizen* (London: Hodder & Stoughton, 1895), 252.
5. *Paulus in Korinth* (Heidelberg: Knecht, 1908), 5. He writes: "Es musste fehlschlagen, denn es war ein Experiment, welches ausserhalb der gegebenen Ordnung lag" ("It [the experiment] had to fail, since it was conducted outside of the normal pattern [of preaching]").
6. Garden City, N.Y.: Doubleday, 1985, 1829. Others who adopt a "negative" view of Paul in Athens are J. Renie, *Actes des Apôtres* (Paris: Pirot-Clamer, 1949), 209; J. Dupont, *Les Actes des Apôtres* (Paris: Duculot, 1953), 157; and M. Dibelius, *Studies in the Acts of the Apostles* (New York: Scribner's Sons, 1956), 63. Dibelius, it should be noted, questions the authenticity of 17:16–34, distinguishing between "the Paul of the Acts" and "the real Paul" on display in Romans (62–63).
7. H. Conzelmann holds the Areopagus speech to be inauthentic, a "free creation" of the author ("The Address of Paul on the Areopagus," in *Studies in Luke-Acts,* ed. L. E. Keck and J. L. Martyn [Nashville/New York: Abingdon, 1966], 218).
8. So L. Legrand, "The Areopagus Speech: Its Theological Kerygma and Its Missionary Significance," in *La Notion de Dieu*, ed. J. Coppens (Louvain: Gembloux, 1974), 338–41.
9. Thus, I. H. Marshall, *Acts*, TNTC (Leicester/Grand Rapids: Inter-Varsity/Eerdmans, 1991), 281.
10. Acts 21:39.
11. The verb ἀνατρέφω can denote physical nurture as well as mental or spiritual training (BAGD, 62).
12. To the ancients, "fatherland" related more to one's city than one's nation.
13. Although banks were found in all commercial cities, Athens was always the leading banking center of the ancient world (H. Koester, *History, Culture, and Religion of the Hellenistic Age*, vol. 1 of *Introduction to the New Testament* [Philadelphia: Fortress; Berlin and New York: W. de Gruyter, 1984], 90).
14. Paul's familiarity with Hellenistic culture in and of itself may account for the knowledge of Greek "poets" seen in his Areopagus address.

196 / The Gospel and Contemporary Perspectives

15. See D. Gill and C. Gempf, eds., *Graeco-Roman Setting,* vol. 2 of *The Book of Acts in Its First Century Setting* (Grand Rapids: Eerdmans, 1994), esp. chaps. 9 and 12.
16. Strabo, however, plays down the notion that Tarsus was an intellectual center (14.5.12–13).
17. S. Berger ("Democracy in the Greek West and the Athenian Example," *Hermes* 117 [1989]: 313) notes that even outside of Greece, Athens became a model of democracy in shedding tyranny from the *polis* during the fifth century B.C.
18. E. M. Blaiklock, *Cities of the New Testament* (Westwood, N.J.: Fleming H. Revell, 1965), 52.
19. Paul quotes from one of Menander's comedies in 1 Cor. 15:33: "Bad company corrupts good morals."
20. *Pro Flac.* 26.62.
21. Strabo 14.5.13.
22. In addition to the Stoic and Epicurean schools, Athens was home to Plato's "academy," the Lyceum, where Aristotle taught, and thousands of initiates into the mystery religions. Koester observes that as late as the early Byzantine era, philosophy students flocked to Athens from all parts of the ancient world (*History,* 99).
23. See E. Mayer, "Apollonius von Tyana und die Biographie des Philostratos," *Hermes* 52 (1917): 371–424.
24. It is worth pointing out that Paul knew two of the three university cities scattered around the Mediterranean region—Tarsus and Athens. Stoic influence in both cities was strong (see M. Pohlenz, "Paulus und die Stoa," *ZNW* 42 [1949]: 69–104).
25. Koester, *History,* 180. Phyla, located near Athens, was the site of a mystery sanctuary.
26. Compare Luke's description in Acts 17:18 and 21.
27. *Charito* 1.2.6 (cited in H. Conzelmann, *Acts of the Apostles* [Hermeneia, Philadelphia: Fortress, 1987], 139).
28. Thus, P. Parente, "St. Paul's Address before the Areopagus," *CBQ* 11 (1949): 144.
29. See J. Ferguson, *Greek and Roman Religion* (Park Ridge: Noyes, 1980), 3–16.
30. Pausanius 1.28.5.
31. A. Aristides 1.40–48. See also Pausanius 1.28.5.
32. The "Council of the Areopagus," ἡ βουλὴ ἡ ἐξ᾽Αρείου Πάγου, in time had come to be known simply as ὁ Αρείος πάγος (K. Lake and H. J. Cadbury, *The Beginnings of Christianity,* pt. 1: *The Acts of the Apostles* [Reprint. Grand Rapids: Baker, 1965], 212).
33. Cicero (*De nat. deo.* 2.29.74) indicates that in the Roman period the Areopagus also had jurisdiction over criminal matters.
34. B. Keil, *Beiträge zur Geschichte des Areopags,* BZAW 71/8 (Leipzig: Teubner, 1920), 59–80.
35. B. Gärtner, *The Areopagus Speech and Natural Revelation* ASNU 21 (Uppsala: Almquist, 1955), 64, 59. B. Keil's 1920 publication, *Beiträge zur Geschichte des Areopags* (see n. 34), remains the most extensive survey of the history of the Areopagus. See also K. Wachsmuth and T. Thalheim, "*Areios pagos,*" PW 2:627–33.
36. D. Broneer, "Athens, City of Idol Worship," *BA* 21/1 (1958): 27.
37. *Mem.* 1.1.1.
38. *De nat. deor.* 1.15.39.

39. E. Plümacher, *Lukas als hellenistischer Schriftsteller. Studien zur Apostelgeschichte*, SUNT 9 (Göttingen: Vandenhoeck & Ruprecht, 1972), 19.
40. See also G. Bornkamm, *Studien zu Antike und Christentum* (Munich: Kaiser, 1963), 93–118.
41. *St. Luke: Theologian of Redemptive History* (Philadelphia: Fortress, 1967), 71–72.
42. Gärtner, *Areopagus Speech*, 29–44; also E. Norden, *Agnōstos Theos. Untersuchungen zur Formgeschichte religiöser Rede* (Leipzig/Berlin: Teubner, 1913), 330–32.
43. See 1:1–2.
44. Lake-Cadbury (*Acts*, 209) observe the following peculiarities in Paul's style before the Areopagus: (1) the neuters ὅ . . . τοῦτο and τὸ θεῖον in vv. 23 and 29; (2) the frequent use of the particle γε; (3) frequent alliteration; (4) frequent use of πᾶς with derivatives; (5) repetition of the participle ὑπάρχων (vv. 24, 27, and 29); and (6) the idiomatic expression πίστιν παρασχών (v. 31).
45. Most helpful in examining the narrative framework of 17:16–34 is Gärtner, *Areopagus Speech*, 73–241.
46. For a discussion of apostolic preaching among the Gentiles, see H. Gebhardt, "Die an die Heiden Missionsrede der Apostel und das Johannesevangelium," *ZNW* 6 (1905): 240–47.
47. See also 19:35.
48. C. F. Evans, "Speeches in Acts," in *Melanges biblique*, ed. A. R. Charne (Paris: Duculot, 1969), 291–92.
49. The verb διαλέγομαι occurs ten times in Acts, and as one would fully expect, in Acts 17:17.
50. In assessing the pagan mindset of first-century Athens, I am indebted to conversations with Dr. Glen Thompson, a classicist who teaches at Saginaw State University and Michigan Lutheran Seminary.
51. Gärtner (*Areopagus Speech*), Dibelius (*Studies*), and Pohlenz ("Paulus") have treated this subject, writing in terms of "natural theology." In this regard, the term "natural revelation" is to be preferred, in order to make the necessary distinction between the Creator's initiation and human attempts at religiosity.
52. See W. Eltester, "Gott und die Nature in der Areopagrede," in *Neutestamentliche Studien für R. Bultmann* (Berlin: Töpelmann, 1954), 202–27. Consider the fact that much of the Jewish view of creation in the OT is formed against the backdrop of a heathen view of cosmic "chaos"; the biblical writer is frequently polemical: e.g., Pss. 73:12–14; 88:9–11; Job 38:8–11; Prov. 8:28–29; Jer. 5:22; 31:35; 38:36.
53. Cf. Rom. 1:18–20. In this connection, see also G. Bornkamm, "Gesetz und Natur: Röm. 2.14–16," in *Studien zu Antike und Urchristentum* (Munich: Kaiser, 1963), 93–118.
54. P. Vielhauer, "Zum 'Paulinismus' der Apostelgeschichte," in *Aufsätze zum Neuen Testament* (Munich: Kaiser, 1956), 13.
55. In Rom. 1:20, τὰ ποιήτα are visible for all to see.
56. Note a critical distinction made by Paul, namely that pagans *possess* this knowledge, not that they can *attain* it.
57. Thus Gärtner, *Areopagus Speech*, 80–82.
58. Zeno, *Frg.* 162, cited in C. K. Barrett, ed., *The New Testament Background: Selected Documents* (New York/Evanston: Harper & Row, 1961), 62.
59. The use of the derogatory term ὁ σπερμολόγος by some in the agora (17:18) may be a Lukan play on words with the Stoic λόγος σπερματικός.
60. A fuller discussion can be found in A. A. Long and D. N. Sedley, *Translations*

of Principle Sources with Philosophical Commentary, vol. 1 of *The Hellenistic Philosophers* (Cambridge: Cambridge University Press, 1987), 158–437; E. Zeller, *The Stoics, Epicureans and Sceptics* (New York: Russell & Russell, 1962), 126–66; and Pohlenz, "Paulus," 69–104.

61. G. Schneider, "Anknüpfung, Kontinuität und Widerspruch in der Areopagrede. Apg 17, 22–31," in *Kontinuität und Einheit,* ed. P. G. Mueller and W. Stenger (Freiburg: Herder, 1981), 173–78; also, Pohlenz, "Paulus," 69–104.

62. H. P. Owen, "The Scope of Natural Revelation in Romans i and Acts xvii," *NTS* 5 (1958/59): 142–43.

63. G. Nauck, "Die Tradition und Komposition der Areopagrede," *ZThK* 53 (1956): 45–46; also, F. Mussner, "Anknüpfung und Kerygma in der Areopagrede (Apg 17, 22b-31)," in *Praesentia Salutis. Gesammelte Studien zu Fragen und Themen des Neuen Testaments* (Düsseldorf: Patmos, 1967), 235–43.

64. Ignorance, not worship, is Paul's emphasis (thus, N. Stonehouse, *Paul before the Areopagus: And Other New Testament Studies* [London: Tyndale, 1957], 19).

65. A vast amount of literature has been devoted to "the unknown god" of Athens. A variety of explanations seeks to harmonize Paul's reference to ἀγνώστῳ θεῷ with ancient sources. Pausanius (1.1.4) and Philostratus (*Vit. apol.* 6.3) describe Athens as the scene of innumerable gods, heroes, and corresponding altars. Tertullian (*Ad nat.* 2.9) writes that Paul chose the singular description— "unknown god"—over the plural, even though the latter is understood. In his commentary on Titus 1:12, Jerome (*PL* 26:572–73) speaks of "all the gods," not the one unknown god. Theodore of Mopsuestia (cited in Lake-Cadbury, *Acts,* 244) relates an Athenian legend in which a demon appeared following defeat in battle. Out of fear, not wishing to exclude any deity, the Athenians erected an altar "to the unknown god." Among the more extensive investigations of the altar inscription are R. Reitzenstein, "Agnostos Theos," *NJKA* 31 (1913): 146–55; T. Birt, "*Agnōstoi theoi* und die Areopagrede des Apostels Paulus," *RheinMus* 69 (1914): 342–92; Norden, *Agnōstos Theos,* 56ff; and Gärtner, *Areopagus Speech,* 242–47.

66. Paul is here engaged in what some might call "pre-evangelism."

67. *Phaen 5.* It is difficult to confine with precision these words to Aratus of Soli alone, given the fact that this language appears in numerous ancient sources. For example, the words of Cleanthes, another third-century B.C. Stoic, are comparable: "You, O Zeus, are praised above all gods. . . . Unto you may all flesh speak, for we are your offspring" (the text is reproduced in M. Pohlenz, "Kleanthes Zeushymnus," *Hermes* 75 [1940]: 117–23). Similarly, the third-century B.C. poet Callimachus, in a hymn "To Zeus," speaks of humankind as "offspring of the earth" (*Hymns, Epigrams, Select Fragments* [Baltimore/London: Johns Hopkins University Press, 1988], 3).

68. Paul's cultural accommodation in Athens should not be misconstrued as syncretization. Paul accommodated himself, not the message, to the level and philosophical assumptions of his audience. See W. J. Larkin, Jr., *Culture and Biblical Hermeneutics: Interpreting and Applying the Authoritative Word in a Relativistic Age* (Grand Rapids: Baker, 1988), 319–21.

69. Thus, debates on creation should be central to ongoing apologetic discourse.

70. Whether acknowledged or not, doctrine lies at the heart of contemporary debates over pluralism, as D. A. Carson reminds us ("Christian Witness in an Age of Pluralism," in *God and Culture: Essays in Honor of Carl F. H. Henry* [Grand Rapids: Eerdmans/Carlisle: Paternoster, 1993], 46–49).

71. No better illustration of this clash can be found than the hostility of cultural anthropologists and sociologists toward the Christian missionary endeavor.

As R. J. Priest notes, in many ways, social theorists and missionaries are opposites: the one advances the notion of original sin, while the other is united in discrediting and undercutting this inconvenient anthropological truth. Evangelical theorists should not compromise on intellectual rigor; they must, however, in the end maintain fidelity to God's revelation. See R. J. Priest, "Cultural Anthropology, Sin, and the Missionary," in *God and Culture*, 85–105.

Chapter 11

1. Mark M. Hanna, *Crucial Questions in Apologetics* (Grand Rapids: Baker, 1978), 63.
2. Ibid., 60. Elsewhere I have accepted this distinction but substituted the terms "trans-cultural apologetics" and "culture-specific apologetics" in an effort to relate apologetics to broader missiological concerns. See Harold Netland, "Toward Contextualized Apologetics," *Missiology: An International Review* 16 (July 1988): 289–303.
3. Much has been written on the subject of relativism. Helpful introductions to the philosophical issues involved can be found in *Relativism: Cognitive and Moral*, ed. Michael Krausz and Jack W. Meiland (Notre Dame, Ind.: University of Notre Dame Press, 1982) and *Rationality*, ed. Bryan R. Wilson (Oxford: Basil Blackwell, 1970). An incisive discussion of the place of relativism in anthropology is found in Elvin Hatch's *Culture and Morality: The Relativity of Values in Anthropology* (New York: Columbia University Press, 1983). Roger Trigg's *Reason and Commitment* (Cambridge: Cambridge University Press, 1973) provides a penetrating critique of various forms of relativism.
4. I use the terms interchangeably.
5. Grand Rapids: Eerdmans, 1978, 185, 190–91.
6. Frame, *Knowledge of God*, 45.
7. Ibid., 125.
8. Ibid., 71; cf. 100. In this connection Frame seems to be influenced considerably by Thomas Kuhn's *The Structure of Scientific Revolutions*, 2d ed. (Chicago: University of Chicago Press, 1970), to which he repeatedly refers approvingly. Unfortunately, he gives no evidence of awareness of the trenchant criticism to which Kuhn's work has been subjected by other philosophers and scientists. See, for example, *Criticism and the Growth of Knowledge*, ed. I. Lakatos & A. Musgrave (Cambridge: Cambridge University Press, 1970); Trigg, *Reason and Commitment*, 99–109; Richard Purtill, "Kuhn on Scientific Revolutions," *Philosophy of Science* 34 (1967): 53–58; and Michael Devitt, *Realism and Truth* (Princeton, N.J.: Princeton University Press, 1984), chap. 9.
9. Frame, *Knowledge of God*, 71–72. See also 106, 114, 119, 121, 123, 333.
10. Ibid., 45.
11. Ibid., 129.
12. Ibid., 128.
13. Ibid., 125.
14. Ibid., 130.
15. Ibid.
16. Ibid. Emphasis in original.
17. Ibid., 131.
18. Ibid. Emphasis in original.
19. Ibid., 303.
20. Ibid., 125.
21. Mention should be made here of a recent development in the epistemology of

religion that is sometimes taken to be a version of presuppositionism—the attempt to argue that belief in God is epistemically "properly basic" and thus does not stand in need of any corroborative support. This position is generally identified with Alvin Plantinga, who has been its most vigorous and articulate spokesman. See Plantinga's "Reason and Belief in God," in *Faith and Rationality,* ed. Alvin Plantinga and Nicholas Wolterstorff (Notre Dame, Ind.: University of Notre Dame Press, 1983), 16–93; "Is Belief in God Rational?" in *Rationality and Religious Belief,* ed. C. F. Delaney (Notre Dame, Ind.: University of Notre Dame Press, 1979); and "Is Belief in God Properly Basic?" *Nous* 15 (1981): 41–51. There are numerous works more or less critical of Plantinga's "Reformed epistemology," including Peter C. Appleby, "Reformed Epistemology, Rationality, and Belief in God," *International Journal for the Philosophy of Religion* 24 (1988): 129–41; Richard Askew, "On Fideism and Alvin Plantinga," *International Journal for the Philosophy of Religion* 23 (1988): 3–16; and William P. Alston, "Plantinga's Epistemology of Religious Belief," in *Alvin Plantinga,* ed. James Tomberlin and Peter Van Inwagen (Dordrecht: D. Reidel, 1985), 289–311. A helpful survey of the discussion can be found in Ronald Nash, *Faith and Reason: Searching for a Rational Faith* (Grand Rapids: Zondervan, 1988), chaps. 5–7. The issues raised by Plantinga's Reformed epistemology are sufficiently different from Frame's theological presuppositionism to warrant not being included in this discussion.
22. Frame, *Knowledge of God,* 109–22.
23. Ibid., 45.
24. Paul Helm, "The Role of Logic in Biblical Interpretation" in *Hermeneutics, Inerrancy, and the Bible,* ed. Earl D. Radmacher and Robert D. Preus (Grand Rapids: Zondervan, 1984), 842–43.
25. Frame, *Knowledge of God,* 243.
26. Ibid., 255.
27. Ibid., 256–57.
28. Particularly helpful here is the work of Edmund Husserl, *Logische Untersuchungen,* trans. J. N. Findley as *Logical Investigations* (London: Routledge and Kegan Paul, 1970), vol. 1, chaps. 4–9. See also Dallas Willard, *Logic and the Objectivity of Knowledge* (Athens, Ohio: University of Ohio Press, 1984) 133–205, and "Space, Color, Sense Perception and the Epistemology of Logic," *The Monist* 72 (January 1989): 117–33.
29. The definition is from the excellent discussion by Mark M. Hanna, "A Response to the Role of Logic in Biblical Interpretation," in *Hermeneutics, Inerrancy, and the Bible,* 861ff.
30. Logical principles can at best provide negative criteria for evaluation. The principle of noncontradiction, for example, provides a negative criterion for truth in that any statement or position that violates the principle cannot be true; but failure to violate the principle of noncontradiction in and of itself does not guarantee the truth of a statement or position.
31. Harold Netland, *Dissonant Voices: Religious Pluralism and the Question of Truth* (Grand Rapids: Eerdmans, 1991), chaps. 4–5.
32. The distinction is made by Nash in *Faith and Reason,* 14ff; George Mavrodes, "Jerusalem and Athens Revisited," in *Faith and Rationality: Reason and Belief in God,* ed. Alvin Plantinga and Nicholas Wolterstorff (Notre Dame, Ind.: University of Notre Dame Press, 1983), 197ff; Brian Hebblethwaite, *The Ocean of Truth* (Cambridge: Cambridge University Press, 1988), 86; Frame, *Knowledge of God,* 348ff; and Paul J. Griffiths, "An Apology for Apologetics," in *Faith and Philosophy* 5 (October 1988): 401ff.

33. Hebblethwaite, *The Ocean of Truth,* 86.

Chapter 12

1. Wllliam A. Quayle, *The Pastor-Preacher,* ed. Warren W. Wiersbe (Grand Rapids: Baker, 1979), 143.
2. John Killinger, *The Centrality of Preaching in the Total Task of the Ministry* (Waco, Tex.: Word, 1969), 28.
3. Phillips Brooks, *Lectures on Preaching* (reprint; Grand Rapids: Baker, 1969), 5.
4. R. E. O. White, *A Guide to Preaching* (Grand Rapids: Eerdmans, 1973), 24–25.
5. Adapted from Clyde Reid, *The Empty Pulpit* (New York: Harper and Row, 1967), 67–74.
6. The case for this view is ably stated by Reid, *Empty Pulpit,* 83–85.
7. It would do every pastor good periodically to ponder the chapter "Demonstration of the Spirit and of the Power," D. Martyn Lloyd-Jones, *Preaching and Preachers* (Grand Rapids: Zondervan, 1971), 304–25.
8. The best discussion of originality in all homiletical literature, in this writer's opinion, is by W. G. T. Shedd, *Homiletics and Pastoral Theology* (Edinburgh: The Banner of Truth Trust, repr. 1965 [of 1867 edition]), 3–32.
9. Homiletics' best discussion of application is still to be found in the century-old text, John A. Broadus, *On the Preparation and Delivery of Sermons* (reprint; New York: Harper and Brothers, 1944), 211–21.
10. Donald Coggan, *Stewards of Grace* (London: Hodder and Stoughton, 1958), esp. 61–64.
11. Another whole approach to this matter of variety in outline structure is suggested by Ilion T. Jones, *Principles and Practice of Preaching* (Nashville: Abingdon, 1956), 103–23. One can further stimulate his thinking by relating Andrew W. Blackwood's fine chapters on doctrinal and biographical preaching to differing ones of these structural styles. See respectively *Doctrinal Preaching for Today* (Nashville: Abingdon, 1956), 184–96, and *Biographical Preaching for Today* (Nashville: Abingdon, 1954), 150–68.
12. This quality of imagination is one of the "most godlike capacities of man," Whitesell insists. Imagination in preaching is the picture-making faculty of the mind always under the control of reality; and without its disciplined use, all preaching is dull: see Faris D. Whitesell, *Power in Expository Preaching* (Neptune, N.J.: Fleming H. Revell, 1963), 103–17.
13. See Donald G. Miller, *The Way to Biblical Preaching* (Nashville: Abingdon, 1957), 142–53.
14. White, *Guide,* 219.
15. Ibid., 220–24.
16. Ibid., 224–28.
17. W. E. Sangster, *The Craft of Sermon Illustration* (Grand Rapids: Baker, repr. 1973 [of 1950 edition]), 26–45. If you have never read this little book's first chapter, "The Place and Use of Illustration," now would be the time to do it.
18. Webb B. Garrison, *The Preacher and His Audience* (Neptune, N.J.: Fleming H. Revell, 1954), 79.
19. Ibid., 81–85.
20. Killinger, *Centrality,* 28.

Chapter 13

1. D. Kelly, *Preachers with Power: Four Stalwarts of the South* (Edinburgh: The Banner of Truth Trust, 1992), 67.

2. Kelly, *Preachers with Power,* 64.
3. J. Stewart, *Heralds of God* (Grand Rapids: Baker, 1972), 73.
4. J. Stott, *Between Two Worlds: The Art of Preaching in the Twentieth Century* (Grand Rapids: Eerdmans, 1982), 125–26.
5. I have tried to unpack this sentence, "God is most glorified in us, when we are most satisfied in him," in two books: *Desiring God: Meditations of a Christian Hedonist* (Sisters, Ore.: Multnomah, 1986) and *The Pleasures of God: Meditations on God's Delight in Being God* (Sisters, Oreg.: Multnomah, 1991).
6. J. W. Alexander, *Thoughts on Preaching* (1864; Edinburgh: The Banner of Truth Trust, 1975), 117.
7. P. Toon, *God's Statesman: The Life and Work of John Owen* (Exeter, Devon: Paternoster, 1971), 171.
8. Stott, *Between Two Worlds,* 222.